Baroque Horrors

Baroque Horrors

Roots of the Fantastic in the Age of Curiosities

David R. Castillo

The University of Michigan Press
Ann Arbor

First paperback edition 2012

Published in the United States of America by
The University of Michigan Press
Manufactured in the United States of America
♾ Printed on acid-free paper

2015 2014 2013 2012 5 4 3 2

A CIP catalog record for this book is available from the British Library.

Library of Congress Cataloging-in-Publication Data

Castillo, David R., 1967–
Baroque horrors : roots of the fantastic in the age of curiosities / David R. Castillo.
p. cm.
Includes bibliographical references and index.
ISBN 978-0-472-11721-5 (cloth : alk. paper)
1. Spanish literature—Classical period, 1500-1700—History and criticism. 2. Baroque literature—History and criticism. 3. Horror in literature. 4. Fear—History. 5. Fear—Political aspects. I. Title.
PQ6066.C365 2010
860.9'64—dc22 2009038396

ISBN 0-472-03491-x (paper : alk. paper)

ISBN 0-472-02668-2 (e-book)

A mi querido hijo Alex

Acknowledgments

This book is the result of nearly seven years of work during which I have had the privilege to discuss my ideas in progress with many colleagues and students at the University of Oregon and at SUNY Buffalo. They are all in a very real sense coauthors of this text. Among the Oregon friends I need to mention Massimo Lollini, with whom I had the pleasure to coedit *Reason and Its Others* (2006), my Golden Age partners in crime Julian Weiss, Leah Middlebrook, Amanda Powell, and Luis Verano, as well as the EMODS gang, including RL colleagues Nathalie Hester and Fabienne Moore. I will never forget our *zesty* sessions of conversation and wine. I am also appreciative to Juan Epple and Leonardo García Pabón for our stimulating team-taught courses.

While this is only our fourth year in Buffalo, my wife and I are fortunate to find ourselves, once again, amidst wonderful friends, many of whom are UB colleagues. Among them, I would like to thank the members of the Department of Romance Languages and Literatures and the interdisciplinary Early Modern Reading Group, including Amy Graves, Galen Brokaw, and Jim Bono. Jim's illuminating comments on an early draft of the introduction helped shape the direction of my research.

I need to thank the Baldy Center for its engaging series of speaker events, including the 2008 presentation by Michigan Acquisitions Editor Melody Herr which led to this publication, the College of Arts and Sciences, and especially the UB Humanities Institute for buying me precious writing time during the most critical phase of my research. Speaking of writing time, I would like to express my deepest appreciation to all my collaborators over the years, including my mentor, Nicholas Spadaccini; my good friend, Bill Egginton; my dear brother, Moisés Castillo; and my current writing partners, Brad Nelson and especially Kari Winter. Kari's dedication to our co-edited volume *What's New About Slavery: Human Trafficking and the Commodification of Life* and her patient and insightful reading of every draft of my *Baroque Horrors* have redefined, in my eyes, the very notion of *intellectual generosity.* I can think of several sections of this book that are literally the result of our conversations.

Finally I would like to acknowledge Edward Friedman, Howard Mancing, Charles Ganelin, Michael Gerli, Anthony Cascardi, David William Foster, and the late René Jara and Carroll Johnson. Their support and professionalism are a true inspiration. Thanks also to my wife, Stephanie, and my family and friends on both sides of the Atlantic for their love and support.

Contents

Preface

The dream of reason produces monsters.
—Francisco de Goya

There is no document of civilization which is not at the same time a document of barbarism. And just as such a document is not free of barbarism, barbarism taints also the manner in which it was transmitted from one owner to another. A historical materialist therefore dissociates from it as much as possible. He regards it as his task to brush history against the grain. The tradition of the oppressed teaches us that the "state of emergency" in which we live is not the exception but the rule. We must attain to a conception of history that is in keeping with this insight.
—Walter Benjamin

This gallery of horrors takes readers on a journey through the early modern roots/routes of the fantastic in miscellany collections, sensationalist news, exemplary narratives, folktales, and legends. It puts the spotlight on a selection of works from the Spanish Golden Age (roughly 1550–1680) that is representative of the pan-European constellation of curiosities. This is a "historiographic" gallery in the critical tradition of Walter Benjamin's "materialistic historiography." As Benjamin writes in "Theses on the Philosophy of History," "to articulate the past historically does not mean to recognize it 'the way it really was' [. . .] but to seize hold of a memory as it flashes up at a moment of danger" (255).[1]

1. Walter Benjamin distinguishes "materialistic historiography" from universal history: "Historicism rightly culminates in universal history. Materialistic historiography differs from it as to method more clearly than from any other kind. Universal history has no theoretical armature. Its method is additive; it musters a mass of data to fill the homogeneous, empty time. Materialistic historiography, on the other hand,

My research is inspired by a desire to turn the current cultural and political conversation away from the familiar narrative patterns that generate self-justifying allegories of abjection and to refocus it on the history of our fears and their monstrous offspring. The urgency to revisit the historical roots of our dreams and nightmares at the present "moment of danger" (to use Benjamin's evocative expression) is made apparent when one reads the highly publicized words of John McCain's spiritual advisor, Christian televangelist Rod Parsley, reflecting on the colonial origins and manifest destiny of America: "I do not believe our country can truly fulfill its divine purpose until we understand our historical conflict with Islam [. . .] It was to defeat Islam, among other dreams, that Christopher Columbus sailed to the New World in 1492 [. . .] Columbus dreamed of defeating the armies of Islam with the armies of Europe made mighty by the wealth of the New World. It was this dream that, in part, began America" (quoted in MotherJones.com/Washington_dispatch/2008).

The echoes of the ideology of the Spanish *reconquista* and the imperial dream of global dominance resonate strongly in these excerpts from Parsley's *Silent No More* (2005). Parsley embraces the legacy of European colonialism that converted the New World and its inhabitants into sources of wealth for the financing of imperial crusades. Reverend Parsley's vision of America as a Christian nation founded on a divinely inspired mission of destruction of Islam is the underside of the banner of freedom and democracy in which the Bush administration has wrapped its "preemptive" war in the Middle East. The mythical imagery of the "war of civilizations" continues to produce sites of horror, such as Abu Ghraib and Guantánamo Bay. Rather than telling us something about the presumed state of exceptionality invoked

---

is based on a constructive principle. Thinking involves not only the flow of thoughts, but their arrest as well. Where thinking suddenly stops in a configuration pregnant with tensions, it gives that configuration a shock, by which it crystallizes into a monad. A historical materialist approaches a historical subject only when he encounters it in a monad [. . .] He takes cognizance of it in order to blast a specific era out of the homogeneous course of history—blasting a specific work out of the lifework. As a result of this method the lifework is preserved in this work and at the same time [sublated/*aufheben*]; in the lifework the era, an in the era, the entire course of history [. . .] A historian who takes this as his point of departure stops telling the sequence of events like the beads of a rosary. Instead, he grasps the constellation which his own era has formed with a definite earlier one" ("Theses on the Philosophy of History" 262–63).

in the political rhetoric of the "war on terror," these two infamous prison camps represent the true legacy of empire.

Baroque Horrors reexamines imperial dreams of national origin and historical destiny as well as fears of invasion and contamination in the age of exploration. A central conclusion of my study is that the shadows that lurk in our closed spaces are symptoms of the baroque horror (vacui) that continues to haunt the architecture of modernity.[2] In this sense, one of the most important lessons we can learn from facing our baroque horrors (fictional as well as historical) is that the monsters come with the house, or as José Monleón put it in his study of the modern tradition of the fantastic, "the monsters were possible because we were the monsters" (23).

Engaging in conversations with various traditions of scholarly inquiry—such as baroque and Spanish Golden Age studies, literary criticism of the fantastic, social and cultural history, and psychoanalytic and feminist theory—this book underscores the productivity of communication between cultural fields that often ignore each other. The national and linguistic borders that have prevented Anglophone and Spanish scholarly traditions from engaging in meaningful interdisciplinary conversations are part of the nationalist legacy of nineteenth-century historiography, but they make little sense when applied to current cultural and historical developments or indeed to the cultural history of the early modern period. My study is thus aimed at specialists, students and readers of early modern literature and culture in the Spanish and Anglophone traditions as well as anyone interested in horror fantasy. It offers new contexts within which to rethink broad questions of intellectual and political history, especially with respect to the origins and meaning of the modern episteme (Foucault). While this gallery of horrors is rooted in and routed through baroque fantasy, a great deal of work remains to be done to illuminate the enduring contact zones that clearly exist between the material culture of curiosities and the literatures (and now the film traditions) of the modern fantastic. At stake is a better understanding of the dreams and fears that condition our perception of the world and the fictional and historical horrors that they continue to produce.

2. My use of the term *symptom* is indebted to Marxist and Lacanian theory. For an explanation of the Marxist concept of the symptom as placeholder of the truth of social antagonism and its connection to the familiar psychoanalytic notion, see Slavoj Zizek's "How Did Marx Invent the Symptom?" in the collective volume *Mapping Ideology* (1995).

This book's journey begins with a discussion of our fascination with curiosities and our quest for the thrill of authenticity in a world filled with simulacra. When life and death are severed from nature and history, "reality" and "authenticity" may be experienced as spectator sports and staged attractions, as in the "real lives" captured on camera in reality TV and the "authentic cadavers" displayed around the world in the Body Worlds exhibitions. Rather than thinking of virtual reality and staged authenticity as recent developments of the postmodern age, I look back at the baroque period in search for the roots of the commodification of nature and the horror vacui that accompanies it. For example, I point out that Gunther von Hagens' postmodern exhibits of peeled-off corpses have much in common with the displays of "monsters" and human remains in the early modern cabinets of curiosities. Von Hagens himself has signaled that his scientific exhibits of "authentic cadavers" share in the sensationalist spirit of early modern anatomical displays, including the baroque compositions of Dutch artist Frederick Ruysch (1638–1731) that were made with human fetuses and body parts adorned with clothes, flowers, and other props.

In chapter 1, I trace the connection between the Renaissance cabinets of curiosities or *Wunderkammern* and the literary miscellanea that emerged contemporarily as textual warehouses of ancient marvels. By the end of the sixteenth century, miscellany collections were turning into baroque journeys that privileged the road over the inventory. This is the case with Julián de Medrano's *La silva curiosa* (The Curious Silva [1583]), a key text for this section of the book. Medrano's macabre travel narrative empties the landscape in the sense in which Marc Augé speaks of the modern traveler's "abolition of place" (89). This bizarre first-person narrative transforms the holy places of antiquity inhabited by relics into baroque ruins devoid of transcendence. I argue that Medrano's grotesque picture of the baroque desert in *La silva* is the first panoramic vista of the modern fantastic.

Chapter 2 studies the instrumentalization of the marvelous and the preternatural in morality tales as well as Cervantes' critical reinvention of literary exemplarity in his *Novelas ejemplares* (1613), especially in the frame tale of the collection, *El casamiento engañoso [y] El coloquio de los perros* (The Deceitful Marriage and the Dialogue of the Dogs). Cervantes disallows the comforts of moral and epistemological certainty while inviting the reader to become coauthor of the text. This section of the book concludes with a discussion of María de Zayas' *El jardín engañoso* (The Deceitful Garden [1637]), a paradoxical morality tale that hails Lucifer as a model of self-control while rewarding those who disregard dominant social mores and codes in pursuit of illicit passions.

Chapter 3 examines María de Zayas' macabre collection of novellas known as *Desengaños amorosos* (Disenchantments of Love [1647]). Zayas' displays of tortured bodies focus our attention on the history of violence that baroque morality suppresses. Zayas' "moral pornography" (to use Angela Carter's provocative phrase) anticipates not only the sensationalist aesthetics of gothic horror but also the critical tradition associated with the literature of terror (Ann Radcliffe). The volume's compulsive repetition of intimate tales of patriarchal violence behind the closed doors of aristocratic houses exposes the dark side of official morality and the nobiliary code of honor. I argue that the mutilated and tortured bodies displayed in *Desengaños* represent the monstrous real of the aristocratic social body hidden behind baroque fantasies of genealogical integrity and blood purity (*pureza de sangre*).

Chapter 4 surveys myths of national origin and religious integrity in the work of Renaissance historiographers to reevaluate their political and cultural legacy within and beyond imperial Spain. These propagandistic notions inform the protoromantic writings of seventeenth-century theologian Cristóbal Lozano, especially his reelaboration of the legends associated with the fall of Spain in *El rey don Rodrigo* (King don Rodrigo) and *La cueva de Hércules* (The Cave of Hercules [1667]). Lozano's baroque vision of the Christian nation as a closed space threatened by ancient shadows and alien terrorists is evocative of the paranoid imagery of horror fiction and the familiar discourse of nationalist politics.[3] *La cueva de Hércules* anticipates Victorian horror fantasies in exposing repressed individual and societal fears while displacing them into landscapes of abjection inhabited by ancestral monsters and alien enemies. By contrast, other paths of baroque fantasy, especially the experimental tales of Miguel de Cervantes and María de Zayas, put the spotlight on the monsters in the mirror.

3. I have borrowed the notion of the "closed space" from Manuel Aguirre's compelling book *The Closed Space: Horror Literature and Western Symbolism.*

Introduction: A Taste for the Macabre in the Age of Curiosities

Body Works, Then and Now

Since the first public showings of plastinated corpses in Japan and Germany in the mid-1990s, audiences the world over have flocked to the controversial exhibits of German anatomist Gunther von Hagens. According to some estimates, von Hagens' galleries of artificially manipulated cadavers have attracted tens of millions of spectators to make his Body Worlds collection the most successful scientific exhibition ever. Arguably, Body Worlds owes some of its popularity to the self-consciously eccentric personality of its creator, known within German and British media circles as "Dr. Death" or "Dr. Frankenstein." Von Hagens himself has invited a certain degree of personality cult and media attention with his adoption of the public image of the rebel artist, reminiscent of famous German artist-performer Joseph Beuys, and with his spectacular publicity stunts. His much-talked-about 2002 public autopsy took place in a London art gallery in front of television cameras and a paying audience, despite warnings from British officials that the dissection was illegal.[1] On a separate occasion, the anatomist "sent the corpse of a pregnant woman—her torso cut open to reveal the fetus—on a bus ride around

1. The NewScientist.com reported the event: "Under the gaze of a 300-strong audience and a battery of TV cameras, the UK's first public post mortem examination for 170 years took place on Wednesday night [. . .] The public autopsy had been justified by von Hagens as demystifying the post mortem examination, which anyone might have to sanction for a dead relative. He likened the medical profession to medieval priests who would not allow ordinary people to read the Bible [. . .] But many doctors criticized the show as a publicity stunt designed to raise von Hagens' profile, rather than that of anatomy. Harold Ellis, an anatomist at Guy's Hospital Medical School, London, left half-way through in disgust: 'I think he is a charlatan. It looked like a butcher's shop'" (November 21, 2002).

Berlin to promote 'Body Worlds'" (*Chicago Tribune*, July 31, 2005). Von Hagens openly admits to embracing sensationalism as a marketing tool: "I need and enjoy sensationalism, because sensationalism means curiosity . . . and this curiosity brings people to museums" (quoted in the *Chicago Tribune*, July 31, 2005). Many theologians and members of the medical, academic, and media communities view this sensationalism as a regrettable trademark of the Body Worlds exhibitions. In their eyes, von Hagens' collection of plastinated cadavers amounts to little more than a thinly disguised "freak show" or "atracción de feria" (Juan Antonio Ramírez) that debases the dead and profits from the lower and darker human passions. While Body Worlds continues to stir emotions ranging from outrage to fascination, much of the criticism springs from the notion that the display of beautified corpses promotes morbid curiosity.[2]

In his contribution to the catalog of the exhibition, von Hagens takes painstaking steps to connect his dissecting practices with the anatomical studies of Leonardo Da Vinci (1452–1519) and anatomist Andreas Vesalius (1514–64) and with the early modern tradition of public autopsies, which are often described as macabre spectacles unfolding in front of crowds of curious spectators in the so-called theaters of anatomy.[3] Media studies scholar José van Dijck explains the intense appeal of these messy performances, which had

2. As Juan Antonio Ramírez writes in *Corpus Solus*, "Parece que su destino es recorrer el mundo entero, como una especie de parque temático itinerante, de explotación indefinida, hasta que pierda interés morboso entre las masas la exhibición exhibicionista del interior corporal, que es la verdadera substancia del fenómeno que nos ocupa [. . .] Es escandaloso, han dicho muchos, o sumamente desagradable, que se exhiban como en una atracción de feria los cadáveres de seres humanos" (191) (It seems that its destiny is to travel the world as a kind of itinerant theme park of indefinite exploitation until such day when the masses will no longer show morbid interest in the exhibitionist exhibition of the interior of the body, which is the true substance of the phenomenon in question [. . .] It is scandalous, many have said, or supremely revolting, that human cadavers should be exhibited as attractions at the fair). Columnist Laura Cummings gets to the heart of the question when she attributes the success of Bodyworlds to its macabre sensationalism: "If Hagens simply showed his flayed corpses as corpses, flat on a bier, his show would hardly have been a sell-out [. . .] The wonders of human anatomy would still be available for all to see, but there would be no theatre to the spectacle. A pregnant corpse, her womb opened to reveal the dead foetus within, is more or less pure data—rather like Leonardo's anatomical drawing of the same. But manipulated into the carefree pose of a reclining dolly-bird she becomes a kind of poster image for Hagens's cabaret of corpses" (*Observer*, March 24, 2002).

3. See Richardson, especially chapter 2.

very limited educational value for anyone other than the anatomist himself: "The naked realism of dead bodies on the dissection table, combined with the public knowledge of their criminal pasts, provided a mesmerizing spectacle for a large audience who paid a substantial fee to attend these anatomy lessons" (van Dijck 103). For his part, the creator of Body Worlds credits the work of Vesalius and the sixteenth-century theaters of anatomy with having "pulled the dead out of their graves and put them back into society" (von Hagens 13). He also mentions the preservation work of Dutch artist-anatomist Frederick Ruysch (1638–1731).

Ruysch's collections of anatomical curiosities (skeletons and embalmed fetuses and body parts embellished with clothes and flowers) are among the earliest examples of anatomical art in line with von Hagens' own work (see Illustration 1). In an age in which the human body was the subject of much investigation, the public was fascinated with dissected corpses, which would begin to be displayed for their eyes in aesthetic poses. As artists and the curious public sought to access "the naked truth" hidden beneath the surface of the body, they could now see for themselves (aut-opsy) in anatomical theaters, museums of curiosities, and illustrations (von Hagens 15).

In the review essay "When Death Goes on Display," the dean of the Lutheran Church of Mannheim warns that the right to see bodies can easily be perverted in social settings in which voyeurism permeates our public life. Fischer hints at sexual exploitation when he states that at Body Worlds "the line separating a free, natural attitude towards the body from prostitution becomes very thin" (Fischer 234). In his view, the success of von Hagens' exhibits of peeled off corpses is comparable to the mass appeal of tabloid journalism, sexually explicit talk shows, and other sensationalist and graphic products of the media culture in our "society of gawkers, onlookers, and of curious people who want to dig up all of the intimate details" (Fischer 234–35).

These issues and questions raised by the debates surrounding the manipulation and exhibition of cadavers (especially the emphasis on the sensationalism of the media culture and the public's curiosity for the odd, the hidden, and the freakish) resonate in familiar tones with scholars working in the early modern period, from historians of art, science, and religion to specialists in European literature and culture. After all, the age of discovery and exploration could just as well be known as the age of curiosity or curiosities, depending on whether we focus on the emerging social type of "the curious" or on the material objects that crowd the famous cabinets of curiosities or *Wunderkammern*, which are characteristic of the period. Curious subjects and ob-

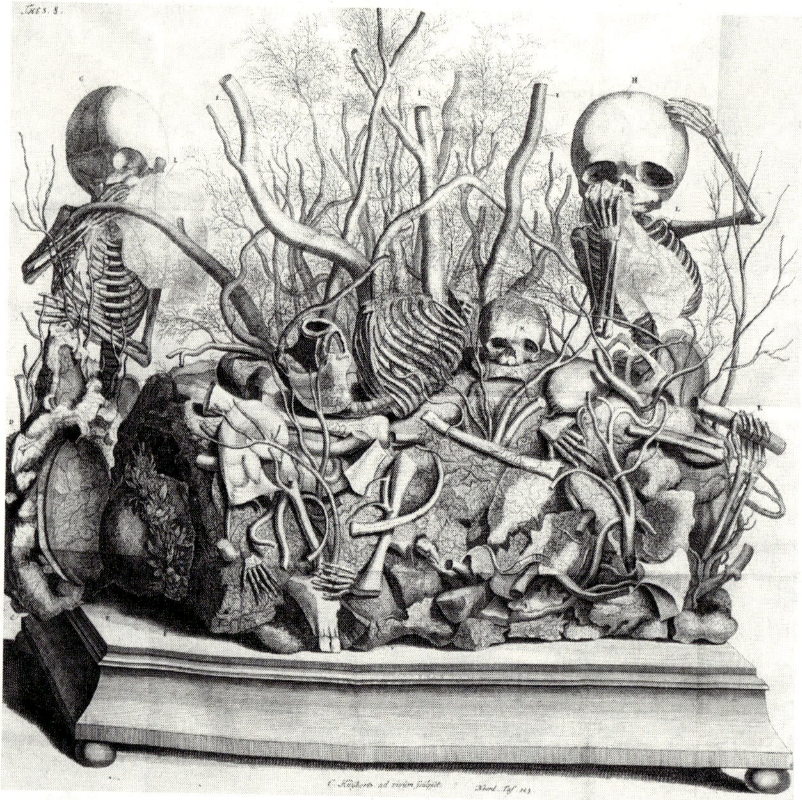

Illustration 1. Engraving reproduction of an anatomical diorama by Frederick Ruysch, "drawn from life" by Cornelius Huyberts. (Image from the Zymoglyphic Museum.)

jects are metonymically bound together at a time when curiosity is taken to be a mark of good taste and refinement.

According to seventeenth-century philosopher Baltasar Gracián, the true men of excellence are those "bizarre subjects" (*sujetos bizarros*) who command the fascinated attention of others.[4] The word *bizarro,* which was once associated with negative moral qualities (ire and a hot or volatile temper), is used in the seventeenth century by authors such as Baltasar Gracián and Luis de Góngora, and also in the context of the theater, to describe curious or peculiar appearance and behavior explicitly aimed at attracting the attention of the public. Paraphrasing Gracián, we could say that those who aspire to shine

4. See *El discreto* and *El héroe.*

in the courtly "theaters of heroism" or "theaters of reputation" (Gracián alternates expressions) must surround themselves with rare, awe-inspiring objects and equally fascinating personalities.[5] While the Jesuit's frame of reference is the Spanish court of the 1600s in which ostentation literally rules the land, his reflections on the functioning of the baroque "theaters of reputation" have found currency in our own postmodern worldly theaters.[6] Thus, an English edition of his *Oráculo manual* conveniently repackaged as a "how to" manual for power executives (*The Art of Worldly Wisdom*) surprisingly made it onto one of the *New York Times* best-seller lists in the 1990s, suggesting perhaps that in matters of fame, political maneuvering, and manipulation of the public, the more things change, the more they stay the same (Spadaccini and Talens).

Cultural historians have pointed out that in the sixteenth and seventeenth centuries, and into the first part of the eighteenth century, the term *curiosity* was at the heart of a series of battles for control of knowledge and behavior across the cultural spectrum. The curiosity culture wars involved traditional subject-oriented meanings, as in Cervantes' "The Curious Impertinent," as well as newer object-oriented uses, as in cabinets of curiosities and printed miscellanies such as Antonio de Torquemada's *Garden of Curious Flowers* and Julián de Medrano's *Curious Silva*. Neil Kenny has put it most succinctly in his recent book on the subject: "[C]uriosity became a key battleground for attempts to distinguish between not only good and bad desire, but also between good and bad objects of desire" (Kenny 5). According to Kenny, the curiosity debates affected neighboring concepts, including wonder, rarity, novelty, difficulty, experiment, and desire for knowledge, and involved naturalists, antiquarians, artists, authors, and commercial publishers, as well as official cultural and religious institutions, from the university to the Jesuit schools and the Church.

To be sure, the echoes of the Augustinian view of curiosity as flesh-

5. As Barbara Benedict writes apropos this early modern fascination with curiosities, "[c]urious texts and displays thus both enhance and shape the reader's power, status, and social value. By watching or reading them, audiences entered the rarefied world of the curiosity-maker: their own interest confers value on the curiosities they witness, as these curiosities, once witnessed, reciprocally raise their status" (43).

6. The late Hapsburgs and their "men of reputation" are under constant pressure to serve up crowd-pleasing novelties, spectacular theatrical performances, religious and secular celebrations, and other forms of entertainment. Cervantes alludes ironically to this situation in several works, including *El retablo de las maravillas* and *El licenciado vidriera* (see my article "Clarividencia tangencial y excentricidad en *El licenciado vidriera:* nueva interpretación de un motivo clásico").

bound, theologically blind yearning resonate as strongly as ever in religious discourse, morality tales, and satires. But by the late sixteenth century, curiosity is also seen, in some quarters, as a healthy passion that may produce legitimate pleasure, even admirable knowledge. The trick now is to distinguish these positive aspects of curiosity from the dangers of *excessive wonder* (Descartes' *Passions of the Soul;* also Bacon's *Novum Organum*); incontinent or impertinent fixations (as in Cervantes' "The Curious Impertinent"); and transgressive passions of inquiry, which are typically associated with female curiosity. Negative views of curiosity are often incorporated into moralistic narratives that discourage the public, especially women, from seeking forbidden knowledge or engaging in transgressive behavior.[7]

We can find a good example of the concern with transgressive "feminine curiosity" in *La pícara Justina,* attributed to Francisco López de Ubeda. The *pícara-narrator,* a self-proclaimed free woman (*mujer libre*), focuses on her role as *curious observer* in describing the circumstances surrounding her own participation in the religious festivities of the city of León: "Por mí digo que esto de *ver cosas curiosas y con curiosidad* es para mí manjar del alma, y, por tanto, les quiero contar, muy de espacio, no tanto lo que vi en León, cuanto el modo con que lo vi" (322) (For my part I say that observing *curious things with curiosity* is for me food for the soul, and this is why I want to tell you, in great detail, not so much what I saw, but rather the way I saw it [my emphasis]). Significantly, the masculine voice of the author bursts into the text to compare Justina's *curious gaze* with the venom of the spider: "[C]omo arañas, que de la flor sacan veneno, y así, Justina, de las fiestas santas no se aprovecha sino para decir malicias impertinentes" (247) (Like spiders, which extract venom from the flower, Justina does not profit from the sacred celebrations, if not to make impertinent and malicious remarks). The type of venomous curiosity that the author attributes to free women, and in general to "ill-intentioned people" ("personas malintencionadas," 247), is viewed as a perversion of the gaze that results not from blindness but rather from piercing insight: "[Justina] no mira cosa / que no penetre" ([Justina] does not set her gaze on anything / that she does not penetrate).[8] This view is consistent with

7. As Kenny writes: "Curiosity was also widely used in narratives to discourage women from trying to know certain things, to try and make them behave in certain ways, or simply to force them to accept a humbling image of themselves" (384).

8. Elsewhere I linked Justina's curious way of seeing ("mirada curiosa") to the "curious perspective" in anamorphic compositions of the sixteenth and seventeenth centuries. See chapter 3 of *(A)wry Views: Anamorphosis, Cervantes and the Early Picaresque.*

Cesare Ripa's iconic image of Curiosity or Curiosità in *Iconología* (1611) as a menacingly alert wild-haired woman endowed with wings. Ripa links curiosity to sharp sight and the desire to seek forbidden knowledge: "[C]uriosity is the unbridled desire of those who seek to know more than they should" (quoted by Benedict 25).

In the eyes of seventeenth-century moralists and conservative social thinkers, such as Cesare Ripa and the author of *La pícara Justina*, curiosity is an essentially feminine passion that threatens the moral and social order. As Barbara Benedict notes, "Curiosity at the start of the seventeenth century was considered an impulse that was thrillingly if threateningly out of control. Unlicensed, undirected, and spontaneous, it seemed to many writers and social thinkers to resemble the madness of the Furies or the hubris of Eve. They often portrayed curiosity as feminine because it was illegitimate, a force that operated outside the world of law and order" (25). The moralists' preoccupation with the dangers of "feminine curiosity" would find continuity in the eighteenth and nineteenth centuries, explicitly converging with female lust.[9] As the early modern period wore on, a sense of "public reason" would become essential in allowing the cultural elite to define the properly masculine and self-restrained uses of curiosity (morally edifying, rational, empirical, scientific, educational) and to distinguish them from the lower passions of the flesh and the mob's (*vulgo*) cravings for sensational oddities.

In the context of Counter-Reformation culture, curiosity is often used to spice up doctrinal lessons and to promote the internalization of moral principles. In Spain and its American colonies, priests and teachers incorporated natural and man-made curiosities in ritual celebrations and pedagogical discourse in order to inspire wonder and awe. According to Maravall, the mobilizing of "irrational drives" (*resortes irracionales*) is characteristic of Counter-Reformation discourse and defines the mass-oriented "culture of the baroque" (*cultura dirigida del barroco*).[10] Indeed, mass-oriented religious spectacles, such as baroque sermons, are carefully crafted to manufacture emotions ranging from astonishment and wonder to suspense and terror. The tradition of the theatrical sermon goes back to Fray Luis de Granada (*Ecclesiasticae Rethoricae* [1576]) and his followers. Gwendolyn Barnes-Karol has studied the spectacular aspects of Counter-Reformation culture, especially

9. As Benedict writes: "Eighteenth-century denigration of women's inquiry into forbidden areas receive parallel treatment in nineteenth-century literature. Victorian poems and novels usually condemn female curiosity as sexual appetite" (250).

10. See especially Maravall's *La cultura del barroco*.

the sermon, in seventeenth-century Iberia. She notes that some preachers converted temples into awe-inspiring theaters in which religious paraphernalia, actual human remains, and other curiosities were displayed on cue to heighten the emotional effect of the performance.[11]

In Protestant Europe, some theologians called for a curiosity devoid of wonder,[12] but wonder and curiosity remained closely linked in Lutheran as well as Catholic contexts throughout the 1600s and well into the eighteenth century, especially in miscellanies and cabinets of curiosities. Lorraine Daston and Katherine Park have traced the history of wonder and curiosity in medieval and early modern thought from the patristic warnings against curiosity (which was viewed as a lustful, blind, and incontinent passion that had nothing to do with proper contemplative wonder) to the modern privileging of scientific inquiry (rational, experimental curiosity) over the sensationalist displaying of oddities, which is characteristic of the material culture of the early modern age. They have shown that wonder, horror, and curiosity were closely linked emotions in the sixteenth and seventeenth centuries: "Wonder has its own history, one tightly bound up with the history of other cognitive passions such as horror and curiosity—passions that also traditionally shaped and guided inquiry into the natural world [. . .] Wonder fused with fear (for example, at a monstrous birth taken as a portent of divine wrath) was akin but not identical to wonder fused with pleasure (at the same monstrous birth displayed in a *Wunderkammer*). In the High Middle Ages wonder existed apart from curiosity; in the sixteenth and seventeenth centuries, wonder and curiosity interlocked" (Daston and Park 15).

These reflections on the cultural history of curiosity and wonder and their convergence in the early modern period shed some new light on the Body Worlds polemics. Much of the criticism that is currently directed against the exhibition of plastinated cadavers focuses on its blurring of the

---

11. Gwendolyn Barnes-Karol has made this point very effectively: "As the seventeenth century progressed, many preachers became masters of theatricality and learned to heighten the dramatic appeal of their persons and the sermon settings [. . .] Terror was routinely produced through the timely display of crucifixes or actual skulls and bones. Astonishment was produced through creative special effects such as the release of white doves adorned with tinsel at a particularly climactic moment" (Barnes-Karol 56–57; see also Sebastián Medrano 188).

12. As Kenny states, "the alignment of curiosity with wonders ran counter to the preference expressed by some Lutheran philosophers for curiosity over wonders, motivated by a suspicion of wonder as redolent of superstitious Catholic miracles" (Kenny 220).

boundaries between proper scientific inquiry and thrill-seeking curiosity and also on the confusion between the natural (God given) wonders of the human body and the artistic ambitions of the show's creator. Hence, the exhibits of plastinated organs have not elicited nearly as much criticism as the aesthetically arranged whole-body displays. Even Lutheran theologian Ulrich Fischer (a relentless critic of Body Worlds) feels compelled to admit that "certain exhibits were extremely informative on a scientific level, such as the lungs of the smoker and the plastinated nervous and circulatory systems" (Fischer 234). In fact, the tar-covered lungs and other samples of self-inflicted physical degeneration exhibited in Body Worlds, from liver disease caused by alcoholism, to enlargements of the spleen, to ulcers and arteriosclerosis, seem closer to the nineteenth-century realist-moralist tradition of anatomical collections than to the artistic anatomical displays of the early modern period. By contrast, the whole-body plastinates are "at least as determined by artistic conventions as by scientific insights" (van Dijck 114).[13]

Significantly, the creator of the exhibition and his supporters in the scientific and philosophical communities have worked hard to distance the "enlightened" Body Worlds project from the "superstitious" preservation of relics and the use of human bodies for artistic, decorative, or symbolic purposes, even as they invoke the work of early modern anatomical artists as worthy predecessors of von Hagens' work. One example of the latter would be Frederick Ruysch's baroque displays of beautified and clothed fetuses and body parts adorned with flowers (see Illustration 1).

Philosopher Franz Josef Wetz provides a good illustration of this paradoxical gesture in his review essay "The Dignity of Man," which is included in the catalog of Body Worlds. Wetz explains that the plastination of cadavers is in the tradition of anatomy that "blossomed for the first time in the Renaissance, and entered into an alliance with art" (Wetz 254). He suggests that von Hagens goes beyond his sixteenth-century predecessors in fusing anatomy and art by "basing the shape of many of his whole-body specimens on paintings and sculptures" (Wetz 254). He notes that the exhibition titled "The Runner" was modeled after the work of futurist painter Umberto Boccioni, while the organic composition "The Drawer Man" was inspired by Salvador Dalí's "Anthropomorphic Cupboard." Other examples of body exhibits arranged to look like works of art include "The Fencer," which is based

13. In the words of Ulrich Fischer, "whole-body exhibits left no room for doubt that von Hagens' artistic ambitions had displaced the interests of scientific enlightenment" (Fischer 234).

on the surrealist erotic pictures of graphic artist Hans Bellmer, and "The Muscle Man" holding his own skin, which evokes the famous rendition of Saint Bartholomew by Michelangelo in the Sistine Chapel.[14] While Wetz is happy to play up the Renaissance connection and has no problem in praising von Hagens for his fusing of art and anatomy, he is also very careful to separate the "enlightened" anatomy art exhibited at Body Worlds, not only from traditional relics (this after all would be expected), but also from such displays as the elaborate decorations of the crypt of the Capuchin Church of Via Veneto in Rome, which were made with human remains (Illustration 2). I see a familiar "modern anxiety" in the overstating of the boundaries between the scientifically instructive specimens exhibited in the Body Worlds galleries and the perceived capriciousness of the displays of human remains in the Roman Capuchin temple, which, according to the German philosopher, "did not fulfill any rationally comprehensible end" (Wetz 255).[15]

This distinction between modern scientific inquiry and premodern, capricious or irrational curiosity informs some scholarly accounts of the evolution of knowledge in the early modern period. According to Krzysztof Pomian, for example, "curiosity was an interregnum between the reigns of theology and science" (quoted by Kenny 165). Pomian's assumption is that the progress of science eventually replaced curiosity. For his part, Kenny argues against Pomian's model and other "grand narratives" (his expression) that tend to overstate the boundaries between science and curiosity. He notes that

---

14. "The Muscle Man" was placed alongside an enlarged reproduction of a Vesalius drawing in the Mannheim exhibition, suggesting an explicit connection between Vesalius' anatomical illustration and von Hagens' organic sculpture (see van Dijck 115). Ramírez noted that this emblematic image of the Body Worlds project is actually adopted from an illustration included in Valverde de Amusco's *Historia de la composición del cuerpo humano* (1556). In effect, the position of the limbs and the placement of the skin in relation to the body seem to have been closely modeled after the illustration in Amusco's volume, even if von Hagens makes no mention of the work of the Spanish anatomist.

15. "To what extent does a plastinated specimen differ from these?" asks the German philosopher. His confusing response to the question shows that the key to shielding the exhibition from familiar charges hinges on a narrowly defined view of education: "these products made from human remains were truly only in fact a means to an end (even though they did not fulfill any rationally comprehensible end). Above all, however, they depicted something that was not human [. . .] Plastinated whole-body specimens such as Gunther von Hagens offers to the public depict the human organism as such in order to educate the individual observer about the inside of his body" (Wetz 255).

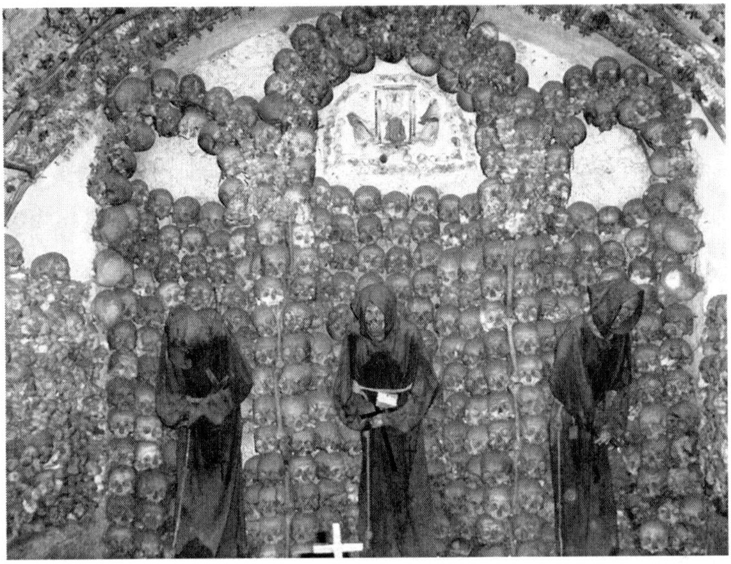

Illustration 2. Crypt of Santa Maria della Concezione dei Cappuccini (Rome). (Image from Wikimedia Commons.)

science "does still include curiosity after all, only now shorn of its object-oriented senses and of its collecting connotations" (Kenny 165). Kenny is especially critical of scholarly approaches that denigrate the sensationalist connotations of curiosity in favor of seemingly more respectable, rational, and scientific forms of inquiry.[16]

Indeed, the perceived need to separate the products of modern science from those associated with irrational curiosity may speak more about the rhetoric and posturing of the Enlightenment, and about our own scholarly biases and blind spots, than about the passions of inquiry of the early modern period or the extraordinary fascination that von Hagens' anatomical displays have elicited in our own time. Significantly, while the creator of Body Worlds insists that plastination is "the most *modern*, lasting, and vivid means of pre-

16. As he notes apropos Daxelmüller's study of curiosity in early modern German universities and learned societies, the privileging of curiosity in the subject-oriented sense over its object-oriented meanings often results in interpretative models that end up "denigrating some of the 'curiosity' family's connotations (such as 'odd,' 'sensational') as degenerate offspring of its supposedly 'true' connotations (such as 'rational,' 'empirical,' 'experimental')" (Kenny 166).

serving specimens of the human body *for educational purposes*" (von Hagens 38; my emphasis), he also recognizes that the tremendous appeal of his anatomy art has more to do with the fascinating authenticity of the cadavers than with the public's appreciation of the technical handiwork of the anatomist or the scientifically instructive potential of the exhibits: "The realism of the specimens contributes greatly to the fascination and power of the exhibition. Particularly in today's media-oriented world, a world in which we increasingly obtain our information indirectly, people have retained a keen sense for the fact that a copy has always been intellectually 'pre-chewed', and as such is always an interpretation. In this respect, the 'Anatomy Art' exhibition satisfies a tremendous human need for unadulterated authenticity" (von Hagens 36).

The irony is that the appealing "realism" and "unadulterated authenticity" of the exhibits are achieved through artificial techniques of manipulation of the bodies and careful imitation of preexisting works of art. At least in this sense, Body Worlds has something in common with other products of the entertainment industry that trade in prepackaged authenticity. The tourist industry, for instance, manufactures "unadulterated authenticity" for crowds of consumers who yearn for an "authentic" encounter with primal nature, albeit a safe and controlled encounter, and for "authentic" cultural experiences through staged participation in native rituals. Some Mexican resorts, for example, have created their own Disney-style theme parks, such as Cancún's Mexico Mágico, in order to display "authentic Mexicanness" for legions of U.S. tourists.[17] Reality TV works on the same premise. As showbiz exposés have revealed, the "authenticity" of reality TV is often staged. Thus, "authentic" contact situations and seemingly natural dialogues are artificially

---

17. Daniel Cooper Alarcón studies the careful staging of "authentic native rituals" and generally speaking "Mexicanness" in Cancún and other tourist sites. As he writes, "a less subtle response to staging Mexicanness has been the creation of Disney-type theme parks within the tourist parks themselves: Cancún now boasts a Mexican theme park called México Mágico" (Cooper Alarcón 174). He concludes that "the greatest tourist construct of all time is [. . .] the concept of authenticity" (169). Interestingly, when confronted with the criticism that Body Worlds might become a kind of Disney World for the masses, von Hagens expresses admiration for Walt Disney's vision, although he insists that Body Worlds educates as much as it entertains (see Ramírez 194–95). For his part, Juan Antonio Ramírez argues that while one might indeed learn a great deal from the display of dissected cadavers in Body Worlds, it seems obvious that most spectators attend the exhibition for its entertainment potential (Ramírez 194).

spiced up to satisfy the public's voyeuristic hunger for intimate secrets. Plainly stated, in the context of the mass-oriented entertainment industry, whether we are talking about tourist resorts or reality TV, Disney World or Body Worlds, "unadulterated authenticity" is, in fact, an effect produced by the simulacrum.[18]

It could be argued that the distinction between fake and authentic has become effectively pointless in our postmodern *culture of the copy* (Schwarz), which continues to produce pastiche after pastiche, endless imitations of imitations.[19] But it is not simply a matter of replication; rather, the order of the

---

18. Baudrillard quotes from *Ecclesiastes:* "The simulacrum is never that which conceals the truth—it is the truth which conceals that there is none. The simulacrum is true" (1).

19. In *Neo-Baroque: A Sign of the Times* (1992), Omar Calabrese reviewed the use of the term *postmodern* in philosophical contexts as well as in the fields of literature, cinema, architecture, and design. He concluded that the term is too vague and equivocal to hold true interpretive value. As he writes, "The first, essentially American, use of the term dates from the 1960s, when it referred to literature and cinema. In this context it simply meant that certain literary products existed that did not base themselves on experimentation (conceived as 'modernism') but on reelaboration, pastiche, and the deconstruction of the immediately preceding literary (or cinematic) heritage. The second cultural context is strictly philosophical and refers to the well-known work by Jean-Francois Lyotard, *The Postmodern Condition,* originally no more than a report prepared for Quebec's Council of State dealing with advanced Western societies and the development of knowledge within them. The adjective 'postmodern' was explicitly picked up by American sociologists during the 1960s, when it was adopted as a concept and reformulated into an original philosophical notion. Lyotard himself writes: 'It describes the state of a culture after transformations undergone in the rules governing science, literature, and the arts since the end of the nineteenth century. These transformations will here be related to the crisis in narrations [. . .] Simplifying to the greatest possible extent, we can consider as 'postmodern' our incredulity when faced by metanarrations.' The third and final context is that of architecture and design. In this field the term has achieved success primarily in Italy and the United States [. . .] In this sector 'postmodern' begins to take on a precise ideological meaning, representing the revolt against the principles of functionalism and rationalism that characterized the Modern Movement. As we can see, although a link between the three cultural contexts clearly exists, it is extremely tenuous [. . .] The term 'postmodern,' in short, continues to be equivocal. For many people, in fact, it has taken the place of a genuine program or manifesto, whereas, according to Lyotard, it was intended to be a criterion for analysis. For many other people it has become a classificatory reference point, under whose banner movements and '-isms' such as the Transvanguardia, neo-expressionism, neo-futurism,

simulacrum works at the level of substitution and erasure.[20] In this sense, von Hagens' anatomy art would seem to close the circle of the culture of the copy by reenacting the interchangeability of copy and original at the level of the flesh. As van Dijck cogently writes, "Whereas before, we wanted the artificial object to look like a real one, we have now entered an era in which we want the real object to look like 'perfected nature' [. . .] The preference for a manipulable body perfectly fits a material, technological culture in which imitation has been replaced by modification. Just like the tulip, the body has become a mixture of organic matter and artifice" (van Dijck 99–100).

Not surprisingly, van Dijck draws an explicit connection between what she sees as von Hagens' "postmodern" free-play with inanimate human bodies and Katherine Hayles' conceptualization of the culture of the posthuman: "The artist-anatomist's plastinated cadavers seem exemplary of a culture that is 'inhabited by posthumans who regard their bodies as fashion accessories'" (van Dijck 125). As we can see, the temptation here is to overstate the historical distinctiveness of our present "end-point of humanist culture," which would have finally and irrevocably erased the distinction between being and

---

and so on have gathered. But is a generic program (a reaction against modernism) sufficient to define such complex groups of artistic, scientific, and social phenomena as those existing today? And is it enough to declare the end of the avant-garde and experimentalism as the characteristic of so-called postmodern objects?" (Calabrese 14). Calabrese proposes the term *neo-baroque* to designate the current taste for what he calls "baroque degeneration," which is grounded on an aesthetic of repetition and replication. Within the field of Hispanic studies, several scholars have also embraced the term *neo-baroque,* albeit from a different perspective informed by postcolonial theory and Severo Sarduy's conceptualization of the baroque. As Mabel Moraña has recently explained: "Severo Sarduy acknowledged in his definition of the Baroque, that in this style, author and work are refunctionalized. In the process of de-auratization of art, the copy (which has been seen as one of the characteristic procedures present in the formation of neocolonial imaginaries) is not inferior to the original, but is rather situated in its own self-supporting epistemological space. The Neobaroque is not, in this sense, a creative art, but an art of citation. Recycling, pastiche, fragmentation, and simulacrum intervene the territory of cultural and historical memory, and reactivate it in combinations that are, at the same time, evocative and parodic" (253).

20. As Baudrillard states, "It is no longer a question of imitation, not of reduplication, not even of parody. It is rather a question of substituting signs of the real for the real itself, [. . .] [a] perfect descriptive machine which provides all the signs of the real and short-circuits its vicissitudes" (2).

appearance, effectively taking metaphysics with it,[21] while dismissing earlier reflections on the confusion of boundaries between nature and artifice as mere rhetorical, allegorical, or ritual gestures designed to redirect our gaze toward the spiritual truth behind worldly deceptions.[22]

By contrast, I would argue that humans were reflecting on the problematic status of the boundaries between art(ifice) and nature, and indeed regarding their bodies as fashion accessories, long before the recent proclamation of our postmodern and posthuman conditions. A case in point is Baltasar Gracián's powerful defense of perfected nature in *El criticón:* "Es el arte complemento de la naturaleza y un otro segundo ser que por extremo la hermosea y aún pretende excederla en sus obras. Préciase de haber añadido un otro mundo artificial al primero. Suple de ordinario los descuidos de la naturaleza, perfeccionándola en todo, que sin este socorro del artificio, quedará inculta y grosera" (*El criticón* I, 8) (Art is the complement of nature, a second being that embellishes it in the extreme, and it even aims to surpass it in its works. It has proudly added another artificial world to the first one. It ordinarily covers the mistakes of nature, perfecting it in such a way that without this aid of the artifice, it [nature] would remain unrefined and vulgar). *El criticón* is in fact a secular allegory of human life conceived as a journey of technological tooling. Along the way, human nature is carefully perfected with prosthetic accessories to ensure worldly success in the baroque "theaters of reputation."

Hence, William Childers thinks of Gracián as the "theorist of the baroque public sphere," a hyperreal realm (if we can borrow Baudrillard's notion) in which performance and "the epistemology of rumor" effectively

21. As Baudrillard writes apropos Borges' well-known cartographic allegory of simulation, "it is no longer a question of either maps or territory. Something has disappeared: the sovereign difference between them [. . .] With it goes all of metaphysics. No more mirror of being and appearances, of the real and its concept. No more imaginary coextensivity: rather, genetic miniaturization in the dimension of simulation [. . .] the age of simulation thus begins with a liquidation of all referentials" (2).

22. As van Dijck writes, "Plastination is a symptom of postmodern culture, just as Frederick Ruysch's anatomical objects were a symptom of Vanitas art [. . .] Cadavers have become amalgams of flesh and technology, bodies that are endlessly pliable, and forever manipulable, even after death. Bodies, like tulips, are no longer either real or fake, because such categories have ceased to be distinctive" (van Dijck 125).

erase the distinction between reality and appearance.[23] Childers speaks against scholarly views that overstate the boundaries between baroque, enlightened, and postenlightened forms of communication in arguing that the baroque is "a kind of modernity—a modernity, moreover, that was always in some respects present beneath the surface of bourgeois culture" (Childers, "The Baroque" 182). He notes that, in the context of the baroque public sphere, social identities (even religious identity) are partly predetermined by birth and partly negotiated through performance, publicity, and rumor.[24] In effect, artifice, performance, and rumor played crucial roles in the social processes of communication and identity negotiation in the baroque period, well beyond the relatively small aristocratic circles of the court. This may explain the recent interest in the work of Gracián in our own age of instant communication and virtual selves. The 1992 appearance of *The Art of Worldly Wisdom* on the *New York Times* best-seller list is striking evidence of the lasting appeal of the Jesuit's principles and recommendations in matters of self-construction and the pursuit of fame and material success through performance and the manipulation of the public.[25] While Gracián's moral philosophy is clearly tied to the aesthetics of baroque disillusion or *desengaño* and the ritualistic aspects of Counter-Reformation discourse, the echoes of his reflections on perfected nature, self-representation, and publicity are not lost in the culture of the posthuman.

Bradley Nelson has recently examined the Jesuit's oeuvre in light of Catherine Bell's work on ritual theory. In his view, the perceived contradiction between Gracián's distinctly modern rationalism and the "ritualistic residue" that permeates his writings can be transcended when we recognize

---

23. "The theorist par excellence of the baroque public sphere is Gracián, whose *Oráculo manual* brilliantly describes the functioning of self-interested reason in the context of theatricalized competition for status [. . .] The epistemology of rumor corresponds precisely to the flexible, evasive play of hiding and revealing that typifies communication in the baroque public sphere" (Childers 169–71). See also William Egginton's "Gracián and the Emergence of the Modern Subject."

24. "Religious identity in the Baroque—like other forms of identity—is partly predetermined by birth and partly negotiated in the public sphere. In this process of negotiation, as we have seen, individuals and groups can achieve a modicum of self-determination through performance. The constant presence of rumor, however, conditions the reception and interpretation of the identities to which they thereby lay claim. Thus the interplay of rumor and performance constitutes a crucial dynamic of baroque publicity" (180).

25. See my "Gracián and the Art of Public Representation."

that this baroque residue did not disappear in enlightened and postenlightened societies.[26] On the contrary, ritual practices are still at the heart of our experience of the world, from religious and secular celebrations, to displays of ethnic and national pride, to our choice of dress codes and body accessories. The (post)modern pressure to assert our uniqueness, while constantly shifting between idiosyncratic modes of behavior, dress codes, and hobbies, is fundamentally ritualistic in nature. As Slavoj Žižek has noted in *The Ticklish Subject*, the injunction to be our true self is paradoxically a call to wear the right mask. Thus, the current cult of extreme individualization may be seen as a paradigmatic form of baroque *horror vacui*, since "what is behind the mask is ultimately nothing, a horrifying void they [postmodern subjects] are frantically trying to fill in with their compulsive activity" (Žižek, *The Ticklish Subject* 373).[27]

From this perspective, one of the most fascinating aspects of the controversy surrounding the Body Worlds exhibitions is the revelation that despite the fundamental skepticism of postmodern culture and its famous proclamation/provocation that there is nothing beyond simulations, we are still passionately attached to the dream of authenticity, however contrived, pathetic, or horrifying this anticipated encounter with "the real thing" might actually be. It is perhaps in this anxious search for the impossible real (the authentic beyond simulations, the *numinous* beyond the moral and rational orders) that we can rediscover wonder, curiosity, and horror, not as cognitive passions of a preceding age but rather as our own passions of inquiry.[28] While Daston

26. Nelson writes, "Gracián's modernity does not emerge by disentangling it from the ritual residue of the Baroque; rather, ritualization is the only way we can approach the lessons that baroque culture holds for modernity [and, indeed, postmodernity]" (Nelson 80).

27. See also my "Horror (Vacui): The Baroque Condition."

28. In his classic study *The Idea of the Holy: An Inquiry into the Non-rational Factor in the Idea of the Divine and Its Relation to the Rational* (1923), Rudolf Otto coined the term *numinous* from the Latin *numen* to describe the human experience or feeling of the Absolute beyond the moral and rational dimensions of the Holy (see especially 1–40). This feeling of the numinous is marked by the dreadful or woeful fascination ("mysterium tremendum") that overpowers the soul in the presence of the awe-inspiring object. This is, of course, reminiscent of the Kantian notion of the sublime. As John Harvey explains in the translator's preface: "The word 'numinous' has been widely received as a happy contribution to the theological vocabulary, as standing for that aspect of deity which transcends or eludes comprehension in rational and ethical terms. But it is Otto's purpose to emphasize that this is an objective reality, not merely a subjective feeling in the mind; and he uses the word feeling [. . .]

and Park are right in noting that the proper "enlightened" attitude toward wonder and curiosities has been skepticism and indifference since the "anti-marvelous Enlightenment," it is also true that we need only browse through the stacks of popular reads and movies at supermarkets, video stores, and airport terminals (from outlandish and sensationalist tabloids, to horror and sci-fi novels and comics, to film and video game fantasies) to realize that "deep inside, beneath tasteful and respectable exteriors, we still crave wonders [. . .] we wait for the rare and the extraordinary to surprise our souls" (Daston and Park 368).

Juan Antonio Ramírez closes his discussion of von Hagens' anatomical theater in *Corpus Solus* by noting that besides making human bodies "transparent," the Body Worlds exhibits result in a totally unforeseen development, that is, a dramatic exposé of modern art and science: "la ciencia y el arte aparecen recíprocamente despellejados" (205) (science and art appear reciprocally peeled off). I would further suggest that our (post)modern shells are also peeled off in these "aut-opsies," allowing our craving for wonders and curiosities to show its "unenlightened" face.

The Monstrous Imagination

The first science museums of the sixteenth and seventeenth centuries were regarded as wonder chambers (*Wunderkammern*) and theaters of nature. These early modern cabinets of curiosities housed heterogeneous collections of singular and sensational objects, including eye-popping artistic and technological novelties such as anamorphic devices and automata, exotic animals and plants, rare books, fossils, and ethnographic oddities. At a time when collections of novelties and curiosities were emerging everywhere in Europe, in museums, art galleries, libraries, gardens, and grottos, a growing number of cultivated men acquired, stored, and exhibited knowledge through the possession and display of admirable objects of nature and art (Findlen).[29]

---

not as equivalent to emotion but as a form of awareness that is neither that of ordinary perceiving nor of ordinary conceiving" (xvi).

29. Findlen underscores the social function of collecting among the cultural elite: "Collecting, in short, had become an activity of choice among the social and educated elite. It filled their leisure hours and for some seemed to encompass every waking moment of their lives. Through the possession of objects, one physically acquired knowledge, and through their display, one symbolically acquired the honor and reputation that all men of learning cultivated" (3).

Collections and exhibitions of curiosities played an important role as aristocratic "theaters of reputation" (to use Gracián's telling expression) in which the social and cultural elites traded in honor and fame.[30] While private collectors would begin to put deformed human beings on display for the entertainment and amusement of the public, "human monsters" (as they were commonly referred to) were still feared in some cultural circles. In Counter-Reformation Spain, as in much of Europe, monstrous births were commonly seen as divine warnings against individual or communal sin and also as signs of ordained calamities or punishments to come.

The authors of printed news or *Relaciones de sucesos*, and those of the popular French *Canards*, often manipulated monsters and other prodigies for political purposes and anti-Turk propaganda. The following account of the birth of a monster in Turkey in 1624 may be considered a paradigmatic case of this type of news coverage in the seventeenth century: "En la cabeza tiene tres cuernos, debaxo la frente tres ojos resplandecientes como Estrellas, las narizes de sola una ventana, las orejas de asno, las piernas, y los pies, lo de atras adelante [. . .] Por los pies y piernas al reves, se manifiesta, la perdición del Estado Otomano [. . .] Conozcan los Principes christianos la ocasion que se les representa, de emplearse unidamente en daño del implacable enemigo comun, pues que su perdición viene declarada en semejante modo, del Cielo" (*Prodigioso suceso que en Ostraviza tierra de el Turco a sucedido este presente año de 1624*) (On the head he has three horns, under the forehead three eyes shining like stars, his nose has only one opening, [he has] the ears of an ass, his legs and feet are inverted [. . .] The inverted feet and legs announce the fall of the Ottoman State [. . .] May the Christian Princes recognize the opportunity they have to unite forces against our unforgiving enemy, since its fall has been prophesied in this way by the Heavens).

It is interesting that monstrous births could still be interpreted as signs of the divine will, even when the deformity of the monster was attributed to natural causes. A good example can be found in the *Relacion verdadera de un mõstruoso Niño, que en la Ciudad de Lisboa naciò a 14, del mes de Abril, Año 1628* (True account of [the birth of] a monstrous child who was born in the city of Lisbon on April 14 in the year 1628). The author of this *Relacion* explicitly cites "causas naturales" behind the birth of a monstrous child covered

30. As Barbara Benedict explains, "Like the cabinets of kings, these private cabinets proclaim their owners' power to reserve objects from circulatory exchange [. . .] This conversion of labor to entertaining display is corporalized in the carnivalesque exhibition of human curiosities" (10–11).

with shells in the city of Lisbon, while simultaneously suggesting possible supernatural interpretations of its meaning: "quiza para pronostico de muchos castigos que se nos aguardan, en pena de tantos y tan graves pecados con que los hombres a su hazedor tienen offendido è irritado; o quiza para pronostico de algunos bienes, que ha de hazer a la Christiandad" (perhaps to announce the punishments that await us for the many and grave sins with which mankind has offended and infuriated God; or perhaps to announce some favors which he plans to grant to Christianity).[31]

The popularity of monsters in news sources and pedagogical literature can be explained, at least in part, by their signifying flexibility, which makes it possible to convey political messages and moral lessons with exemplary effectiveness. But the early modern fascination with monstrosity was not always contained within the bounds of political propaganda and pedagogical discourse. Once devoid of prodigious signification, monsters could be seen as delightful oddities and spectacular manifestations of the glorious variety of God's creation. Hence, in the context of the culture of curiosities, monsters would become "sports of nature," as Daston and Park put it. In the eyes of private collectors, the appropriate reaction to nature's capricious "artwork" is not fear but curiosity and delight. In fact, by the time Antonio de Torquemada published *Jardín de flores curiosas* (1570) (Garden of Curious Flowers), fear of monsters could be considered evidence of superstitious ignorance or a lack of intellectual refinement, at least within some cultured circles: "[L]as monstruosidades que muchas veces se ven, y otras poco usadas, y otras de que no se tiene noticia, en los hombres sabios no han de causar alteración, ni hacerles parecer que tienen causa de espantarse" (Torquemada 106) (The monstrosities that are frequently seen, and others that are rare, and those of which we have no knowledge, must not cause alteration among cultured men, and neither should they be taken as a cause for fear).

This emerging view of monsters as collectable objects of curiosity coincides with the Renaissance revival of Pliny, which would provide a viable alternative to classic Aristotelian and patristic conceptions of nature. Beyond and against the traditional focus on universal categories, Pliny's attention to natural singularities would provide justification for the early modern craving for collectible oddities. Even Aristotelian thought would undergo a series of transformations that made it considerably more accommodating of singular-

31. For more on the *Relaciones de sucesos*, see Redondo's "Les 'relaciones de sucesos.'" See also García de Enterría's *Catálogo de los pliegos poéticos españoles.*

ity.[32] As exceptional (but thoroughly natural) phenomena that went against the known order of nature, monstrous births, hermaphrodites, and other "monstrosities" defied explanation and could potentially undermine the validity of universal axioms and categories. The exceptionality of monsters could lead to a further questioning of norms and social hierarchies, insofar as the social order was grounded on the perceived natural order. Thus, the "monster" could be seen as material evidence or living proof of the inadequacy of inherited knowledge and social structures.

According to Omar Calabrese, the suspension or annulment of categories is the defining characteristic of modern teratology. As he argues in *Neo-Baroque: A Sign of the Times* (1992), "there is a specific character to modern

32. Findlen explains that sixteenth- and seventeenth-century philosophers followed an increasingly eclectic approach, which was largely informed by the Aristotelian conception of nature (albeit modified within humanist and Counter-Reformation contexts) and also by the work of Pliny and other Greek and Roman philosophers. Pliny became an important point of reference among early modern philosophers of nature. The result was increased attention to particular or individual physical phenomena: "By the mid-sixteenth century, natural philosophers had a variety of different approaches to knowledge from which to choose. Most traditional and canonical was the Aristotelian view of nature that favored the collecting of particular data only when directly pertinent to the universal axioms they created and reinforced" (51). On the other hand, it should also be noted that Aristotelian thought underwent crucial transformations in the late Middle Ages at the hands of Albertus Magnus and his disciple Thomas Aquinas. These metamorphoses continued in the sixteenth and seventeenth centuries with such intensity that it seems appropriate to speak of "Aristotelianisms," as Charles Schmitt famously put it. Findlen pays especial attention to these modifications of the philosophical canon as they affect the reception and deployment of Aristotle, Pliny, and others in the early modern period: "Just as Aristotelian philosophy was modified to meet the needs of late medieval Christianity, it underwent a similar metamorphosis in the context of late Renaissance Humanism and Catholic Reformation culture [. . .] Reconstituting Aristotle, they also reinvented Pliny, altering the philosophy of the former and giving the work of the latter greater centrality to the study of nature. Their expansive attitude toward the ancient canon also allowed them to include a variety of other authors who had not previously merited canonical status as philosophers of nature—Aristotle's pupil Theophrastus, the Greek physician Dioscorides, the Roman writers Ovid and Pliny, the mythical Hermes, and so on. This revised and increasingly eclectic list of 'authorities' accompanied the heightened reverence for traditional medical writers who also observed nature, including Avicenna, whose commentaries on Aristotle were the staple of medieval and Renaissance universities, and the Roman physician Galen" (51–52).

teratology. Rather than corresponding to categories of value, our new monsters *suspend, annul,* and *neutralize* them" (94). Rosemary Jackson arrived at a similar conclusion in her well-known study on the fantastic in literature (*Fantasty: The Literature of Subversion* [1981]). Her key suggestion is that the subversive potential of the monster (i.e., the monster's capability to undermine established categories, norms, and certainties) applies to the modern literary genre that houses him or her: the fantastic. While Jackson's best examples of this "literature of subversion" are from the romantic period, classic horror novels such as Mary Shelley's *Frankenstein,* she traces the subversive potential of the fantastic back to the "monstrous aesthetics" of the early English gothic. By contrast, José Monleón sees the literary gothic, and generally speaking the horror genre, as politically reactionary. He notes that the monsters that disturb "our character" come most often from the no-man's land that extends beyond the city walls or from the parasitical edges of the urban center. To be sure, Jackson would agree that some gothic fantasies show a conservative slant insofar as they locate the demonic outside the boundaries and controls of reason, but she emphasizes the progressive internalization of the threat of evil in modern fantasy, which would coincide with the privileging of the uncanny over the marvelous.

I have cautioned elsewhere against progressivist models that do not explain the extraordinary popularity of the marvelous in film fantasies (Castillo, "Horror"). With regard to the political adscription of the marvelous, we must also note that the literary movements associated with "magical realism," "lo real maravilloso," and generally speaking "neobaroque poetics" effectively mobilize the aesthetic of the marvelous against the myths of modern reason in order to subvert the ideology of modernization. Drawing from Carpentier's well-known definition of the marvelous real or "lo real maravilloso," William Childers has recently coined the term *the ambivalent marvelous* to distinguish the critical dimension of Cervantine fantasy from the propagandistic use of the marvelous in the literature associated with official culture in seventeenth-century Spain. The "ambivalent marvelous" would thus leave the reader in a state of unresolved suspense or suspension between alternative worldviews, "a vacillation between two possible, but mutually exclusive systems of explanation" (Childers, *Transnational Cervantes* 69). While Childers works hard to separate the Cervantine "ambivalent marvelous" from Todorov's definition of the fantastic, its effect on the reader would be similar. Thus, the reader would be left in a state of uncertainty that could lead to critical reflection rather than adhesion to the established system of values and beliefs.

Remarkably, the terms of the debate on the ideological dimension(s) of the *baroque marvelous* coincide in part with the ongoing discussions on the politics of the fantastic in modern horror fiction. Thus, José Antonio Maravall and José María Díez Borque focus on the manipulative aspects of religious and theatrical spectacles in baroque Spain while critics such as Severo Sarduy, Omar Calabrese, Fernando R. de la Flor, and Mabel Moraña underscore the destabilizing potential of baroque (and neo-baroque) "monstrosity."

In her recent book *Una era de monstruos: Representaciones de lo deforme en el Siglo de Oro español* (2003) (An Age of Monsters: Representations of Deformity in the Spanish Golden Age), Elena del Río Parra explains that the distinction between portents, monsters, and prodigies, which had been central to ancient and medieval accounts of the monstrous, effectively collapses in the Spanish Golden Age. She quotes from seventeenth-century authors such as Sigüenza y Góngora, Sebastián de Covarrubias, and Rivilla Bonet y Pueyo. Sigüenza y Góngora attributes superstitious attitudes toward the monstrous to ancient paganism. He argues that traces of pagan superstition are present in the etymology of the term *monstrum* and its close relatives ("casi sinónimos" or practically synonyms) *portentum*, *spectaculum*, and *ostentum*.

The entry for *monstro* in Covarrubias' *Tesoro de la lengua* (1611) incorporates an "authentic example" of a monstrous birth from the mid-fourteenth century. This tragic anecdote illuminates the changing attitude toward the monstrous in some intellectual circles: "[C]ualquier parto contra la regla y orden natural, como nacer el hombre con dos cabezas, cuatro brazos y cuatro piernas; como aconteció en el condado de Urgel, en un lugar dicho Cerbera, el año 1343 [. . .] los padres y los demás que estaban presentes a su nacimiento, pensando supersticiosamente pronosticar algún gran mal y que con su muerte se evitaría, le enterraron vivo" (quoted by Del Río Parra 23) (A birth against the norm and order of nature, as when a man is born with two heads, four arms and four legs; as it happened in the County of Urgel, in a place called Cerbera, in the year 1343 [. . .] his parents and the rest of those who were present at the birth, superstitiously thinking that it prognosticated some great calamity that could be avoided with his death, buried him alive). For his part, Rivilla Bonet y Pueyo places the accent on the "rarity" and "novelty" of monstrous births and the "curiosity" and "admiration" that they elicit: "siendo estos partos dignos de admiración por su extrañeza, lo eran también de la curiosidad que los viese y de la novedad que los mostrase [. . .] y en esta acepción se dice monstro hablando más generalmente cualquier cosa admirable, no sólo por exceso de malicia, sino tambien de bondad" (quoted by Del Río Parra 23–24) (these births are worthy of admiration for their rarity, and of the curiosity of those who view them, and of the novelty of their exhibition [. . .] and in this same sense, generally speaking, we call admirable things monstrous, not only for excess of malice but also of goodness).

The echoes of this inclusive definition of the monstrous are present everywhere in the literature of the period. As imitation of nature and the early Renaissance search for classic harmony and proportion are progressively abandoned in favor of artificial modification, metaphoric creation, dissonance, rarity, disproportion, and sensationalist novelty, the monstrous acquires a privileged place at the heart of mannerist experimentalism and baroque literature and culture. The presence of the monstrous is evident in private galleries and collections; essays on natural philosophy; portraits; anamorphic compositions; and illustrations.[33]

In the case of Spain, the *siglo de oro,* or Golden Age, of Spanish letters may indeed be characterized as "an age of monsters," as Del Río Parra has suggested. Besides the obvious appearance of fabulous creatures and other preternatural or supernatural marvels in chivalric and Byzantine romances and teratology treatises (Fuentelapeña, Nieremberg), the monstrous is also central to miscellanies (Mexía, Torquemada, Zapata, Medrano) and *Relaciones de sucesos.* Moreover, when we take into account Bonet y Pueyo's seventeenth-century definition of monstrosity as deviation from the natural norm or "excess," we can see the fascinating face of the monstrous at the level of content or form (frequently both) in the poetry of Góngora and Quevedo; the plays of Calderón de la Barca, Lope de Vega, Tirso de Molina, and Rojas Zorrilla; and the narrative work of Miguel de Cervantes, María de

---

33. The famous portrait of Rudolf II by Alcimboldo, in which fruits and vegetables make up the head of the monarch, effectively illustrates the compatibility of the meaning-producing mechanism of allegory with the "monstrous" imagination cultivated by mannerist and baroque artists and authors. As Daston and Park perceptively write, "Arcimboldo's portrait of Rudolf II was intended both as a display of wit and as an allegorical comment on the eternity and fruitfulness of his reign. The fruits and vegetables that make up the emperor's head come from various times of the year, illustrating his identification with Vertumnus, god of the seasons. The effect is to emphasize the victory of Rudolf's rule over time and to associate it with the eternal spring of the mythical Golden Age" (211). For more on allegory in the baroque see Walter Benjamin's seminal work *The Origin of German Tragic Drama.* As Bryan Turner has explained, the centerpiece of Benjamin's argument is that "allegory, especially allegories about fate, death and melancholy, is the principal element in the aesthetic of modernity and has its archeological origins in the forgotten and obscured past of modernity—the baroque" (7).

Zayas, Céspedes y Meneses, Juan de Piña, and Cristóbal Lozano, among others.[34] Regardless of whether they see monsters as natural curiosities, signs of calamities, or prodigious manifestations of the divine will, storytellers of the Spanish Golden Age capitalize on their shock value, alongside other legendary creatures and preternatural and supernatural prodigies. They use the terms *monstruoso* (monstrous), *maravilloso* (wondrous, marvelous), *prodigioso* (prodigious), *espantoso* (shocking, terrifying), *horrendo* (horrid), and their synonyms and derivatives to qualify all manner of sensational material.

In Cervantes' *El casamiento engañoso [y] el coloquio de los perros* (The De-

34. As Del Río Parra writes, "Si lo monstruoso se expresa como transgresión de la norma natural [. . .] esa excepción, en efecto, pertenece a la figura poética barroca, a la metáfora, a la hipérbole y a la alegoría" (25) (If the monstrous manifests itself as transgression of the natural norm [. . .] this exception, in effect, belongs to the baroque poetic figure, the metaphor, hyperbole and allegory). Julio Baena ("Spanish Mannerist Detours") has recently argued for the need to distinguish the rebellious impulse characteristic of mannerist anticlassicism, which would effectively undermine established norms and certainties, from the moralistic and politically conservative tendencies of vanitas art and baroque *desengaño,* which would seek to reestablish certainty, albeit on a different plane. While Baena's point is well taken, it is also important to recall that the fascination with the odd and the misshapen is central to both mannerist anticlassicism and baroque expressionism, even if it is true that the cult of the monstrous feeds very different, contradictory, and sometimes opposing statements about the nature of the cultural and political order. Baena's approach to mannerism draws from the work of art theorist and historian Arnold Hauser. Ernest Gilman makes a similar point apropos early modern English literature and theater in *The Curious Perspective: Literary and Pictorial Wit in the Seventeenth Century* (1978). Emilio Carilla devoted a monographic study to establishing the distinction between mannerist and baroque aesthetics in Hispanic literatures: *Manierismo y barroco en las literaturas hispánicas* (1983). In his view, the defining traits of mannerism are anticlassicism, subjectivity, intellectualism, aristocratism, refinement, excessive ornamentation, dynamism (movement and torsion), medievalism or gothicism, experimentation, and fantasy. By contrast, the baroque would be defined by a blurring of the lines between classicism and anticlassicism, a predominance of Counter-Reformation values, containment (determined by political and religious boundaries), dynamism (although not as extreme as in mannerism), monumentality, pomposity, realism (with a special inclination toward the ugly and the grotesque), popular appeal, and also (most cryptically) by continuity with mannerism: "continuidad y aprovechamiento de ciertos caracteres manieristas" (154). This concluding remark in a book largely devoted to drawing the dividing line between mannerist and baroque aesthetics illustrates the complexity of the issues and the difficulty of establishing precise boundaries between the two, at least in the context of Spanish literature.

ceitful Marriage [and] the Dialogue of the Dogs [1613]) the terms *maravilla* (marvel), *milagro* (miracle), and *portento* (portent) all serve to describe the same scene involving two talking dogs presumably witnessed by the convalescent soldier Campuzano at the hospital of Resurrection of Valladolid. The dogs Cipión and Berganza, who discuss the circumstances and meaning of their lives; the corruption of their masters; and matters of witchcraft, Aristotelian philosophy, and literary theory, fall squarely *outside the limits of the natural order,* as we are reminded, first by the narrator and later by Berganza himself.[35] For his part, the critical commentary of Peralta, the reader of Campuzano's written account of the events, effectively shifts the focus of the narrative from the marvelous subject matter of the story line (talking dogs, magic spells, ceremonial encounters with the devil) to the monstrous imagination of the narrator and the stylistic novelty of the tale: "el artificio del Coloquio y la invención" (the artifice of the Dialogue and its inventiveness). As with the term *monster,* the word *maravilla* (marvel or wonder) is commonly used in the baroque period to designate anomalous phenomena that deviate from the natural norm and also to qualify the products of stylistic virtuosity, novelty, and unusual creativity. Thus, while Cervantes qualifies his prolific literary rival, the famous dramatist Lope de Vega, as a "monstruo de la naturaleza" (monster of nature), María de Zayas y Sotomayor, another popular novelist of the period, gives the novellas of her first collection the honorific title of "maravillas" because of their originality and artistic virtuosity.

As we noted earlier, the boundaries between the once well-defined realms of the natural, the preternatural, and the supernatural become increasingly porous in the baroque period as shock value and entertainment potential bring theoretically disparate phenomena together. For instance, in *Varia fortuna del soldado Píndaro* (Varied Fortune of the Soldier Píndaro) by Céspedes y Meneses, the formidable but wholly natural strength of the famous Spanish warrior known as Captain Céspedes is alternately described as portentous, monstrous, and shocking or terrifying ("portento," "monstruosas fuerzas,"

35. "—Pues de poco se maravilla vuesa merced, señor Peralta—dijo el Alférez—; que otros sucesos me quedan por decir que exceden a toda imaginación, pues van fuera de todos los términos de naturaleza" (*Novelas ejemplares* 292) (—You marvel at something rather small, my dear Peralta—said the soldier—; for, I have other ocurrances to tell you about which exceed all imagination in that they fall outside the limits of nature); "—Cipión hermano, óyote hablar y sé que te hablo, y no puedo creerlo, por parecerme que el hablar nosotros pasa de los términos de la naturaleza" (299) (—Brother Cipión, I hear you talk and I realize I'm speaking to you, and I cannot believe it, for it seems to me that our speaking goes beyond the terms of nature).

"peregrinas fuerzas," "espantosas fuerzas"). At the same time, the preternatural apparition of the ghost of his antagonist, the baron of Ampurde, is similarly qualified as a shocking or terrifying prodigy ("prodigio espantoso").

In Cristóbal Lozano's *La cueva de Hércules* (1667), those who dare enter the bewitched subterranean palace of the great necromancer ("grande mágico") see and experience marvels (*maravillas*), prodigies (*prodigios*), portents (*portentos*), prophecies of doom (*vaticinios, agüeros, pronósticos de su perdición y de su desgracia*), witchcraft, enchantments (*hechicerías, encantamientos*), phantoms (*fantasmas*), terrifying visions (*espantosas visiones*), and other horrors and curiosities, including images of menacing Arab invaders, moving statues, and a legendary man-eating dog. The "curious reader" ("el curioso") is repeatedly cautioned against the uncritical and possibly impious belief in matters of superstition, even as the authorial voice simultaneously reaffirms the prodigious nature of the cave: "[V]aticinios de más autoridad suelen salir falsos, cuanto y más cosas de superstición y encantamiento [. . .] Estas son las noticias que he podido hallar y descubrir de esta cueva memorable. Crea de ello el curioso lo que le pareciere; que para nuestro intento, basta saber que la hay y que se han hecho experiencias y vístose prodigios" (214–17) (Prophesies of more authority usually prove false, let alone things of superstition and enchantment [. . .] This is the information that I have been able to find and uncover on the memorable cave. The curious reader may believe whatever he wants; for our purpose, it is enough to know that the cave does exist and its prodigies have been seen and experienced).

In another wondrous episode that also takes place in the depths of an enchanted cave in Juan de Piña's *Casos prodigiosos y cueva encantada* (Prodigious Cases and Enchanted Cave [1628]), the terms *portent, marvel,* and *prodigy* serve to qualify an array of monstrosities alongside expressions that underscore their deviation from the norm in every possible way: incoherent, disproportionate, deformed, dissonant (*desconcertados, desiguales, deformes, disonantes*). The incoherent hybridity of the cavernous creatures lavishly described in Piña's tale is mirrored in the monstrous excesses of the narrative style and the inexplicable (con)fusion of a first-person narrative voice with a third-person narrator. The narrative's teasing sensationalism is also evident in the frequent deployment of expressions designed to stir the curiosity of the reader: portentous matters; prodigious adventure; unthinkable prodigy; stupendous case; unseen; unimagined; ignored in maps, books and histories (*cosas portentosas, aventura prodigiosa, no presumido prodigio, no vistos, ni aun imaginados, ignorados del mapa, libros, y relaciones*). Other expressions suggest a (con)fusion between nature and artifice, as we can see in the following passage: "Desangrado el elefante, cayó aquella máquina de cuerpo sobre el dragón [. . .] y yo, entre ellos, envueltos en sangre y polvo, caímos al más profundo valle que se pudo imaginar, entre mayores riscos y peñascos [. . .] de manera que presumí haberse desatado, no sólo la fábrica de aquellas montañas, sino la máquina del orbe, y que al mundo se había dado fin" (70–71) (Having lost its blood the elephant, the whole machine of its body fell on the dragon [. . .] and I, between them, covered in blood and dirt, fell into the deepest valley that anyone could have imagined, amidst the greatest picks and rocks [. . .] Hence, I thought not only that the machinery of all these mountains had collapsed, but the machine of the universe, and that the world had come to an end).

At first sight, the use of the words *máquina* and *fábrica* applied to biological, geological, and cosmic bodies would seem to suggest a connection with the emerging mechanistic view of the universe that, according to Maravall, is reflected in demystifying works of the period, beginning with *Celestina* (Maravall, *El mundo social de* La Celestina). But the machine metaphors do not actually result in a questioning of the marvelous in Piña's pseudo-chivalric fantasy.[36] By contrast, there are other baroque narratives in which the marvelous world of pastoral, chivalric, and Byzantine romances meets problematically with the discourse or discourses of modern rationalism. The discussion of lycanthrope in *Persiles* (1617) apropos Rutilio's autobiographical tale involving a shape-shifting witch is one of the most notorious examples of this type of encounter between the marvelous and what Daston calls "Baconian facts." As Rutilio concludes his outlandish story, another character questions the veracity of the tale. Mauricio claims that shape-shifters are the product of overactive imaginations and superstitions that have no grounding in reality. He adds that those men and women who appear to take on the shape and demeanor of fierce animals are simply suffering from a medical condition known as "mania lupina."

In *El casamiento engañoso [y] el coloquio de los perros*, the problematic encounter of the marvelous with the philosophical tradition of the humanistic dialogue and the secularized landscape of the picaresque results in a form of

---

36. It is important to keep in mind that while the modern understanding of mechanism implies "lifelessness," the notion of the machine in the Greek and Latin traditions (*mechane* and *machina*, respectively) is often attached to images of ingenuity and creativity. At a more general level, the metaphorical blurring of the boundaries between nature and artifice is a common feature of Renaissance and baroque literature, going back to the rhetorical devices of pastoral and chivalric romances and courtly poetry.

epistemological oscillation reminiscent of the uncertainty of the fantastic as theorized by Tzvetan Todorov and Antonio Risco, among others.[37] Even the witch at the center of the story seems unsure as to whether her encounters with the Devil are "authentic" or the product of an overexcited imagination aided by hallucinogens. As far as she is concerned, the distinction is irrelevant; what is important is the intensity of the experience: "Hay opinión que no vamos a estos convites sino con la fantasía en la cual nos representa el demonio las imágenes de todas aquellas cosas que despues contamos que nos han sucedido. Otros dicen que no, que verdaderamente vamos en cuerpo y en anima; y entrambas opiniones tengo para mí que son verdaderas, puesto que nosotras no sabemos cuándo vamos de una o de otra manera, porque todo lo que nos pasa en la fantasía es tan intensamente que no hay diferenciarlo de cuando vamos real y verdaderamente" (Cervantes Saavedra, *Novelas ejemplares* 339–40) (One opinion is that these encounters take place only in our imagination, in which the Devil plants all these fantastical images that we later relate when we recall the events. Others say that we truly experience them in body and soul; for my part, I believe that both versions are true, since we do not know whether we experience them in one way or the other, and all that we experience in our imagination we feel with such intensity that it is impossible to distinguish it from what is real and true).

Another interesting example of the encounter of the marvelous with the rhetoric of modern rationalism can be found in Lozano's *La cueva de Hér-*

37. García Sánchez concurs with Antonio Risco (1987) in arguing that *El coloquio de los perros* ought to be regarded as a manifestation of the pure fantastic (*lo fantastico puro*). They both see *El coloquio* as a paradigmatic product of what García Sánchez calls "the dualism of the baroque mentality" ("el dualismo de la mentalidad barroca" [95]). This "dualism" would result from the conflictive encounter of "un espíritu racionalista en ascenso y un espacio irracional, fantasmagórico, alimentado por un profundo estrato mágico-religioso" (95) (an emerging rationalistic spirit and an irrational, phantasmagoric space which is fed by a deep magical-religious stratum). Other Golden Age texts that would in some measure partake of this "dualism of the baroque mentality" are—according to García Sánchez—*La vida del escudero Marcos de Obregón* (1618) by Vicente Espinel, *Varia Fortuna del soldado Píndaro* (1626) by Céspedes y Menéses, and *La Garduña de Sevilla* (1642) by Alonso de Castillo Solórzano, as well as Cervantes' *Persiles* and *Novelas ejemplares* and Zayas' collections of novellas. For a full list of the texts that Franklin García Sánchez incorporates in his survey of the origins of the fantastic in the Spanish Golden Age, see "Orígenes de lo fantástico en la literatura hispánica" (Origins of the fantastic in Hispanic literature) (89–90). See also "Génesis de lo fantástico en la literatura hispánica" (Genesis of the fantastic in Hispanic literature).

cules. Here the marvelous is allowed to coexist side by side with flashes of skeptical detachment that may be connected with the rationalist push toward the naturalization of the preternatural. The fantastic events that reportedly took place in the underground palace of Hercules on the eve of the Muslim invasion of 711 are never questioned, yet natural explanations are readily provided for the death of the members of more recent expeditions, from diseases caused by the hostile physical environment of the cavern, to irrational fears inspired by preexisting legends and superstitious imaginations.

The coexistence of the marvelous with the probing skepticism of rationalist discourse complicates the epistemological landscape of the early modern period beyond strictly evolutionary or linear models.[38] Carolyn Merchant was right in noting that the emergence of instrumental reason in the 1600s resulted in nature's objectification in scientific and economic discourse,[39] yet recent findings within the field of science studies have shown that our familiar view of the natural world as "inert, passive matter" subject to God's immutable laws was by no means uncontested in the 1600s, even within scientific circles.[40]

---

38. Daston argues that preternatural phenomena progressively swung from the quasi-supernatural extreme of portents to the quasi-natural extreme of Baconian facts: "They began as signs par excellence and ended as stubbornly insignificant. The crucial step in this astonishing transformation was the naturalization of preternatural phenomena" (88–89).

39. See Merchant's provocative and illuminating book *The Death of Nature*.

40. As James Bono has pointed out in his compelling essay "Perception, Living Matter, Cognitive Systems, Immune Networks: A Whiteheadian Future for Science Studies," the Harveian tradition of the seventeenth century opposes the mechanistic conception of the universe that we have come to associate with the birth of modern science. Bono uses the term *vital materialism* to qualify William Harvey's view of nature as "living matter" and to distinguish it from modern mechanism, as well as from traditional animism. He argues that animism and mechanism ultimately agree in regarding matter as passive: "Thus, for both the body was devoid of any inherent activity immanent to matter itself. By contrast, Harvey argues for a view of matter as active" (141). Bono draws a line of contact between the Harveian notion of "living matter" (which would have influenced the work of Francis Glisson, Albrecht von Haller, Diderot, Julien Offray de la Mettrie, and Xavier Bichat, as well as some unsuspected mid-seventeenth-century natural philosophers such as Henry Power, Nathanial Highmore, and Walter Charleton) and Alfred Whitehead's twentieth-century "theory of organic mechanism." Most interestingly, Bono shows that Whitehead sees echoes of a seventeenth-century alternative to the materialistic orthodoxy associated with the New Science in the work of Francis Bacon. The following quote from Whitehead's *Science and the Modern World* (1925) is especially significant:

The conflict between our familiar mechanistic view of nature as passive, inert matter, and the alternative notion of the natural world as "living organism," which is often perceived as a residual worldview, is at the heart of the aesthetics of the fantastic, especially the literature of *cosmic fear* (Lovecraft). This conflict is typically represented in the form of a war between the principles of reason and the Western cultural order, on the one side, and the "archaic" forces of untamed nature, ancient paganism, and oriental monstrosity, on the other; recall such defining narratives as Bram Stoker's *Dracula,* Le Fanu's "Green Tea," Machen's "The Great God Pan," Blackwood's "The Willows," and Lovecraft's "The Call of Cthulhu," among others. Ken Gelder has recently argued that this conflict is in fact the defining feature of horror fiction: "horror is where the archaic (the 'primal,' the 'primitive,' the 'frenzied subject of excess') and the modern (the 'struggling moral subject,' rational, technological) suddenly find themselves occupying the same territory" (3). The question for many horror fiction specialists is whether "the ancient enemies" are reanimated in order to be ritualistically sacrificed in narratives that reaffirm the established sociocultural and moral order (Monleón) or whether the invasion of living (monstrous) nature has the capacity to effectively shake our assumptions and expose the arbitrariness of the walls of the enlightened city (Jackson). Undoubtedly, some strands of horror fiction show glimpses of "the other side" only to reaffirm the barriers that protect our rational world, but the monstrous introduces a disturbance into the cultural and moral horizon that may be difficult to contain. After all, horrors, curiosities, and monsters still fascinate us as much as they disgust us (Carroll).

In approaching the complex issue of the politics of fantasy and horror, it is important to look at where the monster dwells. Caverns are favorite settings for the staging of what Ana Baquero calls "the terrifying fantastic" (*lo fantástico terrorífico*) in the literature of the Golden Age, including some of the darkest and most outlandish passages in Julián de Medrano's *Silva curiosa,* Vicente Espinel's *Marcos de Obregón, Casos prodigiosos y cueva encantada* by Juan de Piña, and Cristóbal Lozano's *La cueva de Hércules.* Uninhabited spaces such as deserts, forests, and mountains are also favored for the staging

---

"Bacon is outside the physical line of thought which finally dominated the century. Later on, people thought of passive matter which was operated on externally by forces. I believe Bacon's line of thought to have expressed a more fundamental truth than do the materialistic concepts which were then being shaped as adequate for physics. We are now so used to the materialistic way of looking at things [. . .] that it is with some difficulty that we understand the possibility of another mode of approach to the problem of nature" (quoted by Bono 138).

of marvels, prodigies, and horrors, especially the exotic lands of Northern Europe (*Jardín de flores curiosas, Persiles*) and the heavily forested and mountainous Iberian regions of Navarre (*El Crotalón*) and Asturias (*La silva curiosa*). The part of *La silva curiosa* devoted to the collecting of epitaphs and "other ancient and curious things" (*cosas antiguas y curiosas*) is especially notable in that it turns the landscape of northern Spain into a museum of macabre curiosities and a privileged site for the exploration and exploitation of the occult for the entertainment and admiration of the curious reader.

Barbara Benedict's observations on the depiction of the countryside in late seventeenth-century miscellanies (e.g., *Admirable Curiosities of England*) seem to apply to Medrano's late sixteenth-century text as well: "[T]hese narratives both turn the countryside into the sentimental site of lost beliefs, and become curiosities themselves that the traveler or reader may collect" (180). In the case of *La silva curiosa,* the narrator's exhibitionist chronicle of his own collecting labors effectively turns both the narrative and the first-person narrator into curiosities. In fact, Medrano's miscellany is explicitly framed as a collection of amusing or "curious things" (*cosas curiosas*) that may be utilized in courtly conversation to enhance our reputation as *bizarre subjects* worthy of admiration.

In discussing the politicization of the landscape in English literature, Benedict establishes a key connection between the representation of space in gothic fictions and the "construction" of the countryside as a reservoir of the marvelous and the occult in seventeenth-century miscellanies: "[T]raditional rural marvels advertise the countryside as a collection of curiosities [. . .] Such wonders locate the occult in the countryside. By politicizing the landscape, these stories, just as gothic fictions do, update a long tradition of wonder tales that in earlier decades dramatized the closeness to God that is purportedly available in the country" (179). Despite its urban setting, the macabre tale of the haunting of Captain Céspedes in *Varia fortuna del soldado Píndaro* may also be connected with the politicization of space in gothic and romantic fiction. The encounter of the heroic Spanish protagonist with the *marvelous* in *Varia Fortuna* takes place in a carefully racialized landscape at the heart of an old *morisco* neighborhood in the new Christian city of Granada.[41]

41. For more on the staging of the marvelous in medieval and Golden Age literature, see the collection *Loca Ficta: Los espacios de la maravilla en la Edad Media y Siglo de Oro,* edited by Ignacio Arellano. The essay by Ana Baquero Escudero, "Los espacios de la maravilla en la novela corta aúrea," included in the collection, is a useful survey of marvelous spaces in *siglo de oro* narrative.

By contrast, the work of Miguel de Cervantes seems to open opportunities to reflect on the arbitrariness of the traditional association of the occult with the space of the other and also on the instrumentalization of the marvelous and the freakish for indoctrinating and commercial purposes. Besides the ironic staging of the marvelous and the occult in the hospital of Resurrection of Valladolid in *El casamiento engañoso [y] el coloquio de los perros*, and similarly burlesque passages in *Don Quixote* such as the Montesinos and Clavileño episodes, one would have to recall the well-known interlude *El retablo de las maravillas* (The Show of Marvels), in which the marvelous is explicitly tied to the manipulation of the public in theatrical spectacles. In *Los trabajos de Persiles y Sigismunda*, the previously mentioned exchange between Rutilio and Mauricio on the subject of the existence of werewolves effectively reverses the directionality of the discourse of the marvelous by disallowing the "exportation" of evil to the margins of the known world. Another example of the critical treatment of the monstrous other in *Persiles* is the self-consciously ironic self-portrait of the *morisca* Zenotia as a powerful witch capable of unleashing apocalyptic calamities.[42]

From this perspective, María de Zayas' *Desengaños amorosos* (Disenchantments of Love) is especially interesting. The collection is rich in preternatural events and situations that seemingly reinforce the traditional association of the religious other with the lurking forces of evil. However, the characters that represent religious, cultural, and social otherness (*morisco* necromancers, lowly prostitutes, etc.) often play the role of "guns for hire" who do the bidding of well-to-do members of Spanish society. While Zayas' second collection of novellas features some of the most shocking, macabre, and graphic passages of *siglo de oro* literature, including a series of gruesome and cold-blooded murders of innocent women, these horrifying events do not typically take place in peripheral, marginal, or exotic landscapes but rather amid the comforts of aristocratic households in populous cities such as Toledo and Seville. It is thus fair to say that the monstrous, the occult, and the horrific are here literally brought home, into the very heart of Spanish society.

A distinctive trait of Zayas' work is the pervasiveness of violence and cruelty throughout the dark social landscape of *Desengaños*. The discussion of masculine cruelty is central to the unifying frame of the novellas (Greer), yet some female characters are also cruel and manipulative. At the same time, a special brand of perverse cruelty is reserved for homosexual males, whose essential "foreignness" is underscored most explicitly in the seventh novella

42. See chapters 5 and 6 of my *(A)wry Views*.

of the collection, which takes place in the Low Countries. The presence of murderous foreign sodomites, *morisco* necromancers, and manipulative and predatory women (often belonging to the lower social strata) would seem to make it difficult to exonerate Zayas from the charge that her novellas reify the conventional demonization of religious, cultural, sexual, and social others. On the other hand, the unflattering portrayal of Spanish aristocrats, who are frequently depicted as heartless murderers, complicates the "political" dimension of these narratives beyond the traditional association of evil with otherness.

For my part, I reexamine Zayas' *Desengaños* in light of its instrumentalization of the monstrous and the macabre. While I draw from the critical work of specialists on the martyriological dimension of the collection (Greer; Jehenson and Wells), its reclaiming of the body (Vollendorf), and its revelation of the fundamental injustice of the honor system (Williamsen; Brownlee), I am especially interested in the graphic exhibitionism of the novellas. I am thinking of their shocking exposés of the dark and dirty secrets of the rich and honorable, as well as their titillating anatomical displays and their "invasive" close-ups of decaying flesh whose vivid pulsion is at once revolting and fascinating. It seems to me that a reevaluation of the sensationalist aspects of the collection in the context of a study of the macabre in Golden Age narrative will complement our understanding of the political dimension of Zayas' writing beyond the commonplace classification of the author as a conservative feminist (Yllera).

While the conventional portrayal of religious and sexual others (*moriscos*, homosexuals) and its overarching preoccupation with moral character (or lack thereof) suggest important connections with the moralistic tendencies of "official culture" in Counter-Reformation Spain, the macabre sensationalism of the novellas would seem to bring them closer, at times, to the exuberant cultivation of morbid curiosity in *La silva curiosa*. But the somber mood of Zayas' work and its tragic dimension have little to do with Medrano's playful cynicism. The unapologetic moral ambiguity of Medrano's *Silva* is nothing short of unique in *siglo de oro* literature. In the case of Zayas' work, the presence of the marvelous, the monstrous, and the macabre, and the teasing eroticism of certain passages, can be explained as a means to an end: the denunciation of the cruelty of men (Greer) or the exposure of the hypocrisy and injustice of the honor code (Williamsen). By contrast, there is no point to make, no lesson to be drawn in *La silva curiosa*. Medrano presents the most outrageously shocking actions and titillating situations with macabre flair as delightful curiosities diligently put together by a self-consciously deviant narrator-collector for the mere entertainment of the reader.

This taste for the occult, the monstrous, and the macabre is also evident in many of Cristóbal Lozano's legends and stories, but in the work of Lozano the shock of horror is often meant to convey moral lessons. This is certainly the case in *Castigo de dos adúlteros* (Punishment of Two Adulterers), an expressionistic and atmospheric tale that is strongly reminiscent of romantic aesthetics. In this and other ghost stories of the baroque period, spectral apparitions serve to warn readers against a life of sin.

In closing this introductory section, I would like to underscore that while the macabre has a prominent role in baroque literature and culture, its function and significance vary considerably from one text or cultural setting to another. Hence, in exploring literary manifestations of the early modern taste for the macabre in imperial Spain, I am not looking to offer a panoramic or exhaustive view. Rather, this gallery of horrors from the Spanish Golden Age is meant as a contribution to our understanding of the roots/routes of the fantastic in the age of curiosities.

A final clarification regarding my use of the term *macabre* in this book: In general, I try to keep the etymological origin of the term in sight. In its strict etymological sense, the macabre is tied to the physical space of the tomb, from the Arabic *maqabir,* as Mercedes Alcalá Galán noted in her critical edition of *La silva curiosa*. At the same time, I think of the macabre in figurative (often metonymic) terms in an effort to account for the sensationalist fixation with (un)dead bodies and the paraphernalia of death in baroque literature and culture.

ONE

Miscellanea: The Garden of Curiosities and Macabre Theater

From the Bibliotheca to the Garden and the Graveyard

The Renaissance hunger for novel objects of knowledge and varied topics of conversation is no doubt responsible for the extraordinary success of miscellanea in the 1500s.[1] As Marcel Bataillon says, "[e]ra el tipo mismo de la olla podrida que deleitaba a los robustos apetitos de la época" (*Erasmo y España* 637) (it is precisely the type of hodgepodge that satisfied the robust appetites of the period). In Spain, the second half of the sixteenth century is especially rich in works devoted to the compilation of all manner of curiosities. Much of this writing is explicitly pitched as entertainment for a mixed audience with a taste for the odd, the shocking, and the rare. In their pairing of knowledge and pleasure, these works would seem to continue on the path of medieval exemplarity. However, the explicit emphasis on entertainment produces an interesting inversion of the terms, as the advancement of knowledge in the traditional sense takes a backseat to the stated goal of providing pleasure to the reader. Thus, pleasure (*delectare*) is no longer viewed merely as a pedagogical tool, which is supposed to make moral teachings palatable (*enseñar deleitanto*), but rather as an end in itself.[2] As the narra-

1. Part of this chapter will be printed in the forthcoming essay "Baroque Landscapes: Traveling West through the Desert of the World," in the collaborative volume *Poiesis and Modernity in the Old and New Worlds,* edited by Anthony Cascardi and Leah Middlebrook.

2. Mercedes Alcalá Galán has made this point in the introduction to her critical edition of *La silva curiosa*. Speaking of the role of admiration (*admiratio*) in miscellany writing, she argues that "[e]l conocimiento es un medio para provocar la admiración, y la admiración constituye un fin en sí ya que el placer producido en el lector es la esencia misma del delectare" (11) (knowledge is a medium to elicit

tor puts it in *La silva curiosa*, "assí como la diversidad de colores conforta y delecta la vista, assí la variedad de discursos y materias curiosas recrea maravillosamente el espíritu" (155) (just as the diversity of colors gives comfort and pleasure to the eyes, the variety of discourses and curious matters wonderfully delights the spirit). More than a simple declaration of intentions, this observation amounts to a programmatic manifesto for the entire corpus of the miscellanea.

In Torquemada's *Jardín de flores curiosas*, the pleasure that the interlocutors receive from the novelty and diversity of the curious topics selected for discussion is metonymically linked to the delightful variety of the flowers growing in the pastoral landscape that serves as the backdrop for the dialogue. As Luis says, "es tanta la variedad de las flores y rosas que están en este pequeño prado, que, mirando cada una por sí, me parece nunca antes haberla visto" (103) (the variety of flowers and roses is such in this little prairie that as I contemplate each one individually, it feels as though I have never seen it before). The topical invitation to pick our favorite flowers from these textual gardens, prairies, or forests (*jardines, florestas, silvas*) is indicative of the specific form of cultural consumption that is at work in the miscellanea, as well as the type of reader to whom these works are directed: "Curiosas invenciones desseando, / Entrad en esta Silva, y descansando / En ella gustaréis dos mil primores. / En ella cogeréis diversas flores, / Si andar queréis en ella paseando (*La silva curiosa* 84) (Wishing for curious inventions, enter into this Forest and rest. In it you shall find two thousand beauties. In it, you shall pick distinct flowers as you walk).[3] Each and every "thing" that can be found inside these essentially heterogeneous texts, regardless of its original source or cultural function, is now offered to the reader as a "curious invention," that is, a novel object of amusement and delight.

A few years ago, Lina Rodríguez Cacho (1993) drew a suggestive picture of the trajectory of sixteenth-century miscellanea, from the early *Silva de*

admiration, and admiration is an end in itself, since the pleasure experienced by the reader is the true essence of delectation).

3. Maurice Molho (1988) examined both the etymology and the history of the term *silva* prior to its conversion into a designator for a specific poetic form. He noted that a common characteristic of the silva is its seemingly careless presentation of a heterogeneous collection of half-baked materials, which in its chaotic structure is reminiscent of a forest (46). Alcalá Galán elaborates on this notion to conclude that the silva and the *selva* (forest) are parallel landscapes, "uno natural y otro literario que comparten su exuberancia y su cualidad silvestre" (12) (one natural and the other literary, both of which share an exuberant and wild quality).

varia lección by Pedro Mexía, first published in 1540, to Antonio de Torquemada's *Jardín de flores curiosas* (1570), Julián de Medrano's *La silva curiosa* (1583), and *Varia historia*, written by Luis Zapata around 1590. She noted that within the pages of Mexía's *Silva*, we never really get the impression of having left a medieval bibliotheca; yet when it comes to Torquemada's *Jardín*, we may feel more like guests in a private backyard gathering than readers at the library. In the case of *La silva curiosa* and *Varia historia*, Rodríguez Cacho imagines herself standing before a group of casual conversationalists at a café.[4] For her part, Asunción Rallo Gruss (1984) looks at the development of the genre from the perspective of its evolution from the encyclopedic display of ancient erudition in the tradition of classical compilations to the more personal or personalized miscellanea that will proliferate in the last three decades of the sixteenth century. Beginning with Torquemada's *Jardín*, miscellany literature will open the door to contemporary sources and folkloric material, as well as personal experience, in an effort to engage new groups of readers who had emerged with the printing press. While most critics, including Rallo Gruss, focus on the works of Mexía, Torquemada, and Zapata, it is perhaps the protonovelistic second part of Medrano's *La silva curiosa* that best exemplifies the subjective impulse of late sixteenth-century miscellanies.

Marcelino Menéndez Pelayo mentioned the miscellanea in discussing the genesis of the modern novel in his classic *Orígenes de la novela* (1905). But only recently do we find critics who examine miscellany literature in relation to the origins of the fantastic. Giovanni Allegra is among the first scholars to grasp the cultural significance of these texts, which are both old (*antiguos*) and new (*modernos*). Sixteenth-century miscellanies stand at the crossroads between the ordered, meaningful cosmos of antiquity and the chaotic and infinite universe announced by Giordano Bruno. As Allegra remarks, these works served as warehouses or textual galleries in which the myths and symbols that once anchored the old world would be compiled and inventoried to satisfy the curiosity of new cultural consumers.[5]

---

4. Rodríguez Cacho uses the expression *charlistas de café* (166). Two decades earlier, Francisco Márquez Villanueva had characterized the implied readers of *Varia historia* in remarkably similar terms in *Fuentes literarias cervantinas* (1973). He noted that Zapata no longer views them as abstractions: "[D]ejan los lectores de ser meras abstracciones incorpóreas para convertirse en un corro de contertulios que se divierten escuchándole sus historias" (118) ([T]he readers are no longer mere incorporeal abstractions but a circle of interlocutors who enjoy listening to his stories).

5. "De la fragmentación de este universo mítico es el *Jardín de flores curiosas* como un almacén o un museo [. . .] Nos encontramos con una 'lectura' degradada de

One can sense the end of the old world as the mythical topoi of antiquity are converted into "curious inventions" to be exhibited in these eclectic literary cabinets, alongside the sensational products of folkloric hearsay and pseudo-autobiographical anecdotes. The transformation of the sense-making myths and symbols of the ancient world into literary curiosities may very well be a first step in the direction of the modern fantastic, as Allegra suggests, but the miscellanies often come closest to the unsettling quality of modern fantasy when they incorporate contemporary folkloric material. Some notable examples can be found in the third treatise of Torquemada's *Jardín*, which includes dozens of anecdotes dealing with monstrous and macabre events belonging to the realm of the preternatural.[6] These popular stories of fantastic occurrences ("cuentos acaecidos," *Jardín* 243) must have inspired Torquemada's contemporary Julián de Medrano, whose own acute sense of the macabre would engender some of the most self-consciously sensationalist passages of the period. The often flippant autobiographical narrative persona that presides over the second part of *La silva curiosa* guides readers into the depths of one of the first genuinely dark landscapes of the modern fantastic.

Before we turn our attention to the macabre content in these fantasies, however, I would like to go over some considerations apropos of an important discussion that takes place at the beginning of the third treatise of Torquemada's *Jardín*. As the interlocutors gather at the customary spot for their third conversation, Luis decides to share his apprehension concerning a widespread rumor that tells of ghostly sightings at the garden (246). This in-

---

mitos, debida especialmente al nivel de laicización en que ya habían entrado los nuevos tiempos [. . .] Ultima fase de lo mítico medieval y entre los primeros éxitos de lo fantástico en literatura, el *Jardín* debe tomarse como registro o inventario de una sabiduría oscurecida en que los símbolos, sin desaparecer completamente, se ofrecen al hombre de los tiempos nuevos en su versión fabulosa, a veces espeluznante, siempre 'curiosa'" (Allegra 79–80) (The *Garden of Curious Flowers* is like a warehouse or museum of the fragmentation of this mythical universe [. . .] We find a degraded "reading" of myths mainly as a result of the level of secularization that the new times had brought [. . .] At the last phase of the mythical medieval, and among the first successes of the fantastic in literature, the *Garden* must be taken as a register or inventory of an obscured knowledge whose symbols do not completely disappear but are passed on to the man of modern times in their fabulous version, sometimes terrifying, always "curious").

6. Allegra calls it subnatural: "reino inferior, demoníaco, caótico, eso es subnatural" (63) (inferior, demonic, chaotic reign, that is, subnatural).

tervention and the resulting exchange with Antonio and Bernardo effect a notable atmospheric change. The tranquil and cheery prairie of previous treatises is now transformed into an uncanny landscape seemingly filled with shadowy presences. This eerily suggestive atmosphere is meant to reset or adjust the mood of readers in anticipation of the topics selected for this third colloquy, which include spectral and demonic encounters, sorcery, witchcraft, and devil worship. Initially, the conversation focuses on the nature of human fear, which is linked to melancholic dispositions naturally impressionable and given to fantasy. We are told that while irrational apprehensions may be treated and ultimately corrected by means of reason and discretion, there are also cases in which our fears are triggered by extraordinary occurrences that fall outside of the common order of nature. As Antonio explains, established authorities draw a distinction between actual spectral apparitions (*visiones*) and false representations fabricated by the imagination, which are called phantoms (*fantasmas*). The trouble is that when it comes to evaluating specific cases, it is often impossible to separate fantasy from reality, as he says in prefacing the first of many recorded accounts of extraordinary occurrences: "Y no sé yo de cual manera de éstas haya sido un caso muy notable que habrá poco más de treinta años acaeció dos leguas de donde estamos" (And I do not know which of these types may have been a notable case that occurred thirty years ago two leagues from where we are).

The difficulty of distinguishing between real events and deceitful appearances will come up again apropos of the contested issue of the witches' flight and their ritualistic encounter with the devil in the infamous witches' Sabbath. We are presented with conflictive evidence, some of which suggests that the witches' ritualistic encounters with the beast are indeed real. In other cases, it appears that the abhorrent flight is nothing but a chimerical fantasy triggered by hallucinogenic substances. Significantly, the power of the illusion may affect not only the witch experiencing the trance but the spectator watching it, "los ojos de los que las miran" (316) (the eyes of those who observe them). Luis attributes this alleged fact to the devil's power to plant false representations in our imagination: "[R]epresenta el diablo en la imaginación y fantasía todas aquellas cosas que quiere" (316) (The devil represents in our imagination and fantasy whatever things he wants).

The terms of the discussion in these passages of the *Jardín* will be echoed almost verbatim in Cervantes' well-known exemplary novel *El coloquio de los perros*, albeit with distinctively ironic overtones. More than a literary or fictional motif, however, the witches' flight is a key issue in contemporary debates and inquisitorial trials and interrogations. The belief in the real nature of the witches' preternatural encounters is widespread in the 1500s and early 1600s and finds its roots in classical and scholastic sources from Pliny and Apuleius to Saint Augustine.[7] Torquemada reproduces both sides of the debate, allowing for the possibility that either version might be true, depending on the case. While the *Jardín* does not go as far as *El coloquio* in linking the potentially deceitful quality of our representations of the physical world in these borderline experiences to broader issues of epistemological uncertainty, the practical result of allowing these manifestly opposite views to stand on equal footing is a blurring of the distinction between fantasy and reality. Thus, it would seem that questions about the true nature of extraordinary experiences cannot be completely separated, at least in some cases, from issues of interpretation. This would be true when we talk about the controversial subject of the witches' flight and also when we attempt to distinguish actual spectral events (*visiones*) from the phantasms (*fantasmas*) engendered by our own irrational fears.

The oscillation between the acceptance of the marvelous and the drive to explain seemingly extraordinary events by means of reason is a common (some would say defining) trait of the modern fantastic. While many theorists of modern fantasy and horror—including Tzvetan Todorov, Rosemary Jackson, Eric Rabkin, and H. P. Lovecraft—focus on antirationalist sentiments in the eighteenth, nineteenth, and twentieth centuries in their drive to substantiate what they see as the countercultural quality of the fantastic, conflictive encounters between reason and its others are germane to the epistemological crisis of the early modern period,[8] a situation brought about by the emergence of a secular and increasingly objectified worldview that stands side by side with different versions of the old finite and ordered cosmos.[9] This is not a linear process by any means, and, of course, the "men of reason" of the Renaissance and baroque periods are not the rationalists of the nineteenth and twentieth centuries. Yet they share in the deep sense of ver-

7. Allegra notes that this is one of the most debated issues of the period, although the majority of those who wrote on whether the witches attended the Sabbath *in somniis* or *corporaliter* ultimately affirmed that the witches' flight was often real (316 n. 118).

8. For a discussion of reason in early modern times, especially in Mediterranean and colonial contexts, see Castillo and Lollini, eds., *Reason and Its Others: Italy, Spain, and the New World* (2006).

9. As Maravall notes in *El mundo social de la Celestina* (The Social World of the Celestina), unlike the world of the ancients (*antiguos*), the nascent world of the moderns (*modernos*) is essentially voided of transcendence (*mundo desdivinizado*).

tigo that results from seeing the world radically change, right in front of their eyes. It would be difficult to exaggerate the potentially seismic effects of the geographical and cosmological discoveries of the age of exploration, especially the appearance of an impossible new continent to the west of Europe and the piling up of evidence that negates the centrality of the earth in an increasingly vast and chaotic universe, from the investigations of Giordano Bruno (1548–1600) to Galileo's careful and detailed recording of his lunar explorations in the *Sidereus Nuncius* (Sidereal Messenger [1610]).

As our view of the cosmos changes, so does our nature. Pascal says it best in his remarkable statement that "our nature is in movement" (quoted by Battistini 24). While the impact of this movement of nature is most often evaluated from the perspective of its advancement of scientific reason, it is also important to point out that the shattering of the familiar and meaningful world of the ancients unleashes genuine forms of epochal melancholia and a profound anxiety about the openness and chaotic structure of the universe.[10] The suggestions that there is nothing motionless in nature and that the universe itself may be ruled by chaos must have intensified the baroque obsession with the fragility of the human condition and the general perception of social dis-

---

10. Andrea Battistini writes, "Human minds were upset by the melancholic sensation that the Earth was deprived of its ancient centrality, lost in the infinite spaces that lacked secure points of reference as there no longer existed anything motionless in the universe" (22). Walter Benjamin made the experience of melancholy a centerpiece of his theorization of the baroque, which he views as the origin of the aesthetic of modernity in *The Origin of German Tragic Drama*. Fernando R. de la Flor revisits the issue of baroque melancholy in the Spanish context in "On the Notion of a Melancholic Baroque" (2005). He poses several important questions at the beginning of his essay, including these two: "Can an epoch or a certain chronological space (or, a geographical one) be melancholic? [. . .] Might it be possible to speak about the secular 'state of sadness' of a whole nation (of an 'illness of Spain,' as was put by Juan Caramuel, one of its most important ideologists)?" (3). He arrives at the following conclusion: "A double crisis is thus installed in modern Spanish subjectivity, which begins to take shape from the end of the sixteenth century. Such crisis implies a break of the harmony between man and the physical world that will later unfold in the insecure relationship of the self with the metaphysical sphere. It is not only life that has become unstable and unsafe, but also salvation, allowing Vieira to conclude: 'temo a imortalidade' (185) (I fear eternity)" (17). See also R. de la Flor, *Barroco; Representación e ideología en el mundo hispánico (1580–1680)* (Baroque: Representation and Ideology in the Hispanic World), especially chapters 1 and 2, which are devoted to discussing depictions of melancholy and death (funerary theaters) and expressions of epochal anxiety associated with the notions of infinity and emptiness (vacuum).

array. These epochal anxieties crystallize in the literature of the period in the recurrent images of the "world upside down" and the fixation with allegories of death and decay.[11] Fernando R. de la Flor examines emblems of melancholy and "funerary theaters" in the Hispanic baroque. He notes that the baroque fixation with death and nothingness (*nihil*), which he traces back to the early 1580s, amounts to a negative ontology. The cult of nothingness would be essentially tied to the discovery of infinity and the idea of the vacuum suggested by Giordano Bruno.[12] The notion of the vacuum and the anxiety that springs from it feed seemingly contradictory views of the human condition, from officially sanctioned spiritualism, to mystical experiences and ascetic movements, to cynical attitudes and expressions of intellectual skepticism.

Galileo's contemporaries coined the expression *nocturnal horror* to describe the ominous feeling that engulfs the soul confronted with the mystery of the starry night described in the *Sidereus* (Battistini 22).[13] The anxious pathos revealed in Galileo's reporting and the astonished terror with which it

---

11. The potentially deceptive nature of appearances is central to the aesthetics of *desengaño* or disillusionment. Images of a deceitful, unstable, and corrupt world are often recalled as a backdrop against which the theological truth will eventually emerge in anamorphic fashion. As I mentioned earlier, baroque religious discourse puts suffering and death on display to remind us about the fragility and precariousness of the human condition and the need to focus on the afterlife.

12. He writes in chapter 1 of *Barroco*, fittingly titled "Emblemas de melancolía, nihilismo y deconstrucción de la idea de mundo" (Emblems of Melancholy, Nihilism, and Deconstruction of the Notion of the World): "Una suerte de ontología negativa se despliega por entonces en un conjunto de nuevas nociones operativas en distintos campos de saber: algo que va desde la mística al saber de una física (sagrada), y de lo que se puede decir entonces que se constituye intencionalmente en un expresivo 'elogio de la nada'. Y es que resulta que hacia 1580 se sitúa tambien el descubrimiento del vacío o del vacuum, asociado indefectiblemente a la gran noción de infinitud, abiertamente sugerida por Bruno [. . .] Vacío cosmológico, infinitud e indefinición de lo creado, que tiene su transferencia en el propio vacío interior (63–64) (A sort of negative ontology unfolds then in a series of new operative notions in different fields of knowledge, from mysticism to (sacred) physics, all of which deliberately converge in what we could call an expressive "praise of nothingness." And it just so happens that around 1580 is also when we can situate the discovery of emptiness or the vacuum, which is inextricably associated with the great notion of infinitude openly suggested by Bruno [. . .] Cosmic vacuum, infinitude, and indeterminacy of creation, which find their counterpart in an interior vacuum).

13. According to Battistini, the expression *nocturnal horror* is used by several poets of the period—notably Francesco Stelluti and Iacopo Cicognini—to refer to Galileo's descriptions of the night of space.

was received in some quarters are strongly reminiscent of the language with which such philosophers as Burke, Kant, and Schiller would come to describe the experience of the sublime. Hence, Anthony Cascardi has recently suggested that the Northern European sublime of the eighteenth century finds its roots in the aesthetics of the Southern European or Mediterranean baroque.[14] Battistini also points in this direction when he asserts, "From the same perspective, man's soul, in perceiving the infinite, discovered itself boundless, and with the revival of Pythagorean motives, there developed an aesthetic of limitless space that assumed the configuration of the sublime. It is precisely this that Edmund Burke realized when theorizing (in the modern sense) this category of aesthetics, which was launched in the seventeenth century and codified in the following century" (24).

In this precise sense, the "nocturnal horror" that is captured in the literature of the baroque period could also be posited as the archaic root of the postenlightened "cosmic terror" evoked in Lovecraft's conceptualization of the classic horror story or "weird tale" (his terminology). Note the distinctive echoes of the shock of infinity and the fear of open spaces in Lovecraft's "The Call of Cthulhu" (1926): "We live on a placid island of ignorance in the midst of black seas of infinity, and it was not meant that we should voyage far. The sciences, each straining in its own direction, have hitherto harmed us little; but some day the piecing together of dissociated knowledge will open up such terrifying vistas of reality, and of our frightful position therein that we shall go mad from the revelation or flee from the deadly light into the peace and safety of a new dark age" (346). As Battistini has suggested, the modern fear of open spaces is a by-product of the discovery of infinity and cosmic chaos in the age of exploration (22). This epochal anxiety was to release an equally strong desire to find refuge from the threats of disorder and meaninglessness (the "black seas of infinity") in a secure citadel or "placid island."

Manuel Aguirre thinks of this compulsion to seal ourselves inside a citadel of reason as the defining trait of modernity. In his view, the idea of the perfectly "closed space" is the most dangerous dream ever conceived by reason.[15] Yet the cosmic (dis)order announced by Giordano Bruno and recorded

14. Revealing in this respect is the title of Cascardi's essay, "The Genealogy of the Sublime in the Aesthetics of the Spanish Baroque" (2006).

15. Aguirre's provocative argument hinges on the notion that for all its inspiring imagery of ever-expanding horizons, modern Western thought is hampered by a constitutive desire to construct the perfectly secured citadel, the "closed space." Of course, the more the West strives to realize this entropic dream of modern reason and to protect it from the unbound forces of unreason (chaos, contingency, meaningless-

by Galileo brought with it not just new walls of reason but also new windows of imagination and, with them, brand new vistas of nightmarish landscapes as well as utopian dreams.[16]

It should not be surprising, then, to see scholars beginning to scout the products of baroque aesthetics and, generally speaking, the early modern culture of curiosities in search for the origins of the fantastic. Specifically, they are looking for signs of encounters between the "residual" world in which magic and miracles seem still possible and the emerging rationalistic worldview. Among them, Antonio Risco and Franklin García Sánchez point to Cervantes' *El coloquio de los perros,* which they consider an example of a Golden Age work that conforms to the most demanding conceptualizations of the fantastic. I discuss the Cervantine text in some detail in chapter 2. Suffice it here to note that the puzzling effect of *El coloquio* and the accompanying frame tale *El casamiento engañoso* has been tied to the problematic meeting of different discursive modes or genres, especially pastoral romances and picaresque narratives (Spadaccini and Talens). For their part, Risco and García Sánchez look at this exemplary novel as a meeting place for opposing worldviews, "un espíritu racionalista en ascenso y un espacio irracional, fantasmagórico, alimentado por un profundo estrato mágico-religioso" (García Sánchez 95) (an emerging rationalistic spirit and an irrational, phantasmagoric space fed by a deep magical-religious stratum).

Among those who have traced the roots of the fantastic back to sixteenth-century miscellanea, Giovanni Allegra focuses on the work of Antonio de Torquemada, which he explicitly qualifies as one of the first success stories of the fantastic in literature (80). As we shall see shortly, some of the folkloric anecdotes gathered in the third treatise of Torquemada's *Jardín* show a distinctive taste for macabre motifs and situations and a certain stylistic affectation reminiscent of the gothic style. However, Torquemada's grotesquerie

---

ness), the more vulnerable it becomes to any real or imagined threats from the outside or even from the inside of the closed space (see Castillo and Lollini).

16. Battistini says, "next to reason, fantasy (which was also rising and mobile) acquired a totally unforeseen positivity, especially when the scientist, facing the infiniteness of the universe, could at any step collide with the unexpected. [. . .] In this sense, the *Sidereus* provided an unintentional incentive for science fiction" (24–27). Battistini further suggests that the "monstrum of space" (he borrows this wonderful expression from Paul Valéry) could also be perceived in some quarters as a wondrous mystery and a potentially "marvelous spectacle" capable of inspiring emotions of admiration and delight (21), much like the oddities displayed in contemporary collections of curiosities.

will be no match for the atmospheric treatment of the macabre in the work of such baroque authors as Cristóbal Lozano and María de Zayas.

More recently, Alcalá Galán has suggested a connection between the aesthetic and themes of modern horror and the "perverse" cultivation of the macabre in *La silva curiosa*. In effect, Medrano's essentially nihilistic funerary theater (to use R. de la Flor's expression) brings us surprisingly close to the horror (vacui) of the modern "weird tale" (Lovecraft). According to Rosemary Jackson, the distinctive feature of the modern fantastic is its foregrounding of meaninglessness, which opens a dark void in the apparent fullness of reality (158). She illustrates this notion with a quote from Poe's well-known tale "The Pit and the Pendulum": "It was not that I feared to look upon things horrible, but that I grew aghast lest there should be *nothing* to see" (quoted by Jackson 109). This quote encapsulates the anxious fascination that readers may experience as they travel through the macabre landscape of the second part of *La silva*. It is not that we fear the spectacle of death but that we grow increasingly anxious about the possibility that there might be nothing behind the funerary theater. To put it differently, what frightens us is not the world of the dead (after all, the dead are treated as amusing grotesquerie in *La silva*) but the creeping sense that the world itself may have lost its meaning and transcendence.

The desolate landscape of the second part of Medrano's work is essentially a hopeless world void of transcendence. This is where the Renaissance garden of curious flowers morphs into a baroque graveyard filled with nothing but tombs and ghosts—funerary theater, night of the living dead. Fittingly, the entire second half of *La silva* is framed by collections of epitaphs, which are of course the literal landmarks of what is not there, that is, the stories of an absence.[17] In its obsessive fixation with absence and its cynical foregrounding of meaninglessness, Medrano's textual graveyard is one of the first expressions of baroque nocturnal horror and is possibly the first panoramic vista of the modern fantastic.

Night Flowers in the *Jardín*

The third treatise of Torquemada's *Jardín de flores curiosas* includes more than twenty allegedly documented occurrences of ghostly encounters. Some

17. In discussing Walter Benjamin's work on baroque allegory, Christine Buci-Glucksmann arrives at the conclusion that baroque aesthetics privilege "feeling, as an

of these cases have been lifted from classical sources with very little elaboration, while others are said to originate from the oral accounts of circumstantial witnesses. These anecdotes are presented as real-life events that illustrate the "scholarly" points made by the interlocutors (especially Antonio, the most authoritative voice of the three) on the nature of extraordinary and unexplained phenomena. Yet the stories sometimes take on a literary life of their own. In this sense, it is important to recall that collections of miscellanea were not read as doctrinal or scientific works, even if they are conceived outside the realm of fiction. Rather, as Alcalá Galán has pointed out, many of these texts present a high degree of literariness ("literariedad") and expression (10). In the case of this third section of Torquemada's book, not all the recorded occurrences reach a notable level of artistic expression or literariness in the sense in which Alcalá Galán uses these terms. Most of the recorded cases are basically short reports presented in a straightforward manner, with little room for the kind of stylistic maneuvering that would have allowed for a meaningful buildup of feelings of anxiety, anticipation, uncertainty, or suspense. We can nonetheless find some examples that come closer to the stylistic affectation and atmospheric feel of the classic gothic tale. I focus here on a handful of the more elaborate reports, which achieve a certain level of independence from the expositive structure of the colloquium.

The first of these recorded anecdotes is framed by the alluded discussion about the practical impossibility of distinguishing between preternatural manifestations and the fantastical images engendered by the imagination. The events in question are said to have taken place thirty years back in the neighboring town of Fuentes de Ropel and would have resulted in the inexplicable death of Antonio Costilla, a prominent gentleman ("hidalgo y principal") known for his strength, determination, and valor. The source of the story is the interlocutor Antonio, who personally vouches for Costilla's bravery and strength: "[P]orque le vi en algunos trances y revueltas de muy gran peligro, de los cuales se libró con muy gran esfuerzo y valor de su persona" (264) ([F]or I saw him in the midst of dangerous events and situations, which he escaped with great labor and personal valor).

In the tale, Costilla is returning home from a business trip in Villanueva when he is overtaken by a pious desire to pray at the entrance of a hermitage

excavation of an absence over reason as domination" (71). I have maintained elsewhere that the baroque horror vacui signals not just a taste for decorative excess but a fundamental feeling of attraction/revulsion concerning open spaces and the idea of absence (see my "Horror (Vacui): The Baroque Condition").

on the side of the road. Costilla is suddenly roused from his devotions by the terrifying sight of three unearthly presences (*tres visiones*) that appear to be coming out of the ground inside the partially lit structure. The man stands there transfixed, seemingly paralyzed by incredulity and fear. Eventually, he turns his horse around and starts home, but no sooner does he look up at the road ahead than the ghouls manifest in front of him. Uttering some words of prayer, Costilla scrambles desperately to leave the three figures behind. As a last resort, the gentleman charges against the ghouls, but the figures somehow manage to keep a constant distance from him, all the way to his home and into the stables. At last, the specters disappear, leaving Costilla in such a pitiful state of confusion and sickly appearance that his wife is certain he must have undergone some tragic ordeal with his enemies. She asks him repeatedly about the trip, but his responses make no sense to her, so she sends for his best friend, a well-regarded man of letters. Costilla confides in his good friend, who tries to console him the best he can, talks him into having a bite to eat, and leaves him to get some much needed rest. The moment the gentleman is left alone in his bedroom, he begins to scream in horror. By his own account, the three specters had come back to throw handfuls of dirt at his eyes. Costilla lost his eyesight as a result of the encounter and died shortly thereafter.

As Antonio brings his story to a close, the other interlocutors offer their own perspectives on the matter. Luis notes that a doctor would surely think of this as a clear case of melancholia. Bernardo agrees that this is indeed a reasonable assumption, which could explain the terrifying visions and even Costilla's untimely death. As he says, we are all subjected to the deceptive power of the imagination, and the terror inspired by phantoms can easily have deadly consequences in a melancholic soul. But the knowledge that a natural explanation might be possible does not persuade Bernardo to reject the view that this is an actual case of demonic persecution: "Y no por esto dejaré de creer también que estas tres visiones serían algunos demonios, que [. . .] viniesen a poner tan grande espanto a ese hombre, que fuese causa de que viniese a morirse" (266) (And not for this reason will I abandon the belief that these three visions were actually some demons [. . .] who put such fear in this man as to cause his death).

It is interesting that none of the interlocutors feels the need to make sense of the haunting of Antonio Costilla in moralistic terms. There is no lesson to learn here, other than the notion that this type of inexplicable phenomena can easily accommodate different and contrary opinions, as Antonio eloquently puts it: "En todas las cosas que no se pueden averiguar de ciencia cierta nunca faltan opiniones diversas y contrarias" (266) (With respect to those subjects of which we do not have certain knowledge, there is never a shortage of diverse and contrary opinions). In fact, there is no stated or even suggested reason for this case of demonic persecution, which would have been prompted not by acts of hubris or contempt for religious symbols (as one might expect) but, most curiously, by the gentleman's sensible display of sincere devotion. Furthermore, Costilla's desperate appeals to the Supreme Judge seem to go unanswered. The bizarre occurrence is thus grouped with other puzzling or inexplicable phenomena whose secret meaning is known to God alone. As for the functional logic of the inclusion of this episode in the *Jardín*, we may do well to turn to Bernardo, who makes the point that exposure to uncertainty and terror awakens feelings of profound admiration: "Muchas cosas acaecen en el mundo semejantes a las que habeis contado que ponen en muy grande admiración, así por ser espantosas, como por no poderse entender la causa de ellas" (267) (Many things occur in the world similar to the events you have narrated, which cause great admiration for their terrifying nature and their unknown origin).

This observation works as a transitional statement with which Bernardo prefaces his own narration of some ghastly events that reportedly took place a few years back in the Italian city of Bologna, involving a Spanish law student by the name of Juan Vázquez de Ayola. Allegra has documented the long-lasting success of this episode of the *Jardín*, which would be quoted and reproduced in curiosity culture circles well into the nineteenth century.[18] The tale is notably lengthier and more elaborate than the previous anecdote. The slower pace, the considerable level of descriptive detail, and the deliberate cultivation of suspense all contribute to the atmospheric feel of the narrative. The basic story line will seem familiar to readers of classic ghost stories.

In Bernardo's tale, a group of young men who seek lodging in a foreign town come across a stately house that has remained uninhabited for many years on account of rumors of demonic possession. Dismissing the persistent rumors and the ominous warnings of the locals, including the owner of the property, the men decide to move into the house. A full month goes by before the students experience anything unusual. This uneventful period comes to an end when Ayola is suddenly roused from his study at the midnight hour by a noise of dragging chains approaching the main staircase. Deeply shaken

18. Allegra points out that this famous case of demonology is quoted in Goulart's *Trésor des histoires admirables* (Treasure of Admirable Stories) and summarized in P. L. Jacob's *Curiosités infernales* (1886) (Infernal Curiosities). According to Allegra, both authors mention Torquemada as their source.

and fearing for his life, the young man places his trust in God, crosses himself fervently, and starts toward the source of the noise, holding his sword in one hand and the candelabra, with a single lit candle, in the other. The dreadful clatter gets progressively louder, as though the chains are being slowly dragged across the floor toward the base of the stairs. At last, a horrifying apparition comes through the door. The hair-raising sight has a paralyzing effect on the poor student, whose body is overtaken by a wholly unnatural rigidity. The vision is described with morbid gusto: "Y estando así vio asomar por la puerta de la escalera una visión espantosa [. . .] porque era un cuerpo de un hombre grande, que traía sólo los huesos compuestos, sin carne ninguna como se pinta la muerte, y por las piernas y alrededor del cuerpo venía atado con aquellas cadenas que traía arrastrando" (269) (And thus standing, he saw coming through the door by the stairs a terrifying vision [. . .], the corpse of a big man with nothing but bones in it, entirely devoid of flesh, as death is commonly depicted, and it was tied around the legs and torso to these chains that dragged behind him). Seemingly unable to move or to avert his eyes from the gruesome spectacle, Ayola masters the courage to ask the ghostly figure who or what he is and the reason behind his present appearance, promising to assist him in whatever way he can. At this, the living corpse signals him to follow toward a field at the back of the house.

The narrator builds up the suspense in this section of the tale, employing stylistic resources that will be familiar to anyone who has ever read a horror story. As Ayola starts to follow the specter, the candle suddenly goes out, leaving him in total darkness: "Ayola la siguió, y llegando al medio de la escalera, o porque viniese algún viento, o que turbado de verse solo con tal compañia la vela topase e alguna cosa, se le mató, y entonces de creer es que su turbación y espanto serían muy mayor" (269) (Ayola followed it, and in arriving at the base of the staircase, a draft must have come through, or perhaps the fear of seeing himself in such dreadful company caused him to stumble and knock the candle on something, but the light went dead, and we have to believe that his confusion and terror must have grown in the darkness). As we can see here, the reader is literally pulled into the scene, asked to put himself or herself in Ayola's place and imagine the character's growing sense of dread as he feels his way through the impenetrable darkness in the company of a living corpse. A few moments later, we are again invited to ponder over a potentially dreadful outcome in a scene in which the student gazes apprehensively at the base of a pit, wondering if this might be the end: "[P]asaron toda la casa y llegaron a un corral, y de ahí a una huerta grande, en la cual la vision entró, y Ayola tras ella, y porque enmedio estaba un pozo, temió que la visión volviendo a él le hiciese algún daño, y paróse" (269–70) (They walked through the house and arrived at the stables, and from there to a large field, which the specter entered, and Ayola behind it; there was a pit in the middle of it, and he began to fear that the figure would turn back and do something dreadful to him, and thus he stopped). After a moment of indecision, Ayola followed the ghoulish figure toward a different section of the field. A moment later, the vision vanished without a trace, leaving the student in a state of intense fear and utter confusion. Eventually, Ayola works his way back to the house and awakens his roommates, who are understandably alarmed at his sickly appearance. His friends force some food and wine into him and lay him down to rest. At last, the young man reveals the details of his ordeal. The story of his nocturnal encounter prompts an official inquiry. Ayola is summoned to provide his sworn testimony and is asked to accompany a team of men sent to dig up the field. The men find a human skeleton at the precise spot of the specter's disappearance. The anonymous remains, which inexplicably fit every detail of Ayola's description, are moved to a church. This puts an end to the dreadful noises, the apparitions, and the whole ghastly affair.

The abrupt ending leaves several important elements of the tale unexplained, such as the significance of the chains and whether or not a murder had been committed. For all we know, the apparitions may have been triggered by an act of improper burial. The lack of a fully satisfying denouement makes it difficult to make sense of the story in moralistic terms. Bernardo's tale is followed by a discussion similar to the one that ensued in response to the Costilla case, although—as Antonio says—the events of Bologna could not be attributed to an abundance of melancholia, since the body that was found behind the house must be taken as confirmation of the vision described by Ayola. Antonio is quick to point out that theologians might disagree over the meaning of the strange affair. Some could feel inclined to blame the whole business on the trickery of the devil, while others might think of it as an angelic vision. Regardless of our opinion, however, it is important to recognize that we do not have access to the whole truth. This is Antonio's last word on the subject: "[C]ada uno podrá creer lo que le pareciere [. . .] y siempre habemos de pensar que nos queda alguna cosa encubierta" (272) (Everyone can believe whatever they will [. . .], and we must always understand that there is something hidden from us). From the perspective of the reader, Antonio's philosophical reflections add a layer of uncertainty to Bernardo's tale, even if we were to believe "the facts of the case" as they have been reported to us. Hence, the unavoidable limitation of our knowledge always leaves room for interpretation with respect to the facts and their meaning.

While the story of the haunted house of Bologna is remarkable for its atmospheric quality and its stylistic cultivation of suspense, other, less elaborate reports of ghostly and demonic encounters are perhaps more significant in that they reveal deep-seated cultural anxieties. I am thinking of the potentially disintegrating threats of excessive or aberrant passions, especially female lust and homoerotic desires, as well as racial or racist anxieties, which literally begin to color the figure of the monstrous other in the cultural production of the period. In this sense, one of the more interesting passages of the *Jardín* is a tale of "unnatural" attachment that Torquemada borrows from the *Genial Days* of Alexander (Alejandro de Alejandro).

In Torquemada's version of the ancient tale, a gravely ill man asks his best friend to accompany him on a trip from Rome to Cumas, where he plans to get treated with curative baths. The two friends take to the road, together with other companions, but because the man's health deteriorates quickly, the group decides to return to their hometown. The man dies shortly thereafter and is buried in a local church. His friends hold the customary funeral ceremonies, with as much dignity and solemnity as they are able to command away from their Roman states. After several days of mourning, the group finally resumes their journey. They travel all day without incident and eventually make it to an inn for the night. At this point, things go horribly wrong for the friend of the deceased. The dead man materializes at the foot of his bed, disrobes, and slips under the covers, looking to embrace him: "El muerto se llegaba a él, dando muestras de querer abrazarlo; y viéndose en este estrecho, y estando ya en lo postrero de la cama, adonde se había retraído, sacando fuerzas de flaqueza y poniendo la ropa en medio para que no pudiese llegar a él, comenzó a resistirle. El difunto, viendo su resistencia, y que se le defendía, mirándole con un gesto airado y mostrando muy gran enojo, se tornó a levantar, y vistiéndose y calzándose, se torno a ir, sin que jamás pareciese" (276) (The dead man approached him, showing signs of wanting to embrace him, and seeing himself in such a tight spot, and having retreated to the very edge of the bed where he had been cornered, he mastered enough strength to resist him, placing the covers between them. Seeing that he resisted and defended himself, the deceased looked at him with a disapproving gesture, and showing a great deal of anger, he got back to his feet, put his clothes and shoes back on, and left to never return).

At the most basic level, this ghostly figure (any ghost for that matter) defies the laws of nature by crossing the boundaries between the world of the dead and that of the living. Specifically, the ghost challenges the notion that death marks the dissolution of all ties ("until death do us part"). But there is another type of boundary crossing at work in this story of passionate attachment beyond the grave. As we can see in the quoted passage, the dead man's unnatural attachment to his friend takes the form of a homoerotic affection, which is strictly forbidden (certainly within the moral and cultural order in which the story is redeployed by Antonio de Torquemada). Of course, moral shock is by no means strange to horror fiction. As the victim of another preternatural assault noted in "Dracula's Guest" (1914), the defiling touch of the monstrous produces "shock, moral as well as physical" (Bram Stoker 157). In the case examined here, the threat of the "unnatural touch" represents a direct challenge to the moral order, as well as the laws of the physical world. On the flip side, the self-defense mounted by the living when confronted with this doubly monstrous love request is by necessity an act of affirmation of the boundaries of the natural and moral orders. We can say that the repulsion that is acted out in this macabre theater is a basic ritual of abjection, in the precise sense in which Julia Kristeva uses the term in her classic study *Powers of Horror:* "It is thus not lack of cleanliness or health that causes abjection, but what disturbs identity, system, order. What does not respect borders, positions, rules. The in-between, the ambiguous, the composite" (4).

Significantly, Bernardo brings in another source of repulsion, a third layer of abjection, in his mention of a similar preternatural assault, which is said to have taken place contemporarily in the house of a prominent Spanish nobleman by the name of don Antonio de la Cueva. Reportedly, don Antonio was reading in his bedroom, late at night, when he heard strange noises. Suddenly, the arm of a naked black man comes out from underneath his bed: "[V]ió salir por un lado de la cama un brazo que parecía ser de algún negro desnudo, el cual tomando la candela la volvió para abajo en el candelero, y la mató, y a esta hora este caballero sintió salir aquel negro y meterse con él en la cama, y tomándose los dos a brazos, comenzaron a luchar y forcejear uno con otro, haciendo tanto estruendo que los de casa despertaron y vinieron a ver lo que era, no hallando sino solamente al don Antonio de la Cueva, el cual estaba tan encendido y sudando como si saliera de algún río" (279) (He saw coming up on one side of the bed an arm, which looked like that of a naked black man who turned the candle over and killed the light. At this moment the gentleman heard the black man come out and slip into his bed, and taking each other by the arms, they began to struggle and wrestle with one another, making such a racket that everyone in the house awoke and rushed to see what it could be, although they did not find anybody but don Antonio de la Cueva, who looked flushed and wet as if he had just come out of the river).

The necrophobic gesture that had been captured in *Genial Days* turns negrophobic in Bernardo's story (if I may be allowed the admittedly silly pun). Thus, the threat of the abject (Kristeva) is now entangled in the racial anxieties that plague the social and cultural fields of imperial Spain. In this sense, the story of the assault of don Antonio by a naked black demon represents a cultural updating of Alexander's tale of unnatural boundary crossing.

Some theorists of the fantastic and critics working on gothic horror, such as Julia Kristeva, Rosemary Jackson, and Eugenia DeLamotte, have underscored the importance of anxieties about boundaries in dark fantasies. They have noted that cultural and moral limits are taken to be coterminous with our nature in horror fiction. Hence, the crossing of limits (moral, cultural, physical, and geographical borders) threatens our individual and communal identity, the "boundaries of self"—as DeLamotte (14) aptly puts it. This is at the very root of the topical witch's flight and of her ceremonial contact with the devil, which is of course an inversion of the Christian ritual of the Eucharist.

Torquemada incorporates several examples of devil worship in this third treatise. In one of the more elaborate episodes, Antonio relates the trials and tribulations of a man of letters (*letrado*) who joined a group of devil worshipers looking to confirm his suspicions about the shady activities of his neighbor. Having witnessed a host of obscene spectacles, including the ritual of the abominable kiss of the beast, the man finally loses his patience and calls on God and the Virgin Mary to protect him. His call is answered by a thunderous clatter that causes him to lose consciousness. The man awakes hours later in a foreign land inhabited by strange peoples. Remarkably, it would take him more than three years, always walking west, to make it back to his homeland. Bernardo's reaction to the episode is most revealing of what is at stake in these tales of boundary crossing: "[E]l se arrepintió a buen tiempo, y le sucedió bien en poder volver a su naturaleza, habiéndole puesto los demonios tan lejos de ella" (314) (He repented at the right time and was fortunate to return to his nature, for the demons had taken him very far from it). The man's eventual return to "his nature" is as much a return to the moral "boundaries of self" as it is a trip back to his homeland from foreign territories inhabited by strange peoples, "gentes tan extrañas y diferentes de las de esta tierra" (313) (peoples so strange and different from those of our land).

While descriptions of devil worship often show men as well as women abandoning themselves to "infernal pleasures" ("deleites infernales," *Jardín* 311), most accounts underscore the danger of female lust. Luis' intervention in the third treatise of the *Jardín* illustrates this point very effectively: "[S]e juntan todos, y muchos demonios con ellos en figuras de gentiles hombres y hermosas mujeres, y se mezclan a rienda suelta, cumpliendo sus desordenados apetitos; y de esta compañía las mas, o casi todas dicen que son mujeres, como más aparejadas, así para ser engañadas del diablo, como para caer en el pecado de la lujuria" (315) (They all get together, with many demons among them disguised as gentlemen and beautiful women, and they all mix wildly, satisfying their disorderly appetites; and most of them are said to be women, since they are more susceptible to being deceived by the devil and to descending into the sin of lust). In their propensity to abandon themselves to infernal pleasures, females are always in danger of overstepping the boundaries of nature.

As Eugenia DeLamotte and Kari Winter have argued, anxieties about boundaries have a special relevance to the psychology of women and their social condition (Winter 23). The pressure to control women's bodies and sexual behavior has much to do with anxieties about the transmission of wealth, the preservation of bloodlines, and the protection of hierarchies and social borders. This may explain the obsession with witchcraft and witches at a time when many ancient boundaries are being pushed or pierced.[19] We can say that the early modern fixation with the figure of the witch emerges as a symptomatic manifestation of the nocturnal horror associated with the disintegration of borders at a time when the world extends out of bounds by land and sea and into space. After all, the witches' Sabbath is an inversion of (moral) order that opens the door to cosmic chaos.[20] The figure of the witch signals a paradigmatic conversion of social structures into natural borders and thus a transformation of history into nature, which is—as Roland Barthes famously put it—"the very principle of myth" (*Mythologies* 129). The punishment or sacrifice of the witch is a performative resealing of the

---

19. For more on the institutional push to control women's bodies and sexual behavior and the treatment of "deviant" women in Counter-Reformation Spain, see the collective volume edited by Anne Cruz and Mary Elizabeth Perry, *Culture and Control in Counter-Reformation Spain* (1992), especially "Woman as Source of 'Evil' in Counter-Reformation Spain," by María Helena Sánchez Ortega; "Magdalens and Jezebels in Counter-Reformation Spain," by Mary Elizabeth Perry; and "La bella malmaridada: Lessons for the Good Wife," by Anne Cruz.

20. As Allegra says, "el aspecto fundamental de la cuestión sigue siendo el de la inversión que la fiesta brujesca alegoriza con su irrupción de lo caótico, monstruoso y abyecto" (312 n. 113) (the fundamental aspect of the question is still the inversion that the witches' ceremony allegorizes with the irruption of the chaotic, the monstrous, and the abject).

social body, a collective return to our nature, and thus a ritualistic reaffirmation of its boundaries.

The last part of the third treatise of Torquemada's *Jardín* includes several episodes of necromancy and witchcraft, most of which are reelaborations of passages from the *Malleus Malleficarum*, the *Tractatus de hereticis et sortilegiis*, *De justa punitione hereticorum*, and other similar works of the period. While the general tone of Torquemada's gallery of curiosities is not admonitory or moralistic, contact with the dark side is certainly not glamorized or presented as desirable. There is no question that sorcery and witchcraft are viewed as novel topics of conversation, or "curious flowers," but it is also true that contact with the dark side is considered dangerous, aberrant, repulsive, and ultimately denaturalizing. In this sense, these episodes are entirely consistent with the logic of abjection, according to which the social body must reject every "thing" that disturbs identity, system, order, borders, positions, or rules (to paraphrase Kristeva). As we shall see shortly, the situation is far more complex in *La silva curiosa*. In his eccentric and highly self-conscious collection of curious horrors, Julián de Medrano engages many of the same subjects—including death, spectral visitations, and the cultivation of the dark arts—with a jovial delectation that has been qualified as morbid, necrophilic, and "nearly pathological" ("casi patológica," Alcalá Galán 31).

A Tour of the Graveyard in *La silva curiosa*

La silva curiosa has received very little critical attention, even among scholars working on sixteenth-century miscellanea. In fact, the first critical edition of the work of Julián de Medrano dates from 1998. Prior to the publication of this edition by Mercedes Alcalá Galán, *La silva* was virtually unknown. In her insightful introductory study, Alcalá Galán underscores the extravagant and outlandish nature of this textual cabinet of curiosities. She compares the heterogeneous components of the work with diverse objects floating in a meandering river (15). Among these free-floating curiosities, we can find seemingly mimetic reproductions of popular discursive forms, such as proverbs, refrains, courtly poetry, and short folkloric tales.[21] But Medrano's cultivation of highly conventional forms of writing, such as the pastoral narrative, devi-

21. According to Alcalá Galán, as many as forty-three compositions included in *La silva* are extracted from Juan de Timoneda's *Sobremesa y alivio de caminantes.*

ates from the norm or standard in important ways. Whereas Neoplatonic literature creates highly stylized expressions of spiritual love, Medrano's treatment of the pastoral genre focuses on the consummation of the sexual act (Alcala Galán 27).

More subtle perhaps, but equally significant, is *La silva*'s deviation from the conventions of the traditional epitaph. The life of the deceased is basically meaningless in Medrano's epitaphs, with the exception of those potentially scandalous occurrences that might add to the shock value of the sensationalist presentation of death. Thus, the majority of the epitaphs included in the collection describe grotesque deaths, "hombres que murieron por muerte cruel o desastrada" (231) (men who died of cruel and disastrous death). One of the few references to the circumstances of somebody's life occurs in an epitaph devoted to a cockled man ("cornudo") killed by a bull. These verses work as a cruel joke: "Cornudo fue en la vida por su suerte; / Otros cuernos después le dieron muerte" (232) (Cockled was he in life by destiny; / Other horns would kill him eventually). The narrator seizes the moment to make his own sardonic remark: "Assí el cuitado dio el alma a Dios con cuernos detrás y cuernos delante" (232) (Thus, the unfortunate man brought his soul before God with horns on the back and horns on the front).[22] While the conventional epitaph is a form of remembrance aimed at capturing the essential meaning of a life that has come to an end, the epitaphs gathered in *La silva* have very little to do with the goal of making sense of (a) life. There is nothing but macabre theater here. In this sense, the collection evokes Fernando R. de la Flor's description of the baroque spectacle of death as funerary theater that signifies nothingness (*nihil*, a vacuum).[23]

I have argued elsewhere that the baroque cult of decorative excess is symptomatic of epochal anxieties that were triggered by a pervasive sense of loss of meaning. As I suggested in "Horror (Vacui): The Baroque Condition," this epochal fixation with emptiness and absence would result in a paradoxical longing for the absolute (87–88). Hence, in the context of Counter-

22. Alcalá Galán writes, "Los epitafios de la Silva tienen la finalidad de divertir con el relato escabroso del final de una vida, y lo que menos importa es la memoria del difunto" (32) (The epitaphs of the Silva are meant to amuse with the shocking details of the end of a life, and the memory of the deceased is of no importance).

23. See especially chapters 1 and 2 of his book *Barroco: Representación e ideología en el mundo hispánico (1580–1680)*. As he writes, "las nociones de vacío, nada e infinito [. . .] son centrales en la construcción de la cosmovisión barroca" (91) (the notions of emptiness, nothingness, and infinity [. . .] are central to the construction of the baroque worldview).

Reformation Spain, official religious discourse and some forms of secular culture work to restore the idea of a meaningful world and thus to (re)situate individuals in relation to social values and structures. The products of what Maravall calls "la cultura dirigida del barroco" (the guided culture of the baroque) are rooted in this drive to fill the blanks of nonmeaning that had appeared in the social fabric as a result of the epistemological crisis of the late sixteenth century.

However, we can also find a host of examples of baroque literature and art that not only do not contribute to fill the gaps in the officially sanctioned worldview but actually call attention to the void at the center of it all. Once we have accepted the essential lesson of the baroque philosophy of *desengaño* (the suspicion that the true face of the world is hidden behind "colorful deceptions," or "engaños coloridos," as Sor Juana Inés de la Cruz refers to them), it takes but a subtle turn of the screw for us to slide from a position of acceptance of the official paradigm that purportedly shows the (metaphysical) light at the end of the tunnel to one from which this shining beacon of "truth" appears as a new man-made deception, another "vain artifice" that must be unmasked and exposed for what it is: "death," "dust," "shadow," "nothingness" (to borrow again from Sor Juana Inés de la Cruz).[24]

24. I have borrowed these expressions from Sor Juana Inés de la Cruz's paradigmatic sonnet of *desengaño* known as "A su retrato" (On Her Portrait). Given the fragile status of certainty and truth in baroque thought and aesthetics, any slight deviation from the light of official dogma may push us toward the edge of the abyss. Among seventeenth-century scientists and philosophers, perhaps no author expresses better the anxious pathos of this paradoxical longing for the absolute than Blaise Pascal (1623–62). As a mathematician, physicist, and religious thinker, Pascal is known for his defense of the scientific method in the face of criticism, for his elaborations on the concept of the vacuum, and for his unfinished *Apologie de la religion Chrétienne* (Apologia of the Christian Religion), which would later be published with the title *Pensées de M. Pascal sur la religion et sur quelques autres subjets* (Thoughts of M. Pascal on Religion and Other Matters). The terror of the dark abyss is never far from Pascal's thinking, even in the midst of his theological work: "When I see the blind and wretched state of man, when I survey the whole universe in its dumbness and man left to himself with no light, as though lost in this corner of the universe, without knowing who put him there, what he has come to do, what will become of him when he dies, incapable of knowing anything, I am moved to terror, like a man transported in his sleep to some terrifying desert island, who wakes up quite lost and with no means of escape" (*Pensées* I.I5.I98h5). Note the echoes of "nocturnal horror" in the following discussion of the ontological place of man between nothingness and infinity: "For after all what is man in nature? A nothing in relation to infinity, all in

In the case of Medrano's work, the multiple faces of death and the unsettling shadows that emerge in the dark section entitled "Parte de los epitaphios curiosos hallados por Julio" represent the original expression of loss of values of an age that has not yet replaced the eroded beliefs of the ancients. This is one of those rare moments in history when the void in the symbolic order becomes visible.[25] In the absence of new symbolic constructs, there is nothing but ruins in the desert of the world. To put it differently, before the emerging discourse(s) of modernity can offer compensation for the loss of the destitute symbols of antiquity, there is a brief ideological vacuum.[26] The pathological indifference of *La silva curiosa* toward symbolic constructs reveals the pits of contingency, arbitrariness, and nonmeaning gaping at the center of the eroded beliefs and values of the ancients before the attempted reconstruction of the symbolic edifice in the cultural products of the high baroque, from sermons and religious theater, to Lopean and Calderonian productions, to the moralistic and/or admonitory picaresque narratives of Mateo Alemán and Francisco de Quevedo.[27]

Fittingly, the final part of *La silva* relates the adventures of an antiquar-

---

relation to nothing, a central point between nothing and all and infinitely far from understanding either. The ends of things and their beginnings are impregnably concealed from him in an impenetrable secret. He is equally incapable of seeing the nothingness out of which he was drawn and the infinite in which he is engulfed" (*Pensées* #72). I am indebted to Kari Winter for these extraordinary quotes from Pascal.

25. Slavoj Žižek makes a similar point apropos of another paradigm-shifting moment in history in *Tarrying with the Negative* (1993), when he talks about the destitution of the old communist symbols that took place in the midst of the disintegration of the Soviet Union. He recalls a scene in which the old communist flags, with gaping holes in the middle, were being waved by enthusiastic crowds of demonstrators. The old symbols had been erased, literally ripped off from the center of the flag. There was still nothing new to replace them. The crowds thus "participated in the unique intermediate state of passage from one discourse (social link) to another, when, for a brief, passing moment, the hole in the big Other, the symbolic order, became visible" (*Tarrying* 1).

26. As Alcalá Galán aptly puts it, "La frivolidad de la *Silva* demuestra un cambio de edad, un tiempo blanco desnudo de creencias" (17) (The frivolity of the *Silva* demonstrates an epochal change, a blank time stripped of beliefs).

27. My use of the term *high baroque* here is analogous to Egginton's notion of the baroque major strategy in "Reason's Baroque House (Cervantes' Master Architect)." Egginton opposes this major strategy to a deconstructionist minor strategy borrowing from Deleuze and Guattari in *Kafka: Toward a Minor Literature* (1986).

ian who travels the desert of the world in search of ancient ruins whose meaning has eroded beyond recognition. Julio writes about one of his many trips, "[F]ui [. . .] donde ai muchas cosas antiguas y curiosas desde el tiempo de los Romanos, como lápidas escriptas, estatuas, Idolos, columnas, Tropheos con diversos lettreros y Epitaphios, que por la grande antigüidad y por ser parte d'ellos rompidos y cubiertos de moho no podía saccarse el sentido de lo que significavan (231) (I went [. . .] where there are many ancient and curious things from the time of the Romans, such as scripted gravestones, statues, idols, columns, trophies with diverse inscriptions, and epitaphs, the meaning of which could not be ascertained due to their great antiquity and because they were in part broken and covered in moss). Julio travels through different regions of Italy, France, Spain, Portugal, and even the Indies, "buscando con trabajo y curiosidad estos epitaphios, antigüidades y otras cosas singulares" (236) (laboriously searching, with curiosity, for epitaphs and other rare and ancient things). Although he says he set aside the bulk of his adventures, including his American voyage, for a second book project, titled *Vergel curioso* (Curious Meadow)—which in all probability was never written—he nonetheless manages to record in *La silva* the chronicle of his pilgrimage to Santiago de Compostela. This central section of "Parte de los epitaphios curiosos" is devoted to Julio's autobiographical account of this journey through the "deserts" of northern Spain.

The narrator uses the word *desierto* to refer to vast strips of terrain stretching from southern France to the northwestern tip of the Iberian Peninsula. The term *desert* appears more than twenty times in a sixty-page spread, rivaling expressions like *curiosity, curious,* and *ancient things. Desierto* is contemporarily defined in Covarrubias as follows: "El lugar solitario, que no le habita nadie ni le cultiva. Allí se retiran los santos padres hermitaños y monges, y en la primitiva Iglesia estaba poblado de santos" (quoted by Alcalá Galán 234 n. 352) (The solitary place, uninhabited and uncultivated where hermits and monks retire. At the time of the primitive Church, it was populated by saints). Apart from the protagonist, his foreign companions, and the occasional group of shepherds, the only other characters that make significant appearances in Julio's travel narrative are aging or dying hermits, demonic specters, and practitioners of the dark arts.

This is consistent with Barbara Benedict's assertion that the early modern discourse of the marvelous turns the countryside into a privileged site for the cultivation of the occult, thus updating (we could say inverting or perverting) a long tradition of wonder tales that represented the countryside as a spiritual reservoir where man could get close to the divine (179). Benedict also mentions that the countryside becomes "the sentimental site of lost beliefs," now viewed as "curiosities [. . .] which the traveler or reader may collect" (180).[28] She draws precise connections between the wondrous countryside of the early modern tale and the fantastic landscapes that would later serve as staging grounds for gothic fiction. Given how closely Benedict's observations fit the representation of the countryside in *La silva curiosa,* it should not be surprising that the tale of Julio's adventures in the curiosity-filled deserts of northern Spain might also be looked at as a precursor of gothic fantasies and, generally speaking, horror fiction. Alcalá Galán writes, "Los ambientes raros, la fantasía, la magia, lo macabro [. . .], el goticismo inherente a ese mundo de aparecidos, espíritus, nigromantes y prodigios convierten de cierta forma la última parte del libro en precursor de algunos relatos fantásticos de temática cercana a lo que hoy conocemos como género de terror" (16) (The rare landscapes, fantasy, magic, the macabre [. . .], the inherent Gothicism of this world of apparitions, ghosts, necromancers and prodigies in some ways turn the final part of the book into a precursor of fantastic tales whose content comes close to what we call today the horror genre).

Beyond "atmospheric" and narrowly defined thematic coincidences, it is important to point out that early modern wonder tales, like gothic fantasies, are discourses of inquiry into the limits of knowledge and morality. In fact, it could be said that these monstrous tales redefine "curiosity" as a new region of the literary imagination, devoted to the testing of epistemological boundaries and the exploration of the forbidden. Benedict says, "[W]onder tales and Gothic fictions [. . .] redefined curiosity as an aesthetic enterprise. This redefinition was exemplified no less by self-conscious literary rarities like *Vathek* than by the Grand Tour or by less grand tourism in both the country side and in literature [. . .] Imaginary literature became the new arena for the exploration of forbidden areas and the testing of truth" (180).[29] These observations resonate strongly with my own reading of *La silva curiosa.* When one examines the

28. Benedict is talking about such seventeenth-century works as *A Wonder in Staffordshire* (1661), *The Hartfordshire Wonder* (1669), and *Admirable Curiosities of England* (1682) and about such eighteenth-century wonder tales as *The Guilford Ghost* (1709), *The Hampshire Wonder, or The Groaning Tree* (1742), and *The Wonder of Surry* (1756).

29. Rosemary Jackson has also pointed out that the drive to test moral and epistemological boundaries and the titillating exploration of forbidden knowledge and prohibited modes of conduct are central to gothic fiction and, generally speaking, the modern literary fantastic.

richly grotesque atmosphere of such foundational gothic narratives as *The Castle of Otranto* and especially *Vathek* side by side with the macabre vistas of *La silva*, it becomes clear that they are all products of monstrous imaginations with deep roots in the early modern culture of curiosities.[30]

Remarkably, Julio uses the term *curiosity* to refer almost exclusively to his unquenchable thirst for morbid mementos and his self-conscious drive to master the forbidden sciences of the occult.[31] In transforming the Renaissance garden of curiosities into a desert filled with crumpling monuments, trophies and tombs, wicked necromancers, and demonic specters, Medrano redirects our pleasures of inquiry to the out-of-bounds regions of the imagination, where the laws of nature and morality can be suspended. Medrano gives us a grand tour of the dark side of the literary imagination, nearly two centuries before the 1782 publication in French of William Beckford's *Vathek* (published in English in 1786). Before the symbolic reconstruction of which Maravall speaks in *La cultura del barroco*, before the time of "the great confinement" (Foucault) and the proclamation of the age of reason, Medrano's unbounded brand of curiosity roams the European countryside

30. Benedict grounds both Walpole's *The Castle of Otranto* and Beckford's *Vathek* in the culture of curiosities. The central themes of *La silva curiosa*, even Medrano's indifferent tone and ambiguous morality, are clearly echoed by Benedict in the following passage: "The violation of literary conventions, [. . .] together with this limpid indifference to shocking scenes, liberates readers to enjoy transgressive amusement at society's expense. Walpole establishes literary curiosity as a space in which readers may safely indulge fantasies of power in alternative worlds. Later Gothics still more openly thematize curiosity as perverse ambition. William Beckford's *The History of the Caliph Vathek* exemplifies a literary rarity created for a mass audience. A collector himself, like Walpole, Beckford threw himself into the acquisition of rarities to decorate his imitation Gothic mansion, Fonthill Abbey [. . .]. *The History of the Caliph Vathek, with Notes* was published first in French, the language of courtly or exotic literature, as befits a work deliberately conceived as a curiosity; something exotic and an example of something tuned for rarefied tastes" (175–76).

31. Alcalá Galán makes this observation in her introductory study: "La palabra 'curiosidad' es un eufemismo que en la última parte de la *Silva* se refiere casi exclusivamente a la muerte. Bajo el término 'curiosidad' hay una obsesión necrófila muy acentuada que nos presenta a un Julio de Medrano recolector de epitafios que narran muertes violentas o extrañas" (30–31) (The word *curiosity* is a euphemism, which in the last part of the *Silva* refers almost exclusively to death. Under the term *curiosity*, there is a very acute necrophilic obsession that reveals Julio de Medrano as a collector of epitaphs that relate violent and strange deaths).

with mad fury.[32] As for the future history of curiosity in the seventeenth and eighteenth centuries (and beyond), I would suggest that despite the modern drive to confine and domesticate this passion of inquiry in the name of reason—suppressing its pathological baggage and redirecting it toward "productive" fields of knowledge—curiosity will keep on reappearing in its original madness in wonder tales, gothic fiction, tales of cosmic terror, and other offspring of the literary fantastic.

Curiosities/Relics/Relicts

As a prelude to a short story titled "Relic(t)s," Kari Winter reproduces the following definitions from the 1996 edition of *Webster's Dictionary:* "*relic:* 1. Something that has survived from a past culture or period. 2. A keepsake: souvenir. 3. An object of religious significance. 4. *relics.* A corpse. *relict:* 1. An organism or species of an earlier era surviving in a changed environment. 2. A widow." Relics and relicts have always been among our favorite curiosities in literature, from early wonder tales and gothic fantasies to contemporary horror stories, novels, and films. We find relics and relicts equally fascinating and horrifying, intriguing and revolting, familiar and strange, and thus essentially "uncanny."[33]

---

32. Foucault sees this key connection between madness and curiosity. Note how they come together in his discussion of the Renaissance view of madness, prior to the "great confinement" of the seventeenth century. I quote from his reflections in *Madness and Civilization* on the temptation of Saint Anthony in relation to the themes of folly and forbidden knowledge: "[M]adness fascinates because it is knowledge. It is knowledge, first, because all these absurd figures are in reality elements of a difficult, hermetic, esoteric learning. These strange forms are situated, from the first, in the space of the Great Secret, and the Saint Anthony who is tempted by them is not a victim of the violence of desire but of the much more insidious lure of curiosity; he is tempted by that distant and intimate knowledge which is offered, and at the same time evaded, by the smile of the gryllos; his backward movement is nothing but that step by which he keeps from crossing the forbidden limits of knowledge; he knows already—and that is his temptation [. . .] This knowledge so inaccessible, so formidable, the Fool, in his innocent idiocy, already possesses" (21–22). The age of reason would aim to undo the link between curiosity and madness, confining madness and redirecting curiosity toward legitimate, productive, rational, and scientific areas of inquiry.

33. Much has been written, from this perspective, on the Freudian notion of the uncanny in "Das Umheimliche" (1919), which is an elaboration of Ernst Jentsch's

In the ideologically saturated Spain of the 1600s, the pagan relic(t)s of Iberian history pose an imminent threat to the integrity of the Christian nation. As we shall see in our examination of Lozano's *La cueva de Hércules* in chapter 4, menacing ancient relic(t)s lurk just below the surface, in the cavernous underground of the symbolic capital of the Counter-Reformation, ready to unleash a new dark age. Lozano's reinscription of history's relic(t)s within the logic of abjection in his refurbishing of the old medieval legends of the cave of Toledo makes perfect sense within the political and cultural horizon of the seventeenth century. As Américo Castro has demonstrated in *De la edad conflictiva. Crisis de la cultura española en el siglo XVII* (Of the Conflictive Age. Crisis of Spanish Culture in the Seventeenth Century [1972]), this is an epoch deeply marked by fears of religious, cultural, and biological pollution. The obsessive preoccupation with the preservation of Christian bloodlines (*cristianos viejos*) would reach its boiling point in the collective paranoia of the 1600s, resulting in the publication of several decrees of Christian purity, or *estatutos de limpieza de sangre;* in the official campaigns of persecution of the Moriscos and their tragic expulsion of 1609–14; and, finally, in the symbolic cleansing of the nation's past.[34]

Yet just a few decades back, it was possible to look at ancient artifacts, including Muslim relics, with delight. Simply put, Lozano's *La cueva de Hércules* is built around the paranoid belief that we must seal the gateway to the pagan and Muslim past in order to protect our Christian nation from its contaminating influence. By contrast, the touch of the ancient relic is not seen as defiling in Medrano's work. On the contrary, the remnants of past cultures are actively sought after in *La silva curiosa*.[35] Julio looks at Roman and Mus-

---

"On the Psychology of the Uncanny" (1906). Julia Kristeva may have best captured the disturbing nature of uncanny leftovers in her theorization of "the abject" in *Powers of Horror* (1982).

34. I discuss the implications of this obsession with biological and cultural purity in the political and sexual economy in the final two chapters, apropos of Lozano's repackaging of the medieval legends of the cave of Toledo as an anti-Morisco diatribe and especially in connection with Zayas' reelaboration of the honor conflict from a feminine (and feminist) perspective in *Desengaños amorosos.*

35. While much of the thinly veiled heterodoxy of *La silva curiosa* might be attributed to Medrano's peculiar biography, his position as a prominent courtier in the court of Margarita of Navarre, and his "francofilia," as Alcalá Galán put it (see the biographical notes in her study), the fascinated attraction of relics and the morally neutral treatment of pagan themes and objects is clearly rooted in the material culture of curiosities (see Daston and Park, especially chapter 7). Incidentally, a pirated

lim ruins and inscriptions with excited curiosity and fascination, even in the depths of a bewitched cavern infested with snakes, rats, and toads: "Luego en estando dentro vimos salir de aquellos rincones dos mil culebras, ratones y sapos que nos saltavan a las piernas, y a los brazos y a la garganta [. . .] El Bretón y yo, curiosos, andávamos mirando por todas las partes de la cueva y gustávamos mucho en ver cosas tan antiguas como eran aquellos letreros y devisas qu'estavan allí escritas, la mayor parte desde el tiempo de los Moros y Romanos" (281–82) (As we entered [the cavern], we saw thousands of snakes, rats, and toads, which came out from every nook and jumped to our legs, arms, and throat [. . .] The Frenchman and I, [who are] curious, were exploring the entire cave and very much enjoying all these ancient things, including the written signs and emblems, most of which dated from the time of the Moors and the Romans).

The metonymic identification of curiosities with the curious subjects who enjoy them is self-empowering in the textual world of *La silva,* even (or perhaps more so) when these curiosities are found in obscure or forbidden realms. The fact that Christóbal Salvage is a wicked monster, a murderer, and presumably a servant of the devil does not deter Julio from seeking to master the necromancer's science: "Y pues mi suerte ha querido hacerme tan venturoso que yo tengo tanta parte en vos, cumple que yo participe en vuestra scientia; porque es uno de los mayores desseos que yo tengo en esta vida" (273) (And since my good fortune has blessed me with your friendship, it is only fair that I should participate in your science, for this is one of the greatest desires of my life). To be sure, Julio will go on to clarify (somewhat cynically) that he is not talking about the diabolical arts: "No quiero yo penetrar tan adelante que vos me mostréis ningún secreto ni experimento de los que tocan a esa scientia negra y tenebrosa, porque yo aborrezco mortalmente las invocaciones y esconjuros de demonios, pues son ennemigos de Dios, nuestro creador" (273) (I do not wish to penetrate so far that you might show me secrets or experiments partaking of the black and sinister science, for I mortally abhor invocations and conjurations of demons, since they are enemies of

version of *La silva* appeared in Zaragoza (1580, Juan Escartilla) before the official (princeps) edition of 1583 (Paris, Nicolas Chesneau). We can think of the apocryphal version published in Spain as evidence of a receptive and avid sixteenth-century market for this type of curious miscellanea. The collecting culture of the early modern period and much of baroque art and literature would continue to treat ancient artifacts as objects of curiosity and fascination. The culteranist poetry of Góngora and his followers, which is often viewed as monstrous, may be considered paradigmatic in this respect.

God our creator). The ironic effect of this meaningless and perfectly ludicrous disclaimer adds insult to injury, especially in light of Julio's eagerness to visit the necromancer's secret chamber.

During his visit, Julio describes the cave of Christóbal Salvage as a curiosity cabinet ("Armario"), which contains a host of diabolical artifacts and inscriptions and a grisly collection of body parts. Even the necromancer gets into the spirit of the curiosity culture. He exhibits his gallery of horrors with the self-conscious pride of a collector of precious rarities. The narrator's detailed inventory of the contents of the cave and his unconvincing disclaimers are certainly worth quoting here: "'Julio mío, agora conosceréis quién soi, agora veréis por experientia que soi raro entre las obras de Natura'. Diziendo esto, teniendo una candela encendida en la mano me lleva al Armario de su cueva, y con tres llaves que tenía abrió tres cerrajas qu'en su puerta o ventana havía. Y, trarme pargaminos vírgines escriptos con sangre y otras tintas diversas. Me muestra imágines de cera, de plomo, de palo y de tierra. Las unas tenían una espina en el ojo, las otras en el corazón, otra tenía un clavo en la juntura de la rodilla, otra en medio d'el pie. El me muestra tambien ciertas ojas de plomo y otras de papel, y otras de pargamino en las quales havía figuras, ruedas y diversos caracteres escriptos, y él llamaba tales ojas Pentáculos o Espantáculos. Passando adelante, y escudriñando más adentro en su cueva, sacca de un rincón un gran puñado de cabellos atados en dos mil lazos. Sacca una calabaza larga llena de dientes de muertos, sacca huessos, sacca cabezas qu'el havía cortado en los sepulchros de los muertos. Yo, viendo cosas tan diabólicas, principié a sentir tal horror y espanto que volvía la cabeza a tras por no ver cosas tan terribles. Y desseando apartarme de la puerta de la cueva quise escaparme; pero no osava" (276) ("'My dear Julio, you will now know me for who I truly am, you will see by your own experience that I am rare among the works of Nature." Having said this, and holding a lit candle in his hand, he takes me to the Cabinet of his cave, and with three keys that he had, he opens the three locks on the door or window, and he shows me some parchment with inscriptions written in blood and diverse inks. He shows me figures made of wax, lead, wood, and clay. Some had prickles in their eyes, others in their heart; another one had a spike in the knee joint, and another in the middle of the foot. He also shows me certain sheets made of lead and some made of paper and some of parchment, in which there were figures, wheels, and different inscriptions, and he called these sheets Pentagrams. Going deeper into the cave, he brings out a fistful of hairs tied up in thousands of knots. He brings a large pumpkin filled with the teeth of dead men; he brings out bones and heads that he had severed from corpses in their tombs. Seeing such diabolical things, I began to feel a great deal of horror and fear and to turn my head the other way to avoid looking at them. And wishing to get away from the door, I wanted to escape but did not dare).

This fascinating passage is exemplary of the moral ambiguity that permeates the textual world of *La silva curiosa*. The narrator may be looking to shield himself from the charges of heterodoxy when he expresses his disgust at the sight of the "diabolical things" contained in the necromancer's chamber, but his show of revulsion is not entirely convincing. Julio had every reason to suspect the sinister nature of the contents of the cave. Also, if he had worked so hard to avoid looking at these dreadful things, how is it that he can describe them in minute detail? Moreover, in a passage that seems inconsistent with his disclaimer, we will later learn that Julio comes to be in possession of the most precious of the necromancer's relics, the secret book of incantations that holds the key to his fabulous powers. We must keep in mind that the narrator imagines a sympathetic audience of curious readers who should be able to appreciate his taste for macabre rarities and his fascination with occult powers.[36]

The richness of detail in the description of the necromancer's gallery of horrors contrasts sharply with the narrator's perfunctory references to the sacred relics of Santiago de Compostela. His hurried and utterly uninterested comments on the church of Saint James and the relics of the patron saint are utterly devoid of curiosity. This is remarkable when we consider that Julio had presented his autobiographical narrative as a pilgrimage story. The church of Santiago de Compostela that contains the remains of the apostle was (and still is) the point of destination of countless pilgrims, the sacred place where their spiritual desire ought to find complete satisfaction.[37] Remarkably, Santiago de Compostela is not the end of the journey for Julio and his companions; it is not even a particularly significant or memorable station. In fact, the narrator devotes no more than a short paragraph to their visit of

---

36. Alcalá Galán says about Julio's disclaimers, "Su situación es la de un hombre que quiere protegerse de juicios morales adversos, pero que ante todo pretende que se le reconozca su pertenencia a un ámbito de dificil acceso y que lo pone en un umbral de poder y conocimiento susceptible de ser admirado" (35) (His situation is that of a man who wants to protect himself from adverse moral judgments; yet, he wishes to be recognized, first and foremost, as someone who belongs to a circle of difficult access which grants him admirable knowledge and power).

37. I am paraphrasing here from "El Persiles" (1980) by Alban Forcione and Tilbert Diego Stegmann. The essay focuses on the religious significance of Persiles' pilgrimage to Rome in Cervantes' *Los trabajos de Persiles y Sigismunda* (1617).

Santiago: "Y entrando en Compostella, la primera visita que hizimos fue visitar la Santa Iglesia donde reposa el cuerpo d'el buen Padrón. Estando allí, después de haver hecho nuestra oration con grande consolatión y contento, y visitando la sancta capilla de los Franceses, deliberamos de confessarnos el día siguiente y recibir en ella el Sancto Sacramento, y assí lo hizimos. Y, después de haver oído nuestra missa muy devotamente, fuimos como es la costumbre a visitar la iglesia d'el Padrón, y las cosas sanctas y antiguas que se hallan en ella y en la montaña de Buratos. Llegados allí y nuestra devotión cumplida, concertamos de partir al día siguiente" (285) (And as we arrived in Compostela, we first paid a visit to the Sacred Church in which the body of our Patron rests. Once there, and after we had prayed with much solace and joy, we visited the sacred chapel of the French and decided to confess on the following day and to receive the Sacred Sacrament there, which we did. And having attended mass with much devotion, we went to visit, as it is customary, the patron's church and other sacred and ancient things, which can be found there and in the mountain of Buratos. Having arrived and complied with our devotions, we agreed to leave on the following day).

The entire two-day visit of Santiago is contained in these few lines. Furthermore, the emphasis on devotional compliance ("nuestra devotión cumplida") and on the perfunctory nature of their actions ("como es la costumbre") trivializes the pilgrims' experience, turning what ought to be acts of profound spiritual significance into a series of virtually empty rituals and meaningless busywork. In fact, the most significant event that will take place in the city of the apostle is the tragic death of one of Julio's companions at the hands of an evil spirit that had been haunting him since before the beginning of the pilgrimage. This outcome is all the more disturbing when we recall that the reason behind the devotional journey of the unfortunate German pilgrim was his desperate hope to escape from the clutches of his demonic tormentor.

The tale of the haunting of the German pilgrim is central to this final part of Medrano's work. The story has all the ingredients of a full-blown gothic fantasy: Faustian motives, visions of damnation, voices from the dead, restless corpses, uncanny surroundings, puzzling actions, suspense, sudden revelations, and occasional jolts of hair-raising terror. Also, as is often the case in classic gothic fiction (beginning with Horace Walpole's *The Castle of Otranto*), this is ultimately a story about the crushing weight of the past. The sense of impending doom is impressed on the reader from the very beginning of the tale, when the German pilgrim is suddenly struck by a vision of death in a remote sanctuary devoted to the memory of Saint James. The description of this dreadful meeting is evocative of the techniques of pictorial anamorphosis, known in the sixteenth century as the *curious perspective:* "Este Alemán sube por la cuesta arriba, llega a la Ermitta, en la qual avía [. . .] una imagen de Santiago, delante la qual el Alemán se arrodilla y haze oration; y levantado, volviendo la cabeza al lado izquierdo, vee un hombre muerto qu'estava en un rincón. El qual (como este peregrino juró por los sanctos de Dios), estando tiesso y derecho contra la pared, abre la bocca y estiende el brazo para asir el Alemán que muy cerca dél estava. El qual tomó tal espanto y terror desto queél cae tendido en el suelo y principia a dar grades grittos" (238) (This German man climbs up the hill and arrives at the hermitage in which there was [. . .] an image of Saint James. He kneels before it and prays; and as he rises to his feet and turns his head to the left, he sees a dead man resting in the corner. As the pilgrim swore before all of God's saints, the corpse, which was resting stiffly against the wall, opened its mouth and extended its arm, trying to grab the German, who was standing nearby. He was overtaken by such dread and terror that he collapsed on the floor screaming).

The devotional image of Saint James is suddenly replaced by a side glance that reveals the terrifying presence of death. The face of death appears as we turn our head and look awry, as in the well-known anamorphic portrait of French ambassadors (1533) by Hans Holbein (see Illustration 3). The anamorphic echoes of the double image that congeals in the frozen gaze of the pilgrim reinforce the suggestion of a symbiotic relation between the sacred and the abject. The anamorphic scene shows that the distance between the third and fourth definitions of *relic* quoted earlier ("an object of religious significance" and "a corpse") is simply the space between the frontal view and the side glance. This is, of course, the place occupied by the gaze, that is, the subject position. Conversely, when we examine this double image as we would an anamorphic picture, we are struck by the revelation that the distinction between the two meanings of *relic* (sacred and abject) is but a matter of perspective.

When we look back at this initial scene from the vantage point provided by the devastating conclusion of the tale, this curious or anamorphic image emerges as a dreadful premonition, a sign of terrible things to come. Indeed, it is within the walls of the city-sanctuary of Santiago that the pilgrim will be eventually claimed by the old enemy: death ("la muerte," 249). Most disturbingly, the death of this contrite sinner and devout believer is prefigured in the narrative as a journey to the place where his soul will join his spectral tormentor in punishment for the sins of his past, ironically on the night of Shrove Tuesday, or Mardi Gras: "[E]ntrando en la cámara hallaron en medio

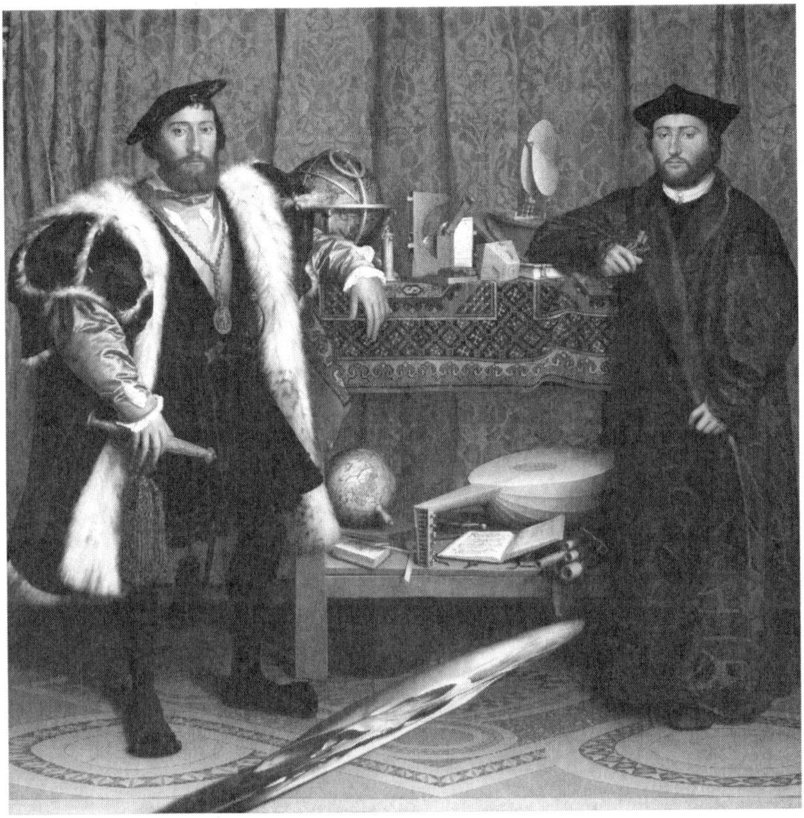

Illustration 3. Hans Holbein's *The Ambassadors.* (Image from the National Gallery, London.)

d'ella el cuerpo d'el pobre Alemán muerto y frío. Y, como Gandalín nos dixo, esto succedió un sábado la noche, que era tres días antes de carnestoliendas, y estonces nos acordamos de lo que el Negromante havía dicho al pobre Alemán quando le dixo que l'esperaría la noche de carnestoliendas debaxo d'el árbol quemado" (286) (Entering the bedroom, they found in the middle of it the cold dead body of the poor German. And, as Gandalín had said, this happened on a Saturday night, three days before Shrove Tuesday; and then we came to remember what the necromancer had said to the poor German when he told him that he would be waiting for him on the night of Shrove Tuesday under the burned tree).

The terrible fate of the German pilgrim is hardly unique among the travelers who cross these mountains. The old hermit refers to the general area as an evil land ("mala tierra," 243), known as the Pass of Ill-Fated or the Pass of the Unfortunate ("el Puerto desventurado o el Puerto de desventura," 243). Among the hermit's stories of terrible events that had taken place in this rough and sterile desert ("desierto qu'es muy áspero [. . .] y estéril," 243), Julio remarks on a tale of two friends who were suddenly overtaken by murderous fury in their crossing of the pass. The memory of the event was preserved on the wall of the hermitage: "Mirando a otra parte, vi en la pared la figura de un demonio pintado qu'estava Escondido entre unas peñas, con una caña y ligna de pescador en las manos; que mirava dos pelegrinos que también estavan allí en figura, los quales se combatían y, como la pintura significava, se divan el uno al otro cruelíssimas puñaladas" (241) (Gazing in a different direction, I saw on the wall the painted figure of a demon who was hiding behind some rocks, with a fishing pole in his hands; he was looking at two pilgrims who were represented in the act of combat, cruelly staving each other, as the painting signified).

This dual image creates a narrative that identifies a hidden (demonic) cause behind the frontal scene of the carnage. In the physical and symbolic space of the hermitage, the life-size figure of the corpse extending its arm toward the living merges with the pictorial representation of the devil fishing for souls. This composite image is the stain in the picture that reveals the true face of the world, like the floating skull in Holbein's portrait of French ambassadors. This is not the joyful union of the soul with the Supreme Lover celebrated by the mystic poets of the previous decades; it is the dreadful fate of the unfortunate, the desperate, and the hopeless. If, as Casalduero, Forcione, and Avalle-Arce have all noted, the Christian journey is an allegory of human life, a search for the final answer of the human condition, the answer suggested by the terrible fate of the pilgrim here is certainly a somber one.[38] Miracles are past, even in the city-sanctuary of Santiago.

In the absence of a proper denouement for this narrative of pilgrimage, we may read the "progression of epitaphs" in the last few pages of *La silva curiosa* as a sort of epilogue. The narrator himself signals a certain narrative continuity when he recalls his visit to the church of Saint James and the city of Santiago at the beginning of the section titled "Progressión de epitaphios." His recollection is an empty gesture that adds nothing to his previous (non)description: "[N]o quiero alargarme más en contarte las cosas singulares y mui antiguas que yo vi tanto en la ciudad de Compostella que

38. See the classic studies on Cervantes' *Persiles* and the Christian pilgrimage by Joaquín Casalduero (1947), Alban Forcione (1972), and Avalle-Arce (1990).

dentro de la linda y devotíssima yglesia de señor Santiago" (287) (I do not want to overextend myself in telling you about the singular and very ancient things I saw in the city of Compostela and inside the beautiful and very devout church of the lord Saint James). The notion that the narrator might "overextend himself" (*alargarse*) in telling us more about the relics of the apostle is quite preposterous when we consider that he has said virtually nothing thus far. In this context, this passage's signaling of a metonymic sliding of devotion from the subject to the object seems hardly accidental. The impression of ironic cynicism is reinforced by the use of the superlative ("devotíssima yglesia de señor Santiago"). The subject has been displaced from the statement. He is literally absent from the scene of devotion. Instead, he occupies the "external" position of the onlooker. Conversely, this superlative display of devotion at the sacred temple takes place without him.

The narrator's (silenced) recollection of the city-sanctuary at the beginning of the section works as a link in the "progression of epitaphs," from the relics of Saint James and the pilgrimage story to the next adventure-epitaph ("Aventura y Epitaphio"), located on the outskirts of the "Ermitta de Finibus Terrae" (287). This hermitage, which sits on a rock formation overlooking the Atlantic Ocean at the edge of the ancient world, marks the end of the line of Continental travel routes ("Finibus Terrae"). This remote and barren land ("lugar apartado y desierto," 287) is the resting place of Orcavella, an ancestral witch who sustained her unnatural life with the help of diabolical arts and the flesh and blood of innocent children. The narrative paints a rich portrait of this ancient vampiric monster: "En el tiempo de las grandes guerras d'España contra los Moros y paganos, apportó en esta tierra de Gallicia una mugger bárbara, vieja, fea y cruelíssima como un demonio. La qual, siendo gran encantadora y mui esperimentada en las artes mágicas, fue tan severa y ennemiga mortal de los hombres y mugeres que aquel monstro de natura persecutó tan cruelmente este pobre Reino de Gallicia con sus artes diabólicas que no havía hombre, mugger ni bruto animal que se salvasse, si ell podía verle los ojos o le tocaba en la carne con su mano. Ella se hazía invisible quando quería, y se transformava en diversas formas. Ella robava de noche y de día quantos niños podía, y con la carne y sangre de aquellas pobres criaturas innocentes mantenía su vida [. . .] Y al fin, viendose ya harta de la sangre humana, y ya cansada y enojada de vivir tanto, escogió por su postrera habitatión y fin este desierto. Y después de haver hecho un encantamiento terrible y cruelíssimo entre las peñas que allí arriba están, hizo en medio d'ellas una tumba o sepulchro en la peña viva con sus propias manos" (288–89) (At the time of the great wars of Spain against the Moors and the pagans, there came on this land of Galicia a barbaric woman—old, ugly, and wicked as a demon. She was a great witch experienced in the magic arts and a mortal enemy of men and women, whom she cruelly persecuted in this poor kingdom of Galicia with her diabolical craft; and thus no man, woman, or wild beast was safe from her if she could look at them in the eye or touch their flesh with her hand. She made herself invisible at will and could take different shapes. She kidnapped as many children as she could, day and night, and sustained her life with the flesh and blood of her innocent victims. At last, tired of life and human blood, she chose this desert for her final resting place, and casting a terrible and wicked spell, she carved her tomb or sepulcher amid these rocks with her very own hands).

This shocking picture of abjection is reminiscent of the horrors inside the necromancer's cave. The detailed description of Orcavella's resting place, which spreads over several pages, contrasts with the strange silence that has fallen over the relics of Saint James. In fact, I cannot help but think that the cursed corpse of the witch buried at Finibus Terrae ("corpo maldito de la encantadora Orcavella") functions as an inverted or perverted image of the sacred relics (corpse) of the apostle, which marks the point of destination of the Christian journey. While the body of the dead saint resting in Santiago de Galicia seems to have no more miracles left in it (the apostle could do nothing to save the devout German pilgrim from eternal death), the powers of Orcavella are evident in the abundance of venomous beasts that are seen guarding her tomb: "[L]a tumba y sepulchro quedan rodeados de una tan grande multitud de culebras, áspides y serpientes que los guardan noche y día" (290) (The tomb and sepulcher are surrounded by a multitude of snakes, vipers, and serpents, which guard them day and night). The deadly presence of Orcavella is felt most severely by those who dare walk about her resting place, for they all perish within the year. The fact that Orcavella's corpse can still intervene with deadly consequences in the world of the living allows us to think of it as both a relic and a relict, an "organism or species of an earlier era surviving in a changed environment."

As we reread "Parte de los epitaphios curiosos" from the perspective provided by the lurking presence of Orcavella, we realize that only old hermits and monstrous organisms or "monsters of nature" seem to have survived the earlier era. The expression *monstro de natura* is used in the narrative to name Orcavella as well as Christóbal Salvage. The witch and the necromancer are surviving relicts of the ancient world in this land of the ill-fated deserted by the divine ("mundo desdivinizado," as Maravall calls it in *El mundo social de "La Celestina"*). This is hardly surprising when we recall that *chaos* is another word for evil. The revered relics of Santiago have become an empty carcass in the changed environment of the late sixteenth century, a pathetic leftover of an age that has come to an end, one more grotesque corpse and one more collectable epitaph. Before the attempted symbolic reconstruction of the high baroque, before the eighteenth-century proclamation of the age of reason, the forces of chaos and contingency (Salvage, Orcavella) rule over the desert of the world. As for the luminous future of modern reason, there is always the danger of someone stumbling upon Salvage's (now Julio's) ancestral book of incantations; someone might accidentally disturb Orcavella's sepulcher; someone might open the door to the ancient (unholy) past and unleash the darkness within.

TWO

Sins of Our Fathers (and Spouses): The Preternatural in Baroque Exemplary Tales

Monsters and Prodigies in the Baroque Landscape

In his classic study *La cultura del barroco* (1975), José Antonio Maravall calls attention to the sensationalist aspects of seventeenth-century Spanish culture. He notes that the directed or guided culture of the baroque mobilizes irrational impulses in the service of values and beliefs that aid in the justification of the social order and the established system of authority. Maravall is thinking of a wide array of cultural products designed for mass consumption, including theatrical spectacles and religious celebrations as well as printed material, from the novellas of María de Zayas to the widespread news of fantastic occurrences and heinous crimes in *relaciones* and all kinds of miscellanea.

Henry Ettinghausen (1993) explains the popular appeal of horrifying images in these early forms of pulp fiction and yellow journalism: "Estas relaciones ostentan poderosas imágenes de impulsos reprimidos convertidos en pasiones desenfrenadas que permiten al lector participar emocionalmente en atrocidades horroríficas, sintiéndose a la vez fascinado [y] escandalizado" (107) (These accounts present powerful images of repressed impulses converted in unbridled passions that allow the reader to emotionally participate in horrifying atrocities, feeling simultaneously fascinated and scandalized). Ettinghausen's conviction that sensationalist and horrifying images ultimately work to reinforce dominant social codes is consistent with a Maravallian understanding of the manipulative and propagandistic character of baroque culture and also with some recent conceptualizations of modern horror, including José Monleón's. As a matter of fact, Ettinghausen draws a direct connection between the sensationalist *relaciones* of the baroque period and present-day tabloids and horror films: "Al mismo tiempo que servían para apuntalar la moral official, las visiones horrendas que proveen estas narraciones poseerían tambien el poderoso atractivo de liberar, sublimándolos, instintos sanguinarios y libidinosos, de manera parecida a como lo hacen hoy día las películas de horror o los sucesos que salen cada día en la prensa y que llenan publicaciones especializadas" (107) (At the same time that they anchored official morality, the horrifying visions that these accounts provide would also possess the powerful appeal of liberating and sublimating violent and libidinous instincts, as in present-day horror films and the sensational stories [*sucesos*] that fill every day the printed pages of specialized publications).

It could be argued that the drive to tap into the emotions and passions of the spectator or reader is not actually new to baroque culture but goes back to ancient Greek tragedy. In medieval times, we could think of oral poetry as a particularly fertile ground for the cultivation of emotional identification with the epic hero, who embodies such social values as loyalty, bravery, and piety. We may recall the heartrending separation of the Cid from his family or the violation and torture of his innocent daughters by the Infantes. This last scene would certainly qualify as a powerful image of "horrifying atrocities" (to use Ettinghausen's words). These catastrophic actions reinforce our passionate attachment to the figure of the hero, ensuring our emotional investment in his quest to reunite his family, punish his enemies, and reclaim his rightful place in the social structure of the Castilian kingdom. We can also find plenty of prodigious signs and supernatural occurrences in the *Cantar de mio Cid*, including the vision of the angel that sends don Rodrigo off on a personal crusade against the Moors.

So, if emotional identification, atrocious actions, and prodigious manifestations are not new to seventeenth-century literature and theater, are we justified in associating the mobilization of irrational wires or *resortes irracionales* (Maravall) with the presumably manipulative impulse of baroque culture? The devil is indeed in the details here. In surveying sensationalist literature of the baroque period—from the *relaciones* of which Ettinghausen speaks, to the popular narratives of martyrdom, to the exemplary novellas of María de Zayas and Cristóbal Lozano's legends—one is struck by the richness of detail with which actions of a prodigious, horrifying, and monstrous nature are consistently presented. It is not that baroque literature invents the manipulation of emotions and the instrumentalization of prodigies and atrocities; what is new is the scale of the cultural investment in the pedagogical potential of the shock value that is associated with rarities, curiosities, prodigies, and horrors.

As William Egginton has recently noted, there is a fundamental shift in the perception of the relationship of the prodigious to everyday reality in the early modern period. In the *Cantar de mio Cid*, for example, the hero's supernatural vision may be seen as an uncommon occurrence and therefore as a sign of the Cid's blessed destiny, but this prodigious event is perfectly in synch with everyday reality in the "medieval world of presence" (Egginton).[1] The matter-of-fact style in which prodigious events are presented in medieval discourse reinforces the notion that the appearance of the supernatural does not produce a rupture in the structure of everyday reality. Rather, without the presence of the magical-supernatural, the picture of the world would be incomplete, incoherent, and essentially meaningless. In other words, the presence of the angel in the *Cantar de mio Cid* does not come as a shock, because it does not disturb the continuity and coherence of medieval reality. On the contrary, prodigious omens, such as the angel and the good-luck birds, are central to the magical worldview characteristic of the medieval epic. Mikhail Bakhtin has explained the functioning of the medieval chronotope of the chivalric romance in very similar terms. He has noted that the normal condition of the knight's world is "the miraculous" (*Dialogic Imagination* 152).

By contrast, what is interesting about prodigies in the increasingly secularized and objectified world of early modernity is precisely their shock value.[2] Hence, the word *espanto,* which denotes admiration or terror or both, is often used in this period to name or qualify prodigious occurrences, along with such derivatives as *espantoso* and *espantable* and such synonyms as *maravilla, maravilloso, monstruo, monstruoso,* and *horrendo.* Events of a prodigious nature, regardless of whether they stir positive or negative emotions (admiration or terror), are typically described in baroque literature as fascinating, shocking, or scandalous insofar as they introduce a disturbance into what

1. See Egginton's *How the World Became a Stage: Presence, Theatricality, and the Question of Modernity* (2003), especially chapter 2, "Real Presence, Sympathetic Magic, and the Power of the Gesture." Egginton's point is that contrary to our familiar experience of the world, which he traces back to the early modern period, magical occurrences and supernatural prodigies are cosubstantial with reality in the medieval world of presence, such that "there was no room for the question, Is this all true?" (44). For more on the medieval experience of the supernatural as it relates to the substantial matter of transubstantiation in the Christian celebration of the Eucharist, see Hans Gumbrecht, "Form without Matter vs. Form as Event," *MLN* 111 (1996): 578–92.

2. For more on the objectification and secularization of the world, see James Burke, *The Day the Universe Changed;* see also José Antonio Maravall, *El mundo social de la Celestina.*

Arthur Machen calls, in "The Great God Pan," "our quiet world." It may be useful to quote here from Clark's reaction to the (impossible) presence of the preternatural in everyday reality in Machen's 1894 classic horror tale: "It is too incredible, too monstrous; such things can never be in this quiet world, where men and women live and die, and struggle, and conquer, or maybe fail, and fall down under sorrow and grieve, and suffer strange fortunes for many a year; but not this [. . .], not such things as this" (*13 Best Horror Stories of All Time* 105). Clark's quintessentially modern mixture of awe and apprehension in the presence of the inexplicable preternatural or "subnatural" (Allegra) is reminiscent of the admiration and terror (*espanto*) with which prodigious manifestations are increasingly viewed in the baroque period.

To say that the modern world is fundamentally devoid of (divine) presence does not mean that the experience of transcendence disappears entirely from modern reality. There are plenty of designated spaces in our world where we can "feel" the ancient presence of the sacred. Egginton refers to these reservoirs of presence in the modern world as "the crypt." While the epistemological shift we are describing is by no means synchronic in the cultural history of early modern Europe, it may be best conceptualized as a general drive toward the confinement and normativization of the sacred, leading to the eventual compartmentalization of lived reality into an "inside" and an "outside" of "the crypt." From this perspective, it is easier to understand the modern logic behind the Church's prohibition of spontaneous unions or "marriage of hands" (*matrimonio de manos*). The prohibition is consistent with institutional efforts to (re)define, regulate, and control our individual and communal ties to the divine. This is also why mystical and ascetic movements are increasingly viewed with suspicion.

The encounter with the "beyond" (the word itself would not make sense, at least not the same kind of sense, outside the modern life experience) must be harnessed, regulated, examined, sanctioned. Miracles are not unavoidably past, but they can no longer be spontaneous or unauthorized occurrences seamlessly connected with everyday reality. To qualify as true miracles, prodigious encounters must be officially sanctioned as extraordinary events; their legitimacy and meaning must be established or "fixed" by the proper authorities. Unsanctioned "miracles" and unauthorized forms of interaction with nature and the spiritual realm are alternately dismissed as the product of superstitious imaginations or condemned as devil worship.[3] Once prodigies

3. Jacques Le Goff has made this point very effectively in *The Medieval Imagination* (1988). He has shown that in the late Middle Ages, the clergy increasingly sought to

have been exiled from everyday reality, they are seen as natural rarities and objects of curiosity; as officially sanctioned miracles that inspire devotion, contrition, moral rectitude, and obedience; or as demonic invasions of "our quiet world," which engender horror and revulsion in spiritually healthy subjects. We are a short step away from the profoundly paranoid horizon of modern horror fantasy.

I am suggesting, then, that the (re)construction of transcendence that takes place in early modern Europe is essentially an institutional response to the rupture of the old substantive "world of presence" that had unleashed the dark forces of chaos, contingency, and nonmeaning. The divine principle is now rebuilt under the careful watch of the Church and the Crown. God no longer inhabits his own creation. Instead, he is represented by earthly ambassadors: the pope, the monarch, and their prosthetic extensions, the Church and the state. Herein lies the fundamental difference between the medieval mappae mundi, which provided a theological picture of the world as the body of Christ, and the political maps of the early modern period, including countless cartographical representations of colonial territories. The miracle of meaning emanates now from the body of the king and his symbolic extension, the royal seal. As Inés says in the first act of Lope de Vega's *Peribañez y el comendador de Ocaña*, "[l]os reyes son a la vista [. . .] imágenes de milagros" (1000–1003) ([t]he monarchs are to the eyes [. . .] images of miracles). The new maps stamped with the royal seal show that, alongside the Church, the Crown has become a source of meaning and transcendence, a symbolic link between us and the sphere of the divine.[4] Thus, royal maps signify the omnipresence of the king in all four corners of his vast colonial empire. They represent the king in his absence, much like Church rituals signify the omnipresence of God.

Percy Schramm has noted that the establishment of the absolutist monarchy in Spain was accompanied by a rush to sell royal paraphernalia, including

---

explain away manifestations of the marvelous that could not be reduced to the status of officially sanctioned miracles. As Childers has noted, this process of "domestication of the marvelous" in European culture culminated in the baroque period (*Transnational Cervantes* 52–53).

4. The map of central Europe commissioned by Charles V in 1560 is a wonderful illustration of this point. The portrait of Queen Elizabeth of 1592 and the image on the cover of Thomas Hobbes' *Leviathan* (1651) convey a similar message. The territory of the state is an extension of the body of the monarch, who takes the place of God as omnipresent source of meaning. For more on the partially divine nature of the monarch, see Ernst Kantorowicz's *The King's Two Bodies.*

ancestral crowns (76–77). At the risk of stating the obvious, the crown can only function properly as a material signifier of royal authority in a relation of visual continuity with the monarch, that is, in his presence. By contrast, the subjects of the king are now being asked to act out their belief in monarchical authority and what it represents *in absentia*. While it could certainly be argued that this is nothing more than a political desideratum of the absolutist monarchy and has little to do with what was really going on in the colonies, for example, the importance of the shift that is signaled here from corporeal continuity to symbolic identification, or (as Egginton would put it) from presence to theatricality, cannot be overstated.[5]

The obsession with religious orthodoxy and the widespread persecution of spiritual dissidents are logical outcomes of this institutional push to control our experience of the divine. As political and religious police, the Inquisition was initially concerned with non-Christian rituals and outward manifestations of cultural difference. By the end of the sixteenth century, however, a more ambitious goal was clearly at play: the control of individual conscience. At issue was no longer cultural homogenization but spiritual normativization. With respect to the situation in Protestant Europe, while some of the central proclamations of the Reformation movement or movements, such as the freedom to privately examine the sacred texts, would seem to run counter to the goal of institutional supervision and control of individual conscience, the successive waves of persecution of witches in Protestant territories suggest that the fear of dissidence and of unauthorized forms of interaction with nature may have been as pronounced there as in Counter-Reformation states. In fact, nature itself is being demoted to the status of passive matter in the field of natural philosophy, because, as Daston and Park put it, "[o]nly a nature consisting solely of 'brute, passive, stupid matter' would not usurp divine prerogatives" (208). The key notion here is not naturalization, as has often been said, but subordination—"the subordination of anomalies to watertight natural laws, of nature to God, and of citizens and Christians to established authority" (ibid).[6] Significantly, in her controversial book

5. See William Egginton's *How the World Became a Stage: Presence, Theatricality, and the Question of Modernity*. See also my "Horror (Vacui): The Baroque Condition" and our collaborative essay "The Perspectival Imaginary and the Symbolization of Power."

6. Daston and Park (210) conclude that such prominent philosophers and theologians as Robert Boyle worked to enslave "nature to God, and God to his own laws."

The Death of Nature, Carolyn Merchant notes disturbing similarities between the scientific terms and methods of inquiry of seventeenth-century natural and political philosophers (Descartes and Hobbes among them) and the language and techniques of inquisitorial interrogations and witch trials.

In Counter-Reformation Spain, while religious authorities call for a tighter control of the spiritual sphere in the name of Christian reason, the discourse of prodigies is very much alive in mass-oriented religious spectacles, such as sermons and sacramental plays, and in the literature of martyrdom. In scientific or pseudoscientific circles, there is clearly an effort to reexamine and classify monsters and prodigies, yet such treatises as Nieremberg's *Curiosa filosofía* (Curious Philosophy [1630]) and *Curiosa y oculta filosofía* (Curious and Occult Philosophy [1643]) and Fuentelapeña's *El ente dilucidado* (The Elucidated Entity [1676]) display a fascination for the novelty of the extraordinary that has more to do with the celebration of singularity, which is characteristic of the culture of curiosities, than with the drive of the new science to subordinate anomalies to immutable natural laws. As Elena del Río Parra suggests in *Una era de monstruos* (2003), Spanish treatises are up to date in their inclusion of known cases and their incorporation of classical and contemporary European authorities, but they are fundamentally contaminated by the narrative of the exceptional. Their accumulation of different and sometimes contradictory notions of monstrosity results in a characteristically baroque plurality of perspectives (44).

Thus, whether we examine scientific treatises, *relaciones*, miscellanea, or other products of popular fiction, monsters and prodigies seem to retain their scandalous potential in seventeenth-century Europe, despite some efforts to explain them as natural rarities, evil spawns, embodiments of sin, or the result of divine punishment. The scandalous dimension of the monstrous is contemporarily discussed in connection with moral perversion, monarchical authority, and the rule of law. Monsters and prodigies are often seen as obstacles in the path toward the modern normativization of nature and the institutional confinement of the sacred.[7] As Jean Riolan writes in a 1614 essay devoted to the discussion of the "perverted" nature of hermaphrodites, monsters represent a defiance of natural, moral, and civil laws, a "perversion of the order of natural causes, the health of the people, and the authority of the king" (quoted by Daston and Park 203).

7. Fittingly, the Greek origin of the word *scandal* (*skandalon*) explicitly conveys the image of an obstacle on the road, "un estorbo, una piedra en el camino" (Baena, *Discordancias cervantinas* 49).

In the case of preternatural events, there is little doubt that spectral apparitions, natural magic, invocations, and incantations are commonly associated with the scandalous monstrosity of evil and sin, yet we can also find instances in which baroque exemplarity comes with an eccentric excess that effectively blurs the borders between the normal and the abnormal. As I mentioned earlier, the distinction between the monstrous, the preternatural, and the supernatural is often lost in baroque fantasy; even the fundamental line between good and evil can become dangerously problematic in exemplary tales that (paradoxically) foreclose the possibility of a total reconstruction of moral certitude. I intend to argue this point shortly, but we should first go over a few examples of pedagogical instrumentalization of prodigious and horrifying images in the propagandistic tradition of which Maravall speaks in *La cultura del barroco.*

Sometimes They Come Back to Teach Us a Lesson

When we look at news stories from the seventeenth century alongside other contemporary forms of entertainment, such as the violent honor plays of Lope de Vega and Calderón de la Barca, the bloody lives of saints, and the graphic *Desengaños* of María de Zayas, it is not difficult to arrive at the conclusion that sensational images sell in the baroque period, whether they are packaged as news, entertainment, devotion, or fiction. Not only do the news stories, or *relaciones,* share in the sensationalist themes and style of baroque fiction, but they are sensationalist fictional narratives that frequently make moral points, sometimes in a direct and explicit manner (Ettinghausen 96).[8] The following admonitions from a 1616 *relación* illustrate the self-conscious exemplarity of many news stories: "Those of you who merrily navigate the arrogant sea of worldly pleasures like unbridled horses [. . .] [l]isten to this case, the rarest that has been witnessed in our own time, so that you may grow fearful of your mad passions" (*Relación autentica y verdadera . . .*). Here is another example from 1672: "And you, prudent reader, must profit from

8. Roger Chartier has also suggested that the difference between fictional tales in print and printed news stories is tenuous at best (*The Culture of Print: Power and the Uses of Print in Early Modern Europe* 4).

this exemplary case in order to correct your vices" (*Relación cierta, y verdadera, del mas estupendo, y espantoso caso que se ha oído . . .*).[9]

This type of moralistic framing is by no means uncommon in seventeenth-century accounts of monstrous crimes, prodigious events, and preternatural encounters in *relaciones,* miscellanea, and other forms of narrative. The anonymous *Libro de cosas notables que han sucedido en la ciudad de Córdoba* (Book of Notable Events That Have Taken Place in the Town of Cordoba [1618]) features two separate and purportedly true accounts of spectral visitations of don Julián, the treacherous count who, according to legend, opened the door to the Moorish hordes in the year 711, condemning Spain to eight centuries of Muslim rule. Navas López and Soriano Palomo refer to these narratives as horror tales, or "cuentos de terror," in their 2001 anthology *Cuentos del siglo de oro.* These stories reinforce the mythical image of Spain as a Christian nation whose evil enemies will be condemned to eternal damnation. This propagandistic view is encapsulated in the specter's own words in the first of the tales: "[S]oy aquel desventurado don Julián por quien se perdió España y estoy padeciendo tormentos increíbles en el infierno" (*Cuentos* 112) (I am the unfortunate don Julián for whom Spain was lost, and I am suffering incredible torments in hell).

This legendary and preternatural material takes on moralistic overtones in the second story, as we can see in the following passage: "—¡Ay!—decía aquel desventurado don Julián—; ¡ay que me abraso!, ¡ay que no tengo esperanza de salir de esta pena!, ¡malditos sean mis pensamientos y gustos! ¿De qué me sirvió ser poderoso en el mundo sino de condenarme?" (*Cuentos* 115) ("Ah!" cried that unfortunate don Julián; "Ah! I am burning! Ah! I have no hope of ever escaping this penance! Damned be my thoughts and appetites!

9. These are my translations of the Spanish original quoted by Ettinghausen (101–5), who offers the following reflection: "Al igual que relaciones de milagros, monstruous, archivejestorios orientales, etc, [. . .] las de crímenes de sexo y violencia suelen ofrecerse, además de como noticias sensacionalistas, como historias amonestadoras y edificantes [. . .] Además, como señala Redondo respecto de las relaciones de bandoleros, el juicio y la ejecución (ritual, ejemplar y pública) de los malhechores [. . .] representan la reimposición del código social vigente" (106–7) (As in the case of accounts of miracles, monsters, and oriental relics, etc., [. . .] the stories of crimes involving sex and violence are often offered not only as sensational news but also as admonishing and edifying narratives [. . .] Besides, as Redondo has pointed out apropos of the news stories about outlaws, their prosecution and (ritual, exemplar, and public) execution [. . .] represent the reimposition of the established social code).

What was the use of pursuing earthly power if I am now condemned?") The exemplary dimension of the tale is effectively underscored in its conclusion, when we are told that the character who witnessed the prodigious visitation of the ghost of don Julián was inspired to abandon his political ambitions and to devote his life to Christian pursuits, for which the entire community rejoices: "Al fin el buen Morales se quitó de alguacilerías y de todo lo demás que le podía ser ocasión de ofender a Dios, a quien de aquí adelante procuró servir como buen cristiano, con mucho ejemplo de los que le conocían, que daban gracias a Dios viendo esta mudanza" (*Cuentos* 116) (At last Morales stayed away from politics and from everything that could present him with the occasion to offend God, whom he served from then on as a good Christian, setting a good example to those who knew him, all of whom thanked God for this sudden change).

Among seventeenth-century writers, the undisputed master of the legendary is Cristóbal Lozano (1609–67), an influential theologian who found much of his inspiration in the medieval Visigoth past and the texts of the Old Testament. Lozano's popular stories and legends contributed to propagating the monarchical myth of gothic origins and the official view of Spain as an essentially Catholic nation. As we shall see in chapter 4, his fictionalized picture of Iberian history in *Los reyes nuevos de Toledo* (The New Monarchs of Toledo [1667]) effectively excludes the "other races" (Muslims and Jews) and demonizes their cultural legacy. Here, I would like to focus on his pedagogical use of the macabre and the preternatural in his short exemplary tale *Castigo de dos adúlteros* (Punishment of Two Adulterers), which was originally published in his collection *De el rey penitente David arrepentido* (Of King David Penitent and Repented [1656]). The story is packed with sensational material—including an extramarital affair; a cold-blooded murder; and a perfectly horrifying, lurid, and gruesome image of damnation—all of which is duly framed with sobering reflections on the blinding nature of passion and the unspeakable suffering that awaits those who give way to their monstrous appetites.

In *Castigo de dos adúlteros,* a young gentleman by the name of Julio courts the wife of his friend Felisardo, a lady of little modesty who quickly succumbs to the ardent passions of the flesh. Armed with the determination of a woman in love, the ungrateful dame murders her husband in cold blood with unrepentant cruelty, clearing the way for the lovers to satisfy their abominable desires. However, their defiance of the heavens does not go unpunished. Soon, their earthly lives are extinguished, and they find themselves at the center of a macabre spectacle of damnation that serves as punishment for the sinful lovers and also as an ominous warning for others ("para castigo suyo y ejemplo de otros," 84). The graphic description of the terrible punishment of the lovers, repeatedly witnessed first by a servant of the count of Nisteria and eventually by the count himself, has much of the flavor of the romantic treatment of legendary and folkloric material by such nineteenth-century authors as Espronceda, Zorrilla, and especially Bécquer: "Sucedió, pues, que habiendo hecho y armado una grande carbonera, y habiéndola ya encendido y estando cuidando de ella, vió una noche, allá, en medio del silencio, que una mujer desnuda venía a todo correr, huyendo de un caballero, que en un caballo negro, con la espada desnuda, la seguía desapoderadamente. La mujer, con tristes ayes, procuraba escaparse, dando vueltas a la carbonera; pero, al fin, habiéndola alcanzado aquel que la seguía, la atravesó de parte a parte con la espada, y habiéndola dejado casi muerta, cogióla y arrojóla en medio de las llamas. Y después que la vió abrasada y casi consumida, sacóla de la hoguera y atravesándola en el arzón de la silla, desapareció con ella" (84–85) (And so it happened that having gathered a great pile of wood and lit it, and as he was attending to it, he saw, in the dead silence of the night, a naked woman running ahead of an armed knight on a black horse, who was chasing her with the utmost zeal. The woman was proffering sorrowful laments as she tried to get away, encircling over and over the wood-burning pile. But her pursuer ultimately caught up to her and run her through with his sword, leaving her for dead. He then picked her up and threw her into the flames, and once he saw her burned and nearly consumed, he extracted her from the fire, tossed her on the saddle and disappeared with her).

This rapid succession of shocking images has a certain cinematic quality reminiscent of the optical experiments associated in the 1600s with the magic lantern. The "great fire" is an important element of the story that completes the circle of the providential punishment of the murderous adulteress, but it is also a perfect source of natural light in the darkness of the night, allowing the count's servant to register every detail of the shocking scene, from the lurid picture of the naked lady running into full view at the edge of the flames to her cruel murder and the gruesome burning of her body at the hands of her lover. The graphic sensationalism of this macabre theater is justified by the moralistic frame that guides the curious reader toward the correct point of view: "Repase, pues, el curioso a la pena cruel a que están sentenciados aquellos que para lograr sus adulterios y maldades cometen semejantes homicidios, tan necios y tan ciegos a la razón, que añaden yerros a yerros" (87)

(The curious should examine the cruel punishment that awaits those who, in order to consummate their adulteries and evil deeds, commit such crimes; they are fools who are blind to reason and add error to error).

The narrator describes the scene as a horrifying spectacle ("un espectáculo horrendo," 85) that stirs a range of emotions, including curiosity, confusion, melancholy, admiration, and terror. Indeed, the shocking images possess the kind of appeal of which Ettinghausen speaks: "the powerful appeal of liberating and sublimating violent and libidinous instincts, as in present-day horror films" (107). Our position as readers is scopically identical to that of the servant and the count who repeatedly witness the voyeuristic spectacle (up to five times in the case of the servant). They are shocked, scandalized, and horrified, but also fascinated; and so are we. Readers thus participate in the libidinal economy of the text, reenacting in their consumption of the scandalous spectacle the redemptive cycle of sin and punishment. As Maravall would put it, Lozano's exemplary tale pulls on the emotional wires of the reader and mobilizes irrational drives in the direction of dominant social codes and values.

The story of Captain Céspedes in *Varia fortuna del soldado Píndaro* (1626) by Gonzalo de Céspedes y Menéses may be seen as another example of this type of exemplary literature. The atmospheric quality of the narrative is also reminiscent of romantic aesthetics, but the treatment of the macabre and the prodigious is significantly more complex in these passages of *Varia fortuna* than in Lozano's *Castigo de dos adúlteros*. The multilayered narrative frame and the anticlimactic ending of the tale of Captain Céspedes leave room for different and possibly contradictory interpretations. The story is further complicated by the ultimate impossibility of disentangling the signs of providential reason and justice from the passionate excesses of the human will and the scandalous contingencies of history. While this is not the place to go into the details of the picaresque adventures of the protagonist prior to the episode in question, it is important to point out that the *pícaro*-soldier relates the tragic end of the legendary Céspedes as told by another character in the story, a priest.

The priest's tale is meant to serve as a warning against the foolishness of skeptics who are blind to the powerful presence of prodigious forces in our human world. Ironically, the one character who appears to need convincing is actually convalescing from an encounter with just such magical powers. In this sense, the framing of the story is reminiscent of Cervantes' *El coloquio de los perros*. There are also inconsistencies between the stated goal of the tale and the narrated events. The discussion that frames the story focuses on preternatural forces, that is, the diabolical shadows permitted by the heavens (169), but the prodigious events of the narrative are interpreted as either natural (the portentous strength of the captain) or supernatural (spectral signs of things to come in accordance with the divine will). The specter of the French antagonist seems to overstep his boundaries as providential messenger in order to inscribe his own (pathological, perhaps even diabolical) will into the very form of the divine message. Finally, the narrative coda does little to justify the exemplary framing. If anything, the priest's enigmatic mention of alternative explanations of the events adds to the ambiguity of the tale. His brief but poignant political commentary offers a glimpse of the true face of history, outside the comforts of the aesthetically structured reality of exemplary discourse. To be sure, the priest's somewhat unguarded remarks at the conclusion of the story are by no means unbiased; they certainly share in the propagandistic view of Spain as a Christian nation that must be defended against the lurking enemies of God. However, the momentary dissolution of the discursive boundaries of the exemplary tale exposes the reader to the cold world "out there" where people suffer and die, perhaps for no good reason at all.

The story begins with a portrait of don Alonso de Céspedes, a knight of the order of Santiago who served under Charles V and Philip II in the battlefields of Italy, Flanders, Germany, and France. The news of his extraordinary bravery and especially his rare and monstrous strength ("monstruossas y peregrinas fuerzas") afforded him the legendary status of a human prodigy or portent ("ilustre portento") capable of the most extraordinary feats: lifting a millstone, breaking five horseshoes with a single blow, crushing a horse with the pressure of his legs, killing a thousand enemy soldiers with nothing but a sword. Yet his prodigious strength could not protect him from the sin of ire and the desire for vengeance that would ultimately cause his downfall. Blinded by rage, the captain denies his French enemy, the baron of Ampurde, the rite of confession. The priest put it in characteristically moralistic terms: "Nunca la ira y el desseo de venganza executaron mejores obras [. . .] tales pasiones indignas son del corazón magnánimo" (172) (Never did ire and the desire for vengeance achieve better results [. . .] [S]uch passions are unworthy of the magnanimous heart). Don Alonso would soon meet his ordained punishment in the new Christian province of Granada during the Morisco uprising of the Alpujarras. But before we get to the historical site of the hero's demise, the story takes a decisive turn in the direction of the fantastic.

A veiled woman comes out of a church and privately begs don Alonso to follow her into the Morisco area of Granada known as Albaicen (today Albaicín), where two beautiful damsels await, with the utmost anticipation, their chance to meet the famous captain. The servants are left behind at San Cristóbal, halfway up the Albaicen, at the request of the mysterious woman, who continues to lead don Alonso through meandering streets bordering a cemetery. As darkness falls, the woman signals toward some windows at the top of a house and leaves the captain awaiting further developments. About a half hour later, two heavenly beauties appear at one of the windows, their celestial faces illuminated by candlelight. It does not take long for the determined captain to climb up the wall. Yet as he sets foot into the ladies' quarters, the walls of the house close behind him with a thunderous clatter. A puzzling and terrible scene suddenly materializes inside the gloomy room. The richness of detail in this macabre theater merits quoting at some length.

> Entró por la ventana, mas no lo uvo bien echo quando, cosa es que atemoriza, con un grande y furioso estampido se juntó la pared, y sin quedar señal de puertas ni ventanas, mugeres ni otra cosa, se halló metido en una larga y anchurosa quadra. Estava ésta vestida de presagios funestos, paños y bayetas oscuras, lo mismo todo el suelo, y en la mitad un túmulo, vassa de un ataúd, a quien también cubría un tapete negro; a la cabeza y pies tenía dos achas encendidas; con que unas cosas y otras representavan tristemente un trágico y fúnebre teatro [. . .] pasmado y atónito, contemplándose entre quatro paredes, casi tragó la muerte [. . .] apenas comenzó a descubrir el trágico tapete de la tumba, quando dando tristes gemidos, vio que yva poco a poco saliendo della un espantoso hombre—y doile tales títulos, no porque su persona fuesse monstruossa o desigual a los demás comunes, sino por el prodigio lastimoso que representavan en su cuerpo infinitas heridas, de las quales venía acrevillado y roto, desde el pálido rostro a la punta del pie. Suspenso quedó el animoso Céspedes viendo tan impensado y sangriento espectáculo; [. . .] el horrendo güesped, en puniéndose en forma, bolviéndose al capitán la encarnizada vista y notando su grande suspensión, con ronca y triste voz le dixo desta suerte:—¿Qué miras, arrogante español? Abre mejor los ojos y conóceme; que aun tienes causa y obligación de hazerlo: Obras son de tus manos las que tienes delante [. . .] yo soy aquel francés varón a quien impío y cruel diste en París la muerte. Allí te pedí entonces la vida de merced, y no quisiste dármela; confessión te pedí, y no me concediste término para hazerla. Grandemente irritaste la justicia divina; tales echos y acciones la están clamando siempre por venganza;

más mientras ésta llega librada en las moriscas lanzas de las vezinas Alpujarras, no estemos assí los dos ociosos, vengamos tú y yo otra vez a los brazos; quizá podrán los míos, despedazados y sangrientos, executar aora lo que sanos y enteros no pudieron entonces. Con esto, dando un terrible salto, le llevó de boleo al mismo punto que apagándose las achas, dexaron en lóbregas tinieblas el aposento y el corazón magnánimo de don Alonso no sin algún horror de tan estraña y temerosa empresa. Flacos y débiles estavan los quebrantados miembros del herido, mas no assí le parecieron a Céspedes sus espantosas fuerzas [. . .] mas ¡qué mucho, si es el poder humano tan limitado y corto y el sobrenatural tan disconforme! (176–78) [He entered through the window, yet no sooner had he achieved this when, and this is something that inspires terror, the walls came together with a great and furious clatter, and he saw no trace of doors, windows, women, or anything else as he found himself in a large and spacious ward. The room was dressed in funereal garb, with dark palls and rugs covering the length of the floor; there was a tumulus right in the middle of it, with a casket on top, covered with a black cloth and illuminated by two lit torches at its head and foot, all of which gloomily represented a tragic and macabre theater [. . .] Dumbfounded and aghast, he felt engulfed by death within these four walls [. . .] As he lifted the lugubrious cloth that covered the tomb, a horrid man slowly emerged from underneath, proffering sorrowful laments, and I refer to him in this way not because he was monstrous or dissimilar to other, normal men but because of the pitiful prodigy of his body, riddled with infinite stab wounds from the discolored face to the tips of his feet. The brave Céspedes contemplated this unthinkable and bloody spectacle with the utmost astonishment [. . .] The horrid host rose up and turned his fierce gaze in his direction, acknowledging his bewilderment with a hoarse and sorrowful voice: "What do you see, arrogant Spaniard? Open your eyes wider and recognize me, for you have good reason and obligation to do so. What you see before you is the work of your own hands [. . .] I am the French baron of Ampurde whom you impiously and cruelly murdered in Paris. It was there that I begged for your mercy and you denied me. I asked for confession and you did not permit it. You greatly angered the Divine Judge. Such words and actions cry out for vengeance, but while it arrives at the armed hands of the Moriscos of the neighboring Alpujarras, let us not be idle, let us battle one more time, perhaps my torn and bleeding arms will accomplish now what they could not do when they were healthy and whole." With this, he leapt grotesquely and flew through the air as the torches went out, leaving the lugubrious room in total darkness and the heart of the magnanimous don Alonso filled with dread in the middle of this strange and horrifying undertaking. The broken members of the wounded man were feeble and weak, but this is not how his terrible strength felt to Céspedes [. . .] But why should we marvel at this when our human power is so limited and minuscule and the supernatural so incomparable!]

There is little doubt that the narrator of the tale works hard at generating suspense and horror in these passages. The oppressive atmosphere of the windowless and gloomy room is reminiscent of the architectural enclosures characteristic of classic gothic fantasies, while the expressionistic quality of the language and the narrative attention to the thought processes and emotions of the main character may be considered protoromantic. But we should also note that the use (and abuse) of expressionistic language and the cultivation of "suspense" (*suspensión* is the expression used in the seventeenth century) are often cited among the defining traits of baroque art and literature. Moreover, the focus on intense feelings of dread and the experience of astonishment and terror in the presence of awesome forces (whether natural, preternatural, or supernatural) is as central to the baroque worldview as it is to the modern aesthetics and philosophy of the sublime.[10]

The carefully staged appearance of the bleeding specter of the French baron marks the climactic moment of the tale. The ghost prophesies the imminent death of don Alonso at the hands of Morisco rebels in the neighboring region of the Alpujarras. This tragic end(ing) has seemingly been preordained by the Supreme Judge ("la justicia divina"). Yet the final triumph of divine justice is incongruously qualified in the lugubrious voice of the undead as a much-awaited act of revenge. This is all the more confounding

10. I mentioned earlier that Andrea Battistini and Anthony Cascardi have posited strong connections between the baroque marvelous and the modern sublime. James Mirollo has also argued that the aesthetic of the sublime at work in romantic fiction finds its roots in the "age of the marvelous" ("The Aesthetics of the Marvelous: The Wondrous Work of Art in a Wondrous World" 39). For his part, José Antonio Maravall resorts to Schiller's theory of the sublime in explaining the baroque sense of doom and its fixation with the most shocking, dreadful, and terrifying aspects of reality (*Culture of the Baroque* 212–13).

when we take into account that the entire episode has been framed by the priest as a warning against the dark passions of ire and vengeance. Surely, there is no place for vengeance in the infinitely magnanimous heart of God. Rather, it would seem as though the specter's misuse of the word *venganza* in place of *justicia divina* is a sort of Freudian slip that provides a window into his own murky motivations. Thus, the baron's vengeful drive pollutes the providential message, infusing a sort of perverse enjoyment into the very form of divine justice. Indeed, the specter's physical attack on the captain is a gratuitous act that serves no other purpose than the fulfillment of his (not God's) "unnatural" desire for vengeance. This is little more than the acting out of an irrepressible passion that has survived death—a leftover emotion trapped in the preternatural realm.

The superimposition of sacred and profane spaces seems to reinforce this sense of a confused and confounding overlapping of divine signs and dark unnatural or preternatural forces. The veiled woman who leads don Alonso through the streets of the Albaicen is said to come out of a Christian temple, yet she is most at home in the space of the demonized other. The encounter of the captain with the ghost of the French enemy had taken place inside a house in the Morisco neighborhood, but his unconscious body is eventually found in the Catholic church of San Cristóbal, where his servants had been told to await his return. What about the radiant (presumably Morisco) beauties whose angelic faces had so utterly suspended don Alonso's senses ("dos soles hermosíssimos, cuyo bello semblante [. . .] le dejó suspendido," 175)? They had vanished with the windows as the walls of the house closed behind the captain. Were they angelic presences or demonic illusions? Were they doing God's work in attracting don Alonso to the place where the specter of the baron awaited him? Why is the Albaicen the designated place for this prodigious encounter? Why are the Morisco rebels of the Alpujarras the chosen hands to administer the punishment of don Alonso for actions that took place in French territory? More important, is the death of Captain Céspedes at the hands of the Moriscos a preordained punishment for the sins of his past, an act of spectral vengeance, or a contingent vicissitude of history?

In his treatise *De verdadera y falsa profecía* (Of True and False Prophesy [1588]), respected author Juan de Horozco y Covarrubias had explained the doctrinal position on the question of how to distinguish true prophesies from the false prognostications of the devil, which are designed to plant the seeds of discord, chaos, and sin in our souls and the Christian body. He concluded that God alone knows the future and sometimes communicates portions of it to chosen recipients in prophesies whose truth is certified by their source.[11] The key issue here is whether or not the source may be considered legitimate. Only reliable or "authorized" sources are eligible to speak the true word of God. Simply put, to distinguish prodigious signs of divine wisdom from false illusions inspired by the devil, we need to make sure we are dealing with "authorized" sources. The truth of the divine message is thus certified by the preestablished authority of the messenger.

Indeed, the credibility or legitimacy of the source of the prophetic sign would seem to take precedence over questions about the proper executor or executors of ordained punishments. As we know from reading the Old Testament, God had routinely made use of his enemies to carry out some of his harshest punishments on his own people. This Old Testament logic of sin and punishment is also at the core of the official explanation of the reason behind the eight centuries of Muslim domination of Christian Spain.[12] We should not be surprised, then, if the punishment of the legendary Captain Céspedes is ultimately carried out by enemies of "our nation" and the Christian faith. Hence, it would seem that the problematic dimension of the narrative has more to do with the questionable source of the prophetic message than with the fact that the execution of God's punishment is left to the

---

11. Jorge Checa refers to this important work of Horozco y Covarrubias in his essay "Cervantes y la cuestión de los orígenes: Escepticismo y lenguaje en *El coloquio de los perros.*" He summarizes the contribution of the author to orthodox doctrine as follows: "Resumiendo la doctrina ortodoxa, El tratado de verdadera y falsa profecía, publicado en 1588 por Juan de Horozco y Covarrubias, estipula cuándo las formulaciones proféticas pueden considerarse fidedignas. Covarrubias afirma que sólo Dios conoce los eventos futuros y los comunica a veces mediante profecías cuya verdad viene garantizada por su fuente; pero, frente a las verdaderas profecías divinas, Covarrubias distingue las falsas que inspira el demonio para sembrar el pecado y el desconcierto" (310) (Summarizing orthodox doctrine, *The Treatise of True and False Prophesy,* published in 1588 by Juan de Horozco y Covarrubias, explains when prophetic formulations may be considered reliable. Covarrubias states that God alone has knowledge of future events and that he sometimes communicates it in prophesies whose truth is certified by its source; but, in contrast to the true divine prophesies, Covarrubias distinguishes the false ones that are inspired by the devil to plant the seeds of sin and discord).

12. Incidentally, Jerry Falwell, Pat Robertson, and other leaders of the Christian Right have recently employed a similar logic in claiming that the terrorist attacks of 9/11 at the hands of Muslim fundamentalists had been "permitted" by God as a way of punishing the United States for its abandonment of foundational Christian ideals and its fostering of secularists, abortionists, feminists, gays, and liberals.

Morisco rebels of the Alpujarras. We could certainly ask ourselves whether the specter of the French baron whose own undead heart is filled with revenge is the right messenger to deliver the news of the divine indictment of don Alonso for his careless abandonment to the dark passions of ire and vengeance. It would seem that the baron's own vengeful inclinations could disqualify him as a legitimate vessel of the divine sign.

On the other hand, the story's denouement seems to open the door to a different type of explanation of the tragic events: "Tales postrimerías tuvieron el valeroso Céspedes y sus monstruosas fuerzas, indignas ciertamente de sus merecimientos; si bien ya uvo quien dixo que fueran desta suerte apresuradas por no acudirle, como pudiera, don Antonio de Luna; mas no es de aqueste cuento su calificación. Recibid, don Francisco, mi buen desseo y admitid este exemplo" (181) (Such was the end of the valorous Céspedes and his monstrous strength, certainly unworthy of his merits, though some have argued that this end arrived prematurely because don Antonio de Luna failed to come to his aid, as he could have; yet this story is not the place to discuss the merits of their view. Receive, don Francisco, my best wishes, and admit this example). The priest alludes to an alternative version of the events that has no place in his narrative. This other view must remain untold simply because it does not fit the exemplary mode. These final passages hint at the sacrifices that must be made in order to make proper (exemplary) sense of the contingent vicissitudes of history. Perhaps the ultimate lesson of this tale of the fall of Captain Céspedes is the revelation that the greatest enemy of exemplary discourse is not immoral or evil words or deeds but the raw life content "out there" that literally makes no sense. Contingency and chaos are, in fact, the dreaded monsters. These are the true obstacles on the road to exemplarity, the scandals, or *skandalons,* that the symbolic system must fend off and guard against. To again quote Machen's "The Great God Pan," "such things can never be in this quiet world." There must be a proper reason for everything, and everything must happen for a reason.

Exemplarity Gone Awry

From the classic Aesopian fables and Lucianic satires to the seventeenth-century picaresque novels of Mateo Alemán and Francisco de Quevedo, literary exempla were supposed to help us make sense of human life from a watchtower position, as Alemán eloquently expresses it in the subtitle of his *Guzmán de Alfarache: Atalaya de la vida humana* (Guzmán de Alfarache:

Watchtower of Human Life).[13] We expect exemplary narratives to build and fortify our (moral) character. By contrast, Cervantes' collection *Novelas ejemplares* (1613) explicitly problematizes the ways in which edifying or character-building discourses make sense of life, art, and their relationship. Hence, the prologue invites the reader to look at the novellas not as life lessons but as open-ended narrative experiments resulting from the writer's "table of tricks" ("mesa de trucos").[14] This is especially true of its frame tale, *El casamiento engañoso [y] El coloquio de los perros*, which is incoherently split into two novellas and a disjointed in-between.

In his compelling essay "Cervantes, Freud, and Psychoanalytic Narrative Theory," E. C. Riley notes that the Cervantine frame tale has more in common with the literature of the modern fantastic (as theorized by Rosemary Jackson) than with the tradition of fables and satires, within which "fantasy serves the ends of moral and satirical commentary on human behavior" (4). For our purposes here, I would like to underscore Riley's keen understanding of the fundamental line of contact between *El coloquio de los perros* and Jackson's conceptualization of the fantastic, which Riley traces very closely in the following passage: "One of the functions attributed to modern literary fantasy seems entirely appropriate applied to the *Coloquio*. It is to 'interrogate the category of character—that definition of self as a coherent, indivisible and continuous whole which has dominated Western thought for centuries and is celebrated in classic theatre and realist art alike'" (4).[15]

Franklin García Sánchez has examined *El coloquio* in light of recent theorizations of the fantastic by such critics as Todorov and Antonio Risco. Sánchez focuses on the uncertainty that results from the coexistence of the

13. Part of this section is forthcoming in an essay titled "Exemplarity Gone Awry in Baroque Fantasy," in a special volume of the *Revista Canadiense de Estudios Hispánicos*, edited by José Jouvé-Martín and Renée Soulodre La France.

14. For a suggestive discussion of the collection, including the prologue, as a self-consciously failed container, see Julio Baena's "Spanish Mannerist Detours in the Mapping of Reason: Around Cervantes' *Novelas ejemplares*" (2006). Baena elaborates there on María Rey López's notion that the novellas "shatter the box" (quoted by Baena 210). In their illuminating 1993 book on Cervantes, Nicholas Spadaccini and Jenaro Talens examine the frame of the *Novelas ejemplares*. They compare it with the rhetorical techniques characteristic of the Italian novella and conclude that the "Italian narrative frame played a role that was fundamentally literary, but in Cervantes the frame dealt with the relationship between art and reality" (131).

15. For a discussion of "character" that builds on Jackson's and Hélenè Cixous' reflections on character-building narratives in the context of early modern literature and culture, see my "Horror (Vacui): The Baroque Condition."

marvelous with a modern rationalism that is supposed to explain it away. Instead of guiding the reader in the direction of a preestablished set of beliefs in line with a secured view, Cervantes' twist on exemplarity reveals the endemic weaknesses in the fortresses of reason and morality, the *skandalons* (scandals, obstacles) of sense making. For all of Berganza's righteousness and Cipión's entrenched defense of the principles of well-measured, harmonious, and reasoned discourse, "it is the messiness of narration which is shown up" (Riley 6). There is no safe way out of the textual labyrinth; there is no universally valid solution; whatever (re)solution we may be inclined to endorse is always already tainted by the polluting or constructive presence of our interpretive gaze, unmasked by the self-reflective language of the narrative as our own arbitrary choice.

In other words, the Cervantine text shows the seams in the storytelling process and also the unavoidably dialogical structure of the process of narration. According to Spadaccini and Talens, this is, in fact, the paradoxical basis of Cervantine exemplarity: "[T]he text contains gaps and silences, conflicts and contradictions, which shift to the reader-critic the obligation of investing it with meaning [. . .] Therein resides the most important aspect of their exemplarity" (124).[16] In this context, the shock of the preternatural, the monstrous, and the marvelous adds to the ambiguity of the text and its resistance to monological views.[17] This playful sense of puzzlement and indeterminacy leads to a further questioning of the boundaries between reason and imagination and between fantasy and reality. This is the polar opposite of the "shock and awe" strategy employed by baroque moralists who coach (or advise or warn) readers to accept their assigned place in the world in accordance with the secured view of the watchtower of human life.

---

16. Spadaccini and Talens are not alone in claiming that one of the most innovative aspects of the Cervantine style in general and the tale(s) of *El casamiento engañoso* and *El coloquio* in particular has to do with the fact that "Cervantes demands that his reader assess critically opposing positions and arguments and gives less help than they [other authors of his time] usually do" (Thomas Hart 201). See also Rey Hazas' "Género y estructura de *El coloquio de los perros*" and Blanco Aguinaga's pioneering study "Cervantes y la picaresca: Notas sobre dos tipos de realismo." For more on the experimental nature of the *Novelas ejemplares*, see the studies of the collection *Cervantes's Exemplary Novels and the Adventure of Writing* (especially the essays by Alban Forcione and Michael Nerlich) and the more recent essays by Julio Baena and William Egginton in *Reason and Its Others.*

17. As Checa says about the witch at the center of the textual labyrinth of *El coloquio*, Cañizares represents the perplexity associated with the extraordinary (306).

The ironic tone of the Cervantine narrative contributes to the overall parodic effect, especially in those passages that mimic traditional forms of discursive exemplarity in classical literature and biblical sources. When we finally get to the heart of the mystery of the talking dogs, the explanation we crave comes in the form of some equivocal recollections of a half-recovering witch who, by her own admission, has trouble distinguishing reality from the fancies of her monstrous imagination. Cañizares recalls the dying confession of her elder, the legendary Camacha, in the presence of the dog's mother (Montiela), including the enigmatic prophesy that might explain the dog's sudden gift of speech: "Llegóse el fin de la Camacha y estando en la última hora de su vida llamó a tu madre y le dijo como ella había convertido a sus hijos en perros por cierto enojo que con ella tuvo; pero que no tuviese pena: que ellos volverían a su ser cuando menos lo pensasen; mas que no podía ser primero que ellos por sus mismos ojos vieren lo siguiente: Volverán en su forma verdadera / cuando vieren con presta diligencia / derribar los soberbios levantados / y alzar a los humildes abatidos / por poderosa mano para hacello" (338) (The end of Camacha had come, and during the last moments of her life, she called your mother and told her how she had transformed her sons into dogs for reasons that had to do with some grudge she had held against her; but not to worry: for they would return to their original being when they least suspected it; yet this could not happen before they saw with their own eyes the following: They shall return to their true shape / when they see with agile diligence / fall down the towering proud / and rise the fallen and dejected / by the hand with the power to do it).

Following the internal logic of the narrative, we could conclude that Camacha's verses belong to the phantasmatic realm of false prophesies inspired by the devil himself.[18] After all, it is common knowledge that the fallen angel delights in mimicking Christian rituals and dogma, even divine language. But whether directly or by way of a diabolical (or devilish) degree of separation, the witch's prophesy mocks the solemn language of redemptive exemplarity. Contemporary readers would not have failed to grasp the echoes of the Gospel of Luke in these verses, unfamiliar as some may have been with Virgil and other potential classical references for this passage.[19]

---

18. See Checa's commentary on Horozco y Covarrubias' treatise on true and false prophesies in connection with these Cervantine passages (310).

19. For more information on potential classical references for this passage, especially Virgil, see Alban Forcione's *Cervantes and the Mystery of Lawlessness: A Study of "El casamiento engañoso y El coloquio de los perros."*

The dog's discussion of different interpretations of the prophetic message intensifies the parodic effect of the text. Cipión first considers an allegorical reading but ends up favoring what he calls "the literal sense." His reasoning reaches a hilarious climax in the following passage.

> [S]us palabras se han de tomar en un sentido que he oído decir se llama al[e]górico, el cual sentido no quiere decir lo que la letra suena, sino otra cosa, que, aunque diferente, le haga semejanza, y así [. . .] tomándolo en el sentido que he dicho, paréceme que quiere decir que cobraremos nuestra forma cuando viéremos que los que ayer estaban en la cumbre de la rueda de fortuna, hoy están hollados y abatidos a los pies de la desgracia y tenidos en poco de aquellos que más los estimaban. Y asimismo, cuando viéremos que otros que no ha dos horas que no tenían deste mundo otra parte que servir en él de número que acrecentase el de las gentes, y ahora están tan encumbrados sobre la Buena dicha que los perdemos de vista; y si primero no parecían por pequeños y encogidos, ahora no los podemos alcanzar por grandes y levantados. Y si en esto consistiera volver nosotros a la forma que dices, ya lo hemos visto y lo vemos a cada paso; por do me doy a entender que no en el sentido alegórico, sino en el literal, se han de tomar los versos de la Camacha [. . .] pues muchas veces hemos visto lo que dicen y nos estamos tan perros como ves; así, que la Camacha fue burladora falsa, y la Cañizares embustera, y la Montiela tonta, maliciosa y bellaca, con perdón sea dicho, si acaso es nuestra madre, de entrambos o tuya, que yo no la quiero tener por madre. Digo, pues, que el verdadero sentido es un juego de bolos, donde con presta diligencia derriban los que están en pie y vuelven a alzar los caídos, y esto por la mano de quien lo puede hacer. Mira, pues, si en el discurso de nuestra vida habremos visto jugar a los bolos, y si hemos visto por esto haber vuelto a ser hombres, si es que lo somos. (346–47) [Her words must be understood in a sense that I have heard called al[le]gorical, in which sense they do not mean what the letters say but something else, which, although different, it would be similar, [. . .] and thus, looking at it in the said sense, it seems to me that it would mean that we would recover our form when we saw that those who were at the top of the wheel of fortune yesterday are today fallen and dejected at the feet of disgrace, despised by those who used to esteem them, and also when we saw that others who, not two hours ago, were nothing to this world but numbers to increase the total population figure, and now they are standing

> so high up on their good fortune that we can hardly see them; if they could not be seen at first for their small and shrunken size, now they cannot be reached in their towering greatness. And if our returning to the shape you speak of were to consist of this, we have already seen it, and we see it at every step. This is why I am beginning to think that it is not in the allegorical sense but in the literal that Camacha's verses must be interpreted [. . .], for we have seen what they say many times and remain as dogs as you can see; and so Camacha was a deceitful impostor, and Cañizares a liar, and Montiela a malicious and wicked idiot, with my apologies if she turns out to be our mother, or at least yours, for I will not have her for a mother. Thus, I say that the true meaning of it is a game of bowling, in which those standing are toppled with agile diligence and the fallen are picked up by the hand that has the power to do it. Look back, then, to see if we have seen in the (dis)course of our lives a game of bowling, and consider if we have for this reason turned back into men, if this is what we are.]

Cipión arrives here at a perfectly logical, if preposterous, conclusion about the meaning of Camacha's prophesy. The dog's reasoning progresses from the kind of allegorical interpretation that we would have expected (at least within conventional forms of exemplary discourse) to his sense of the true literal meaning, which turns out to be something as random (again, from the point of view of the reader of a traditional exemplary tale) as a game of bowling. As Checa says, Cipión's interpretive choice trivializes and parodies the solemn tone of a language saturated with classical and evangelical echoes (309). But just as important, this passage shows not only the "messiness of narration" and how untidy the storytelling business really is underneath—to paraphrase Riley (6)—but also the inescapable messiness of the business of interpretation. While we may be inclined to think of Cipión's reading of the witch's prophesy as erroneous and even preposterous, who is to say that we are better off than the dog? Indeed, the joke may be on us when we consider the insurmountable obstacles that we face as readers of *El coloquio* and professionals of the business of interpretation, especially if we believe that the Cervantine exemplarity "shifts to the reader-critic the obligation of investing [the text] with meaning" (Spadaccini and Talens 124).

To put it in perspective, we are being asked to "make sense" of a Satanic prophesy that Campuzano may have overheard from the mouth of a talking dog, who had heard it from a witch, who says that his mother had said that the dying Camacha had related it to her. As for the reliability of the links in the chain, Camacha, Montiela, and Cañizares are devil worshipers. Campuzano is a roguish figure who claims he has written the true dialogue of the dogs, word by word, before handing the text over to his good friend Peralta. The convalescent soldier was suffering from life-threatening fever when he apparently overheard the dialogue of the dogs from his hospital bed. By his own admission, the cause of the fever was a sexually transmitted disease that he had contracted in the course of his failed attempt to cheat a seemingly respectable lady of her wealth (which incidentally had turned out to be fake). The talking dogs (partners and perhaps brothers) could be characters in Campuzano's fantastic story (which is how his friend Peralta wants to see them), the result of a nightmarish hallucination caused by fever, a prodigious sign (as the dogs themselves suggest at the beginning of their colloquy), the product of a diabolical curse (if we uphold the view attributed to Cañizares), exemplary characters in a collection of exemplary tales, or something else entirely, since Campuzano and Peralta end up walking out of the frame before the narrative arrives to any kind of (re)solution: "—Vamos—dijo el alférez. Y con esto, se fueron. FIN" (359) ("Let's go," said the soldier. And with that, they left. THE END).

This is the frame tale that is supposed to help us make sense of the collection of exemplary novels, yet this monstrously amorphous fantasy underscores not the secured propositions of morality and reason but their arbitrariness and the holes in the meaning-producing machine. As Manuel Aguirre has suggested in his provocative book *The Closed Space: Horror Literature and Western Symbolism* (1990), the perfectly secured citadel or "closed space" is the impossible ideal of reason and morality. Much of Western fiction has helped to construct and propagate this ideal in the name of self, character, honor, and country, but in the fictional world of the *Novelas ejemplares*, "the self-protecting enclosures that guarantee the stability of our social identity do not hold up well" (Castillo and Lollini).

El celoso extremeño (The Jealous Extremaduran) and *La fuerza de la sangre* (The Force of Blood) are among the novellas that deal most explicitly with the (de)construction of self-protecting enclosures. In *El celoso extremeño,* Carrizales erects the ultimate fortress to safeguard his honor. He builds a prison-house to protect his virgin wife from potentially defiling contact with the world. Not surprisingly, however, Carrizales' baroque house fails, as containers often do in Cervantine narratives, and his wife's virtue is compromised. The point here—as Egginton has perceptively noted—is that virtue and honor are spoiled not despite the protecting walls erected by Carrizales but because of them (191). The following passage from the novella is eloquent in this respect: "Uno destos galanes, pues, que entre ellos es llamado virote [. . .] asestó a mirar la casa del recatado Carrizales, y viéndola siempre cerrada, le tomó gana de saber quien vivía dentro; y con tanto ahínco y curiosidad hizo la diligencia que de todo vino a saber lo que deseaba. Supo la condición del viejo, de la hermosura de su esposa y el modo que tenía en guardarla; todo lo cual le encendió el deseo de ver si sería posible expuñar, por fuerza o por industria, fortaleza tan guardada" (107) (One of those young men who among them is called *virote* [the word emphasizes the virility of the young bachelor] [. . .] began to watch the house of the cautious Carrizales and, seeing it always closed, got the urge to find out who lived inside; and he completed the task with such determination and curiosity that he came to know everything he desired. He learned of the condition of the old man, the beauty of his wife, and the ways in which he guarded her, all of which ignited his desire to see if he could conquer, by force or diligence, such a well-guarded fortress). As we can see, the *virote*'s desire is ignited by the impenetrable walls of the house and by the obsessive diligence with which the old man protects his wife's virtue. The built-in failure of fortresses of character and honor is also the theme of *El viejo celoso*, a short theatrical piece that reworks the topic of the "excessively" jealous husband in the comedic format of the *entremés*, or interlude. Once again, the old man's fears would be realized not despite but because of the walls he erects around the body of his wife to protect her virtue and the integrity of his honor. The difference is that in *El viejo celoso*, "the attack" comes from the inside of the fortress. Thus, his young wife succeeds in bringing a boy toy into her bedroom with the help of two other women who readily recognize the urgency of her physical needs. In a way *El viejo celoso* is the feminine version of *El celoso extremeño*, that is, a (de)construction of the baroque house from a feminine perspective.

While these two works underscore the hopeless futility of the dream of honor, which is parodied in the figure of the impotent old man forced to guard the virtue of a wife he cannot satisfy, *La fuerza de la sangre* offers a tragic view of the inside of the aristocratic vault where women are silently victimized. The "conflict of honor" is a familiar one in baroque narrative and theater. As in many Lopean and Calderonian plays, rape is treated in this Cervantine exemplary novel as "a family affair," a private disgrace that must be kept from the public eye. *La fuerza de la sangre* explores one of the theoretical (re)solutions of the conflict of honor caused by rape, that ultimate breach of the walls. The infamy of dishonor is kept secret to avoid public exposure. The perpetrator goes unpunished and eventually agrees to repair the tear in the familial and social fabric by marrying his victim.

At first glance, the final reunification of the rapist and his victim would seem to uphold the propagandistic view of which Maravall speaks in *La cultura del barroco,* but then we have to contend with the characteristically Cervantine mudding of the waters. Thus, the central passage, in which the victim is coached to keep quiet for the sake of preserving in public the honor that she has lost in private, is effectively strained to the point of contradiction: "Y advierte, hija, que más lastima una onza de deshonra pública que una arroba de infamia secreta. Y pues puedes vivir honrada con Dios en público, no te pene de estar deshonrada contigo en secreto: la verdadera deshonra está en el pecado y la verdadera honra en la virtud" (84) (And beware, my daughter, that an ounce of public dishonor does more damage than a load of secret infamy. And since you can live honorably in public with God, don't worry about being dishonored with yourself in secret: true dishonor is sin, and true honor is virtue).

The first part of the statement locates (dis)honor on the side of appearances and public opinion, while the final moral truism resituates both dishonor and honor in reference to notions of sin and internal virtue. It would not be difficult to find statements that support the view on either side of the colon in baroque literature and theater, often in the same work. The contradiction is, in fact, inherent to the concept of honor, since honor is both the "patrimony of the soul" ("patrimonio del alma," as Pedro Crespo famously put it in Calderón's *El alcalde de Zalamea*) and dependent on public opinion and the system of familial and social obligations. Hence, the consistency of the baroque notion of honor can be sustained only as long as these inherent contradictions remain unconscious at the level of the utterance. But this is directly disallowed in the Cervantine passage, which places honor as virtue side by side with honor as public opinion, both united and separated by a colon. As Egginton argues in his illuminating reading of the novella, the text "establishes a relative equality between honor and dishonor": "There is, in other words, no such thing as honor, only the fear of exposure, a fear obviously enough, coterminous with enclosure and secrecy" (198). Thus, Cervantes' handling of the popular honor motif breaks the container: the walls of the baroque house crumble, and failed junctures protrude.

In this sense, we can read the broken and unfinished final tale of the *Novelas ejemplares* as a conclusion of sorts, a final "shattering of the box" (to use the eloquent image coined by María Rey López and quoted by Julio Baena). As Baena concludes, the Cervantine "*mesas de trucos* deconstruct what *tabula rasa* so painfully tried to build" (213). In effect, the "table of tricks" of the *Novelas ejemplares* can be seen as an alternative to the tabula rasa on which missionaries and educators inscribed their edifying lessons packaged in airtight containers.[20] While the official educational institutions of the baroque period work to secure the prized possessions of the Spanish aristocracy (honor, lineage, virtue) inside fortresses of reason and morality, Cervantes' texts show the cracks in the walls of the baroque house. Against the secured view of the watchtower, *El coloquio* and, by extension, the rest of Cervantes' exemplary novels offer the monstrous "insecurity" of a multiplicity of perspectives. In the same way that the aesthetics of the fantastic open alternative points of view that interrogate the categories of character and self and ultimately our fortified notion of reality, the Cervantine "table of tricks" invites us to reexamine, from eccentric (off-center) perspectives, the foundations of baroque culture, the shifting ground on which the modern house is built (Egginton 199).

The echoes of the epistemological uncertainty of the fantastic are most evident in *El coloquio*'s programmatic blurring of the boundaries between reality, fantasy, and art. In some ways, Peralta's solution would seem to be the safe way out of the epistemological labyrinth of *El coloquio:* "Aunque este coloquio sea fingido y nunca haya pasado, paréceme que está tan bien compuesto que puede el señor Alférez pasar adelante con el segundo" (359) (Even if this dialogue is fictional and never took place, it seems to me that it is so well written that you may go ahead with the next one). Peralta wants to confine the dog's dialogue to the sphere of art, where it could be properly shelved as fiction. As modern readers, we can certainly understand his discomfort: "Yo alcanzo el artificio del Coloquio y la invención y basta" (359) (I understand the artificial nature of the dialogue and its inventiveness, and that's enough). Yet Campuzano's "authorial" interventions explicitly disallow the comfort of this safe (re)solution down to the very end, when the two friends literally leave the frame of the novellas to go for a drink.

This radical openness of the tale certainly allows for the plurality of perspectives of which Spadaccini and Talens speak. But there is another manifestation of "the multiple eye" that is, strictly speaking, internal to the structure of the self. Riley has picked up on this possibility in his Freudian reading of the narrative. For him, the dogs constitute a "split character" that chal-

20. Baena reminds us that the emergence of the modern schoolteacher is associated with the notion of the child as tabula rasa. He paraphrases from Maravall's *La cultura del barroco:* "Maravall traces the figure of the teacher as an important landmark in the series of reconfigurations undertaken by the broken Christian corpus of the Reformation/Counter-Reformation, a time when the schoolteacher starts to compete with the priest [. . .] The Baroque idea of education, however, presupposes a child as tabula rasa" (211–12).

lenges not only the monological structure of exemplary language but the basic unity of self, that is, "the definition of self as a coherent, indivisible and continuous whole" (4). In this sense, one of the most compelling passages of *El coloquio* is Cañizares' confession of her inability to distinguish between different versions of her own experience of demonic encounters: "Hay opinión que no vamos a estos convites sino con la fantasía en la cual nos representa el demonio las imágenes de todas aquellas cosas que despues contamos que nos han sucedido. Otros dicen que no, que verdaderamente vamos en cuerpo y en ánima; y entrambas opiniones tengo para mí que son verdaderas, puesto que nosotras no sabemos cuándo vamos de una o de otra manera, porque todo lo que nos pasa en la fantasía es tan intensamente que no hay diferenciarlo de cuando vamos real y verdaderamente. Algunas experiencias desto han hecho los señores inquisidores con algunas de nosotras que han tenido presas, y pienso que han hallado ser verdad lo que digo" (339–40) (One opinion is that these encounters take place only in our imagination, in which the devil plants all these fantastical images that we later relate when we recall the events. Others say that we truly experience them in body and soul; for my part, I believe that both versions are true, since we do not know whether we experience them in one way or the other, and all that we experience in our imagination we feel with such intensity that it is impossible to distinguish it from what is real and true. Our lords the inquisitors have gathered some evidence of this from some of us whom they have had in prison, and I believe that they have found what I say to be true).

In this statement, Cañizares summarizes the terms of contemporary debates on the witch's experience of demonic manifestations in the course of their ceremonial celebrations. The treatment of the issue is reminiscent of similar passages in Torquemada's *Jardín* that also resist the comforts of a definitive answer. As we saw in chapter 1, Torquemada attributes the theological confusion to the difficulty of distinguishing between visions of spectral events and phantasms, or creations of our own imagination. Both texts would seem to call attention to the fact that, at least in some borderline experiences, the truth is a matter of interpretation. The difference is that the witch's borderline experiences in *El coloquio* are part of a much larger interrogation of the frontiers between reality and fantasy (and reason and unreason) in life and art. Moreover, while the focus in Torquemada's *Jardín* is on the existence of different opinions in a contested field of theological discussions, Cañizares' autobiographical account brings the conflict home, inside the very structure of the self. In fact, the Cervantine witch explicitly suggests that the distinction between reality and fantasy is not only problematic but irrelevant, since what we perceive in our imagination is, in fact, our reality. Once again, the Cervantine handling of containers and borders has caustic effects: boxes are shattered, and lines are not only crossed and blurred but erased. This is, in effect, where *El casamiento engañoso [y] El coloquio de los perros* comes closest to the irresoluble uncertainty of the fantastic in its subversive version.

Even the soul-saving distinction between good and evil falls into the Cervantine whirlpool. Thus, Cañizares draws a portrait of herself as a nonrepentant half-recovering witch who cares for the sick and the destitute (while stealing from the dead) to clear her name (and perhaps her soul) with public acts of charity and prayer that hide secret sins. Her moral self-portrait culminates in a paradoxical confession of hypocrisy: "Quisiera yo, hijo, apartarme deste pecado y para ello he hecho mis diligencias [. . .] vame mejor con ser hipócrita que con ser pecadora declarada: las apariencias de mis buenas obras presentes van borrando en la memoria de los que me conocen las malas obras pasadas. En efecto: la santidad fingida no hace daño a ningún tercero, sino al que la usa" (340) (I would like, son, to separate myself from this sin, and for that I have made some arrangements [. . .] [T]o be a hypocrite works better for me than to be a sinner in the open: the appearances of my present good deeds are slowly erasing in the memory of those who know me my past evil work. In effect: pretend sanctity harms no one [literally, "no third party"] but those who use it). This confession of hypocrisy is reminiscent of the classic paradoxical statement "I am lying." If Cañizares' confession of hypocrisy is sincere, she is not really a hypocrite, in which case she would be lying when she says she is a hypocrite; if her confession is hypocritical, she is telling the truth about being a hypocrite, and therefore she is not one; and so on. Whatever the case, Cañizares' confession that her good deeds are an effective cover up for her sinful activities (past and present) defies clear-cut distinctions between good and evil in the same way that her experience of demonic manifestations blurs the line between fantasy and reality.[21]

21. In his classical reading of *El coloquio* in *Cervantes and the Mystery of Lawlessness*, Alban Forcione arrived at the conclusion that the text is structured by the Christian narrative pattern of "sin and redemption." My own reading focuses on the ironic distance with which this narrative pattern is reproduced in this paradigmatic example of Cervantine exemplarity. While Forcione's notions are both informative and illuminating, I would nonetheless agree with Childers when he makes the point that "the pattern of sin and redemption established through the generic hybridity of fable, picaresque novel, and sermon does not achieve the release of completion, and we are left instead *en suspensión*, faced with the negative impression of an unredeemed, perhaps irredeemable, world" (*Transnational Cervantes* 67).

We can find a similar blurring of the boundaries between reality and appearances, especially between good and evil, in *El jardín engañoso* (The Deceptive Garden) in María de Zayas' collection *Novelas amorosas y ejemplares* (Amorous and Exemplary Novels [1637]). Here, too, magic and fantasy, even Faustian motifs, elude the traditional moralistic treatment. As Marina Brownlee has recently argued, Zayas exploits preternatural themes "for the purposes of generating further indeterminacy, further polysemy" (*Cultural Labyrinth* 95). *El jardín* is also (coincidentally perhaps) the concluding narrative of the collection and therefore the frame tale that should help us to make sense of the rest of the novellas in exemplary terms. The story line is a variation of Boccaccio's treatment of magnanimity in *Decameron* X, 5, but Zayas' seventeenth-century reelaboration of the tale is scandalously refractive of exemplary interpretations. In Zayas' baroque garden of deceptions, one can literally get away with murder.

In *El jardín*, Teodosia falls in love with her sister's suitor Jorge and determines to win his affections at any cost. The unintended result of Teodosia's cunning deceptions is Jorge's killing of his own brother Federico, whom he thinks a traitor. After the murder of his brother, Jorge flees the country. Honoring the etymology of her name, Constanza remains faithful to Jorge, despite his inexplicable absence, until a new suitor, Carlos, woos her into marrying him, by pretending to be a dying wealthy man. Carlos eventually confesses his despicable double deception (he was not dying, and he is not wealthy), and Constanza forgives him. Surprisingly, she considers herself fortunate to have a husband capable of such elaborate trickery for the sake of love. Meanwhile, Jorge returns and attempts to regain Constanza's affections. Constanza rejects him, as any good wife would, except that, oddly, her rejection comes in the form of an impossible and somewhat random request: should he be able to create a sumptuous garden overnight, she would favor him over her husband. One could certainly read Constanza's request for this impossible garden as a manifestation of her inexpressible (perhaps unconscious) desires. With the devil's help, Jorge succeeds in producing the fabulous garden. Carlos then frees Constanza from her matrimonial obligations so that she can keep her word, in a show of magnanimity that can only be rivaled by Jorge's own renunciation of Constanza, so impressed is he by her husband's generosity. At this point, the devil jumps in to throw his own spectacular show of magnanimity into the ring, as he frees Jorge's soul. Jorge then marries the deceptive Teodosia (etymologically "divine gift"), and they all live happily ever after in the company of their children. Teodosia tells no one about the tragic end of Federico until after Jorge's death.

The story of Federico's murder would only be publicly known after Teodosia's own death.

Members of the internal audience, all of whom listen most attentively to this final story of the collection, end up arguing over which of the characters may have exhibited the most magnanimity: Jorge, Carlos, or the devil. One thing they all come to agree on, however, is that the devil had outdone himself, since good deeds are most uncharacteristic of him. Shockingly, the devil becomes the mouthpiece of traditional Christian morality, when he proclaims: "[N]o quiero alma de quien tan bien se sabe vencer" (420) (I do not want the soul of a man who is capable of conquering himself). With respect to the issue of poetic justice, Jorge's murder goes unpunished, while the deceptions of Carlos and Teodosia are rewarded with happy marriages. Meanwhile, nobody seems to care about the sacrifice of Federico, which makes the happy ending possible. As Brownlee rightfully concludes, "Zayas is decidedly uninterested in following the path of predictable exemplarity" (*Cultural Labyrinth* 98).

When we compare the fate of the central female characters, both sisters end up married with children, but there is little doubt that Constanza's modesty and "discretion" had left her exposed to the trickery of men. The virtuous Constanza is by no means in charge of her destiny. Her reason for accepting Carlos as a husband is not so much love—and certainly not passion—but pity. The final show of magnanimity between Jorge and Carlos (with the devil as chaperone) dramatizes the extent to which Constanza's exemplary virtue and the reliability of her word serve only to ensure her absolute objectification in the patriarchal system. She is literally up for grabs, subjected throughout the novella to the whims of the men who will have her. The cunning Teodosia, in contrast, takes charge of her own destiny. Her refusal to play her assigned role of the modest and virtuous lady in the traditional patriarchal script is not punished by the gods of poetic justice in this exemplary novel. On the contrary, her unladylike licentiousness, her deceptive words, and her Machiavelian tactics are rewarded with the acquisition of her love object. Teodosia's triumph and the hailing of the devil by the cheering audience as an example of magnanimity and Christian virtue (the conquering of the self) make a mockery of the language of exemplarity in this Zayesque garden of deceptions.

El jardín engañoso is deservedly one of the most revisited tales of Zayas' first collection of novellas, due to the eccentricity of its labyrinthic plot, its daring moral ambiguities, and its "festive" incorporation of black magic. Yet a growing number of Golden Age specialists are currently focusing on the novelist's second volume, aptly titled *Desengaños amorosos* (Disenchantments of Love). These dark novellas that deal with issues of domestic violence, torture, and murder have proven particularly attractive to scholars working in the area of early modern feminism. The collection offers a dramatic exposé of the honor society of the 1600s, reminiscent of the Cervantine treatment of rape in *La fuerza de la sangre*. Yet the morbid flavor of Zayas' volume is virtually unmatched in the novelistic production of the seventeenth century.

Chapter 3 is devoted to the examination of some of the most graphic and macabre passages of *Desengaños amorosos*. I hope to demonstrate that the oppressive view of the house that is characteristic of Zayas' second collection of novellas goes beyond the image of the failed aristocratic fortress that emerges in *La fuerza de la sangre*, *El celoso extremeño*, and other Cervantine works. In *Desengaños*, the lavish houses of aristocrats serve as prisons, torture chambers, and tombs where countless women waste away in silence. These behind-the-walls images of the aristocratic house have much in common with the unsettling representations of architectural enclosures in the tradition of gothic horror, from Horace Walpole's *The Castle of Otranto* to Edgar Allan Poe's "The Fall of the House of Usher" and Charlotte Perkins Gilman's "The Yellow Wallpaper," to mention some of the best-known examples of this gothic fixation with sinister structures. As we shall see, Zayas' relentless exploration of the evil that comes with the house adds another dimension to the exemplary treatment of virtue, duty, sin, desire, and monstrosity as these notions relate to questions of honor, gender, and subjectivity in the aristocratic culture of crisis of the mid-1600s.

THREE

Zayas' Bodyworks: Protogothic Moral Pornography or a Baroque Trap for the Gaze

The Body Inside Out

The sensationalist aspects of María de Zayas' second collection of novellas, especially the extreme close-ups of tortured female bodies, have been linked to the manipulative aesthetics and propagandistic aims of official culture in baroque Spain (Maravall). Recently, Yvonne Jehenson and Marcia Wells have noted that although the repulsiveness of the Zayas' portrayal of women's bodies may distance it from sexual arousal, "its objectification approximates it to how images mean in pornography" (187). They quote from the Minneapolis Dworkin-MacKinnon Antipornography Civil Rights Ordinance, which defines pornography as the enacting of "scenes in which women are portrayed in scenarios of degradation, injury, abasement, torture, shown as filthy or inferior, bleeding, bruised, or hurt in a context that makes these conditions sexual" (quoted by Jehenson and Welles 187). They conclude that with the exception of the final words, "these descriptions fit Zayas' images of women" (187). From this perspective, the absence of "a context that makes these conditions sexual" would seem essential for an interpretation of *Desengaños amorosos* as a work that promotes sympathetic identification with the victims instead of the kind of voyeuristic objectification that we associate with pornography; and this is precisely the direction of the Jehenson and Welles argument.

Others disagree with this view of Zayas' anatomical displays as scenes of violence "devoid of titillation or calculated eroticism" (Jehenson and Wells 187). A particularly pertinent example would be Judith Whitenack's study of *La inocencia castigada* (Innocence Punished), in which she argues that Zayas makes use of the conventional motif of the erotic enchantment in Desengaño 5 precisely because it presents an opportunity "to describe in titillating detail the night's sexual adventures" (Whitenack 174). Whitenack looks at the logic behind the ancient motif of the erotic enchantment, from Odysseus' encounters with Calypso and Circe to similar episodes in Arthurian and chivalric literature, to conclude that the amorous enchantment "provides an excuse for the hero's sexual dalliance" (173). Applying this logic to doña Inés' entranced visits to don Diego's bed, Whitenack argues that even if it is obvious that the married lady is "to be regarded as a victim of diabolical magic" (175), one of the lessons of *La inocencia castigada* is precisely that a wife deprived of sexual attentions ("lo que ha menester") might be "vulnerable to seduction" (186). Regardless of whether the reader is willing to take doña Inés' "guilty conscience" as evidence of the fact that there is something other than black magic at work here (as Whitenack does), we still have to contend with the powerfully suggestive scene of an exceedingly beautiful young lady wandering the city streets at night in nothing but a shift while a gentleman awaits her arrival in the privacy of his bedroom with lustful anticipation. It seems difficult to deny that readers might approach such scenes with voyeuristic fascination.

In this chapter, I revisit the central issues of this debate. I draw from Angela Carter's reflections on pornography in the work of the Marquis de Sade and Kari Winter's commentary on the gothic aesthetics of Ann Radcliffe and the so-called "female terrorists."[1] At the same time, I try to not lose sight of the baroque genealogy or genealogies of Zayas' expressionism and the sensationalist motifs and situations that are the trademark of *Desengaños.*

Gilles Deleuze noted that one of the defining features of baroque art is an expressionistic treatment of the body that turns it inside out. The inside-out body signifies the intensity of the spiritual forces that mold its inner surfaces. The extraordinary folds of the tunic of Bernini's Saint Theresa, which represent the moment of her mystical ecstasy, would be the quintessential expres-

---

1. This notion can be traced back to Radcliffe's reflections on the distinction between tales of terror and tales of horror in her article "On the Supernatural in Poetry" (1826). Winter explains: "Ann Radcliffe defended the morality of her writing by distinguishing it from other types of Gothic fiction. She reacted against the tales of romantic horror written by men like M. G. Lewis by asserting that she wrote tales of terror, not horror. In her article 'On the Supernatural in Poetry,' she argued that 'terror and horror are so far opposite, that the first expands the soul, and awakens the faculties to a high degree of life; the other contracts, freezes and nearly annihilates them' (150). In tales of terror, she continues, 'the dreaded evil' is 'uncertain' and 'obscure' (151); the imagination of the protagonist and the readers is awakened and they may be stimulated to positive action. In this way, terror may be life-affirming and liberating, whereas horror is paralyzing and deadly" (53–54).

sion of this baroque spiritualization of the body. As Deleuze writes, "[these folds] cannot be explained by the body, but by a spiritual adventure that can set the body ablaze" (*The Fold* 122). The ghostly human figures characteristic of El Greco's painting would also work as examples of this type of baroque expressionism. El Greco's bodies are unnaturally (or supernaturally) elongated by a spiritual force that stretches them upward toward the celestial plane. Even the highly conventional pictorial genre of the still life would be invested in this baroque search for a new harmony between matter and spirit, between earthly finality and celestial eternity. This is what Deleuze calls "the fold to infinity": "The usual formula of the Baroque still life is: drapery, producing folds of air or heavy clouds; a tablecloth, with maritime or fluvial folds; jewelry that burns with folds of fire; vegetables, mushrooms or sugared fruits caught in their earthly folds. The painting is so packed with folds that there results a sort of schizophrenic 'stuffing.' They could not be unraveled without going to infinity and thus extracting its spiritual lesson" (122–23).

The echoes of the spiritual lesson of the baroque fold that turns the body inside out resonate strongly in Zayas' *Desengaños,* most notably perhaps in *El traidor contra su sangre* (Traitor against His Blood), one of the bloodiest and most shocking novellas of the collection. The insides of the body of doña Mencía, murdered in cold blood by her brother don Alonso, literally spill to infinity in order to provide a spiritual lesson. As the still bleeding body of the unfortunate lady is transported to the chapel of a convent a full year after don Alonso had stabbed her to death, a crowd congregates to witness the prodigy: "[H]abiendo muchos testigos [. . .] que, con haber pasado un año [. . .] estaban las heridas corriendo sangre como el mismo día que la mataron, y ella tan hermosa, que parecía no haber tenido jurisdicción la muerte en su hermosura" (385) (There were many witnesses [of the fact that] a year later [. . .] her wounds were spilling blood as the day she was killed, and she looked so beautiful that death did not seem to have jurisdiction over her beauty). Inside and outside, body and soul, are fused in this beautified cadaver that bleeds saintliness.

The image of the beautified body would be familiar to readers of Christian narratives of martyrdom. As Margaret Greer has noted, narratives in which the body of a deceased shows signs of incorruptibility represent death as a spectacle of salvation. She quotes the description of the good death of Saint Theresa by Ribadeneira: "Her death completed, her face stayed most beautiful, white as alabaster without a single wrinkle [. . .] All her members became beautified with clear signs of [. . .] innocence and sanctity" (quoted and translated by Greer 268–69). It is not difficult to see a connection between Ribadeneira's picture of the beautified cadaver of Saint Theresa and the quoted passage from *El traidor contra su sangre.*

This is by no means the only time that grotesque actions, gruesome events, and macabre situations are turned into spectacles of martyrdom and saintliness in Zayas' work. In fact, we find a similar progression in the same novella: don Alonso beheads his wife at the dinner table, stuffs her headless body down a well, and buries the head in a cave. This macabre scene is encoded in the language of sacrificial rituals, as are many other violations, debasements, and killings of innocent wives, sisters, and daughters who are referred to throughout the collection as "martyrs," "lambs," and "innocent doves." The sacrificial dimension of the scene is enhanced by the narrator's use of the term *sacrificio* to refer to the decapitation of doña Ana (394). When the head of the young lady is unearthed six months later, it is as fresh and beautiful as ever ("fresca y hermosa," 398). There is little doubt that the prodigious beauty of the severed head of doña Ana is offered as textual evidence of her sanctified innocence. But what about the detailed description of the folds of clothing that cover her headless body? "Tenía vestido un faldellín francés con su justillo de damasco verde, con pasamanos de plata, que como era verano, no había salido con otro arreo, y un rebociño negro que llevaba cubierto, unas medias de seda nacarada, con el zapatillo negro que apenas era de seis puntos" (*Desengaños* 395) (She was wearing a French-style overskirt with a green brocade bodice adorned with silver braid. As it was summer, doña Ana had worn no other garment except for a small black mantilla to cover her face, iridescent silk stockings, and black slippers scarcely six inches long).

Close-ups of garments and intimate apparel commonly contribute to the voyeuristic objectification of the female body in sentimental novellas as much as they do in pornography. As we shall see, Zayas herself uses this technique to produce eroticized images of the female body in other passages of *Desengaños.* So it seems fair to ask whether the expressionistic excesses of the narrative might not be approaching the dangerous terrain of necrophilia when the reader is offered such an intimate view of the exquisite clothing that covers but also reveals the anatomical surfaces of doña Ana's mangled body. This clothing includes traditionally eroticized garments, such as silk hosiery. Yet when we look closely at the context of the reemergence of the headless body, we realize that the seemingly out of place inventory of garments is included here as material support to help establish the identity of the victim in the absence of her face. Furthermore, I would propose that the articles of clothing that cover the body of doña Ana may also be seen as outward signs of her noble status and even as metaphors of her innocence. Thus, as we connect this remarkable passage with the scene of the recovery of the beautified head, the narrator's detailed description of the mutilated cadaver (clothing included) seems suggestive of a spiritualization of the body that would be fitting of the Christian narrative of "the good death" as a spectacle of salvation.

Again, Deleuze's notion of the baroque fold as the imprint of spiritual forces on the outer surfaces of the body may be useful here. As he writes, "folds of clothing acquire an autonomy and a fullness that are not simply decorative effects. They convey the intensity of a spiritual force exerted on the body" (Deleuze 122). In accordance with the aesthetic logic of the baroque fold underlined by Deleuze, we could say that doña Ana's innocence is imprinted on the clothing that covers her body, in the same manner that the incorruptible beauty of her face signifies her saintliness. The proliferation of diminutive suffixes (*faldellín, justillo, rebociño, zapatillo*) reinforces this impression that the childlike purity of her soul might indeed be revealed in the folds of her clothing. From this perspective, the small black shoe whose size would be more fitting for a child than an adult woman could be read as a metaphorical marker of doña Ana's innocence.

Beyond the fields of baroque aesthetics and Christian hagiography, images of violated and mangled bodies, especially female bodies, abound in gothic literature and painting. As Todorov and others have observed, the sudden conversion of eroticized feminine bodies into grotesque cadavers is a common feature of horror narratives, down to the latest wave of *Halloween*-type films.[2] In fact, the punishment of female immorality is the theme of countless baroque and gothic morality tales, going back to the news coverage of crimes of passion in the seventeenth century. Lozano's *Castigo de dos adúlteros* (discussed in chapter 2) is also a fitting example of this type of redemptive narrative that provides both the thrill of transgression and the grotesque spectacle of its brutal punishment. As we saw earlier, the pornographic dimension of Lozano's story is most evident in the compulsive repetition of the punishment scene, a voyeuristic spectacle of the hunting, piercing, and burning of the naked body of the female temptress.

The notion that the female victim could be responsible for her own suffering is often present—at least momentarily—in baroque dramas, including such well-known plays as *El castigo sin venganza*, *El alcalde de Zalamea*, *El*

2. As Kari Winter writes about M. G. Lewis' treatment of this gothic motif, "women who are at all self-assertive in *The Monk* are tortured or killed," and "Lewis suggests that the victim is to blame for her own suffering" (27).

médico de su honra, Peribañez y el comendador de Ocaña, La estrella de Sevilla, and others. This assumption is still integral to the plots of many horror films of the so-called splatter variety, which convey the message that "transgression"—in particular, female promiscuity—leads to torture and death. *Friday the 13th* comes to mind here. With regard to the historical gothic, Winter argues that while the male-authored tradition tends to blame the victims for their own suffering in narratives that help naturalize dominant values and social structures, the gothic narratives of such women authors as Ann Radcliffe and Mary Shelley reveal the terrors of patriarchy from the point of view of its female victims. Hence, the institution of marriage is often the target of the critical eye of female gothic novelists well into the twentieth century.[3]

Seen in this light, María de Zayas' second collection of novellas would seem to anticipate not only the expressionistic sensationalism characteristic of the original male gothic tradition but also the critical stance of the "female terrorists." This is possible insofar as Zayas and, later, Radcliffe, Brontë, and others reflected on and reacted against similar practices of familial and social (de)structuring of the female body. This is where Zayas' martyrs, lambs, and doves who are sacrificed on the altars of aristocratic honor meet the madwoman in the attic (to evoke the telling title of Sandra Gilbert and Susan Gubar's classic study of nineteenth-century women's writing). Along these lines, Marcia Welles, Elizabeth Ordoñez, Marina Brownlee, and Amy Williamsen have all noted a connection between Zayas' oppressive and virtually claustrophobic view of the house as an instrument of confinement and what Gilbert and Gubar called the "architecture of patriarchy," in reference to the gothic obsession with enclosures. Indeed, in the claustrophobic world of *Desengaños,* the house works as "an instrument of torture employed against women" (Williamsen 144).

There is possibly no better or more horrifying illustration of the sinister workings of the architecture of patriarchy than the tragic tale narrated by doña Laura in *La inocencia castigada.* The unfortunate protagonist of this novella is doña Inés, a virtuous young lady who sternly resists don Diego's advances despite the careless neglect of her often absent husband. Blinded by

3. Winter writes, "[N]o well-known Gothic novel written by an English woman between 1790 and 1865 presents its readers with a sustained picture of a happy marriage [. . .] Later nineteenth-century female Gothic tales like *The Yellow Wallpaper* often follow the pattern of Jane Eyre: the frightening patriarch is the lover or husband. In twentieth-century mass-produced Gothics, this pattern becomes formulaic; the heroine fears that 'somebody is trying to kill me, and I think it's my husband' (Russ 32)" (62–66).

passion, don Diego resorts to the forces of darkness and, with the help of a Moorish necromancer, gains access to the body, though never the soul, of doña Inés. Don Diego's diabolical spells turn doña Inés into a human puppet who sleepwalks to his bed in a trancelike state. When don Diego is finally exposed and prosecuted for his crimes, the innocence of the victim of his vile scheme is publicly acknowledged by her spouse and sanctioned by the legal system. Secretly, however, doña Inés' husband, brother, and sister-in-law conspire to punish the lady for her (seemingly involuntary) desecration of the family honor. They imprison her inside a wall of the house, where she is kept alive in horrifying confinement for six years. It would be left to her decomposing body to tell the story of her cruel imprisonment: "En primer lugar, aunque tenía los ojos claros, estaba ciega [. . .] Sus hermosos cabellos que cuando entró allí eran como hebras de oro, blancos como la misma nieve, enredados y llenos de animalejos, que de no peinarlos se crían en tanta cantidad, que por encima hervoreaban; el color, de la color de la muerte; tan flaca y consumida, que se le señalaban los huesos, como si el pellejo que estaba encima fuera un delgado cendal [. . .]; los vestidos hechos ceniza, que se le veían las más partes de su cuerpo; descalza de pie y pierna, que de los excrementos de su cuerpo, como no tenía dónde echarlos, no sólo se habían consumido, mas la propia carne comida hasta los muslos de llagas y gusanos, de que estaba lleno el hediondo lugar" (287) (In the first place, although her eyes were clear, she was blind [. . .]; her lovely tresses, which when she entered were strands of gold, white as the very snow, tangled and full of little animals that breed in such quantity when hair is not combed that teemed on top of it; her color, the color of death, so thin and emaciated that her bones showed as if the skin on top of them were but a thin veil [. . .]; her clothes turned to ashes so that most parts of her body were visible; her feet and legs bare, because the excrement from her body, since she had nowhere to dispose of it, had not only eaten into them, but her very flesh was eaten up to the thighs with wounds and worms, which filled the stinking place).

Graphic images of "death in life" abound in baroque art and literature associated with the *vanitas* and *memento mori* motifs, but Zayas' treatment of the spectacle of decaying flesh is not framed here by philosophical reflections on the transitory nature of earthly life or the spiritual truth behind worldly deceptions. Instead, the extreme close-up of the entombed body of doña Inés, covered in excrescence and penetrated by maggots, is contextualized within a story (indeed, a history) of patriarchal violence in *La inocencia castigada*. The fact that blameless women or innocent lambs, as they are presented throughout the novellas, are systematically tortured and murdered by their own husbands, fathers, uncles, and siblings in response to the pressures of honor suggests that the code of honor is "a death trap" for women. The graphic image of an innocent woman literally buried alive in a wall in the name of honor exemplifies most tragically the confining aspects of the architecture of patriarchy.

We find a similar situation in Desengaño 6, *Amar sólo por vencer* (Love for the Sake of Conquest). Deceived and abandoned by her lover, the young and naive Laurela lives with her aunt and uncle for a full year, until the day her uncle and her father (Don Bernardo) decide that it is time to finally remove the stain in the family name. Significantly, the patriarchs' weapon of choice for this honor killing is a wall of the house, which they had carefully dislodged so that it would fall on top of the young lady and one of the maids as they were having lunch. The description of Laurela's death is particularly revealing of the crashing and suffocating weight of the architecture of patriarchy: "[L]a pared le había abierto la cabeza, y con la tierra se acabó de ahogar" (330) (The wall had split her head open, and the rubble asphyxiated her). This is a powerfully emblematic image of the blind violence of patriarchal structures. We should thus note that the murderous monsters in these stories of terror are not evil spawns invading our quiet world from mysterious and sinister lands outside the boundaries and controls of respectable society; rather, they are the suffocating walls of the patriarchal fortress erected to protect the aristocratic body from contamination. The monsters come with the house in Zayas' baroque tales of kinship and terror. At the end of the last Desengaño, *Estragos que causa el vicio* (Ravages Caused by Vice), we are left with nothing but dead bodies and ruins everywhere. This is an implosion of the aristocratic house not unlike Poe's vision of decay and destruction in "The Fall of the House of Usher." These are ultimately stories about patriarchal institutions and values turning predatory. The protective patriarchs are compulsively unveiled as wolves in shepherds' clothing.[4]

If, indeed, the code of honor may be seen as a "fortification" in service of the aristocratic dream of self-containment, then *Desengaños'* nightmarish parade of tortured and suffocating bodies and mangled corpses is a shocking reminder of the code's monstrous face. The dream of honor engenders monsters. This is literally the case in Desengaño 2, *La más infame venganza* (The Most Infamous Revenge), another tale about an innocent woman who is unjustly punished by her husband. The poison administered by don Carlos fails

4. In this sense, one could also draw a connection with the treatment of monstrosity in Mary Shelley's *Frankenstein*.

to kill his wife. Instead, Camilla's body swells up to an enormous size. The victimized lady remains in this monstrous state for six long months, at the end of which she is finally summoned by God himself: "Y fue el caso que no le quitó el veneno luego la vida, mas hinchóse toda con tanta monstruosidad, que sus brazos y piernas parecían unas gordísimas columnas, y el vientre se apartaba una gran vara de la cintura [. . .] Nunca se levantaba de la cama, y en ella estaba como un apóstol, diciendo mil ejemplos y dando buenos consejos a sus criadas. De esta suerte vivió seis meses, al cabo de los cuales, estando sola en su cama oyó una voz que decía: 'Camila, ya es llegada tu hora.' Dio gracias a Dios porque la quería sacar de tan penosa vida; recibió sus sacramentos, y otro día en la noche murió, para vivir eternamente" (195) (And as it happened, the poison did not kill her immediately; instead, it made her whole body swell monstrously; thus, her arms and legs looked like huge pillars, and her stomach distended the length of a rod down from her waistline [. . .] She never left her bed, and there she laid like an apostle, offering pious examples and advising her maids. She lived in this state for six months. One day, as she rested alone in her bed, she heard a voice that said: "Camila, your time has come." She thanked God for rescuing her from such a wretched life; she took the sacraments and died to this world on the following night to find eternal life).

This passage may have been influenced by seventeenth-century discourses of monstrosity and crime in teratology treatises and *relaciones de sucesos*, but the anatomical description of Camila's victimized body is here framed by a narrative that once again reveals the monstrous aspect of the code of honor and elevates its victim to the status of a Christian martyr who is destined to find in heaven the justice she is denied on earth. The horribly deformed body of Camila is a literal embodiment of the monstrosity of the patriarchal system as well as a living relic or devotional object. The same may be said about the recasting of the ritual murder of the wife in Desengaño 3, *El verdugo de su esposa* (The Executioner of His Spouse), which focuses not on the tragic dilemma of the husband, as was the case in the Calderonian model (*El médico de su honra* [The Surgeon of His Honor]), but on the unspeakable cruelty of a deceitful don Pedro who uses the honor code as a cover for the cold-blooded murder of his innocent wife Roseleta.

Thus, while Zayas' close-ups of beautified cadavers, decomposing flesh, and tortured bodies must have been inspired by conventional representations of the body in contemporary discourses of martyrdom, *vanitas*, and monstrosity, these graphic images are reinscribed within narratives of female victimization. Don Pedro, don Carlos, don Bernardo, and don Alonso, among many other murderous husbands, fathers, brothers, and uncles represent the honor society of seventeenth-century Spain. They are the enforcers of the honor code, the human faces of a vampiric monster that feeds on the blood of countless innocent victims. The heartless indifference of the aristocratic honor system may be best illustrated by the reaction of don Alonso's father upon hearing the news of his son's execution for the savage killing of doña Ana in *El traidor contra su sangre*. Don Alonso had carried out his father's murderous designs with surgical diligence, yet don Pedro barely interrupts his game of cards to proudly declare, "[m]ás quiero tener un hijo degollado que mal casado" (398) (I'd rather have an executed son than an ill-wedded one).

Anatomy Art and Body Politics

It could be said that Zayas' baroque bodyworks have something in common with von Hagens' postmodern or neobaroque anatomy art. Both Zayas and von Hagens offer graphic presentations of beautified cadavers. Their anatomical displays and careful arrangements of bodies are often modeled after preexisting artwork. As we have seen, Zayas draws from contemporary literary and theatrical models, especially Calderonian dramas, Christian narratives of martyrdom, and the well-established artistic traditions of the *vanitas*. With respect to von Hagens' anatomy art, it is no secret that many of his whole-body exhibits are organic copies of anatomical illustrations and sculptures from the sixteenth and seventeenth centuries. Other displays are inspired in twentieth-century art pieces, including the work of futurist painter Umberto Boccioni and artists Salvador Dalí and Hans Bellmer (Wetz). When we take the long historical view, it would seem as though the Spanish writer and the German anatomist might even be placed within the same Western tradition of human exhibition, if anthropologist Uli Linke is correct in establishing a genealogical link between von Hagens' exhibits and a "history of human exhibition, in which the themes of death, dissection, torture and martyrdom are intermingled" (9).

At the same time, Linke is careful to distinguish von Hagens' Body Worlds from earlier traditions of anatomical display, insofar as "its galleries of plastinated corpses do not attempt to inspire horror or fear by dramatizing mortality" (9). This distinction is consistent with what we know about much of baroque anatomical art, including the organic tableaux created by Dutch artist-anatomist Frederick Ruysch and the Catholic displays of skulls and bones in the crypt of the Capuchin Church of Via Veneto in Rome (see introduction), but we could also point out that in the work of Zayas, as in the tradition of Christian hagiography, the horror of mortality is often transcended by the promise of eternal life that is imprinted onto the face of death. Thus, the unspeakable horror with which the reader witnesses the murders of doña Mencía and doña Ana in Desengaño 8 (to mention a paradigmatic example of the exhibition of dead bodies in Zayas' work) appears to be transcended when we take the providential perspective into account. Conversely, the horror and revulsion inspired by the original scenes of senseless violence are seemingly displaced by the final spectacle of salvation, which turns the mutilated bodies into beautified repositories of saintliness. Could it be that in adopting the aesthetics of martyrdom, Zayas would be guilty of the kind of mystification that such cultural critics as Juan Antonio Ramírez see in postmodern anatomical displays, from von Hagens' plastinates to the organic compositions of Damien Hirst?

Critics of Body Worlds have made the point that the displacement of revulsion in the whole-body exhibits must be seen as part of an aesthetic program that provides the illusion of life after death by suppressing evocations of violence, victimization, and history. Linke sees a masculine and masculinist project at work in what she calls "the German exhibit": "[T]his exposition of bodies is driven by an aesthetic that seeks to transform the male corpse into an heroic figure. The cadavers are arranged so as to emphasize physical strength, virility, athletic prowess, and muscular vigor" (10). While von Hagens' plastinates may indeed be seen as the culmination of a long masculinist tradition that seeks to improve on the works of Mother Nature (Baltasar Gracián's notions of perfected nature and heroic immortality come to mind), perhaps nothing expresses the illusion of the triumph of man's artifice over nature's corruptibility better than Damien Hirst's most famous creation to date, a real eighteenth-century skull encrusted with nearly nine thousand diamonds, with a price tag of ninety-eight million dollars. The diamond-encrusted skull is explicitly meant to laugh in the face of death. In a May 2006 interview, Hirst himself said about his work in progress, "I just want to celebrate life by saying to hell with death [. . .] What better way of saying that than by taking the ultimate symbol of death and covering it in the ultimate symbol of luxury, desire and decadence? [. . .] [T]his will be the ultimate two fingers up to death" (*Observer*, May 21, 2006). In his description of his yet unfinished sculpture, Hirst offered a postmodern or neobaroque reversal of the *vanitas* motif and the aesthetics of *desengaño*. Hence, Hirst's piece would be fittingly titled *For the Love of God*.

Hirst's obscenely expensive skull is no longer the placeholder of the spiritual truth of the cosmos or the stain in the picture that reveals our true face hidden behind layers of worldly deceptions. Rather, it is a pathetic leftover of a remote history of human suffering that has nothing to do with us. *For the Love of God* is thus a tribute to the commodification of life and death in our culture industry, a celebratory totem of the illusion manufactured by the economic and political forces of global capitalism—the cynical promise of a universal triumph of wealth and luxury over suffering and death.

With respect to the baroque bodyworks of María de Zayas, it is true that the aesthetics of martyrdom employed by the seventeenth-century novelist are anchored in the Christian promise of individual immortality and the belief in the ultimate triumph of providential law over man's injustice. But it is also important to note that the providential view adopted by Zayas does not hide the miseries of man's history in the way that the diamonds cover over the face of death in Hirst's composition. Rather, Zayas seems to bring in the providential perspective to make a point about a man-made history of victimization and injustice. We could say that Zayas stakes claim to the providential vantage point in order to expose the inadequacy of prevailing views on gender and gender trouble and to denounce individual and institutional practices of victimization of women in her aristocratic society. Thus, while Hirst's diamond-encrusted skull and von Hagens whole-body plastinates "suppress evocations of violence, victimhood (sic) or history" (Linke 10), Zayas' bodyworks are framed within narratives that not only do not suppress traumatic memories of man's history of violence but dare to offer intimately graphic close-ups of the oozing wounds of its victims.

When we compare the dramatic treatment of the theme of the honor killing in the tragic plays of Calderón de la Barca and Lope de Vega with the presentation of the same material in *Desengaños,* it is clear that Zayas brings the reader closer to the bodily reality of violence. The violence of the act of the honor killing is certainly present in Lope's *El castigo sin venganza* (Punishment without Revenge) as well as Calderón's *El pintor de su deshonra* (The Painter of His Dishonor) and *El médico de su honra* (The Surgeon of His Honor), which is—as I mentioned earlier—the direct model for Desengaño 3. But the tragic death of the lady in these and other baroque dramas happens at a safe distance from the reader's gaze, even from the victimizer's touch. Jehenson and Wells have perceptively noted, "The victims become abstract entities, spectacles viewed through the frame of a door or window. The husbands/executioners, in turn, become spectators of victims they do not touch even at the moment of death, and whose death always occurs off-stage"

(190). But is this not precisely the point of those who warn against the sensationalist techniques of official propaganda? Would Zayas' graphic close-ups of the intimate act of violence on the female body not be closer to the objectifying and manipulative nature of pornography than is the distanced stylization offered by Lope and Calderón?

Angela Carter has studied the detailed representation of violence against women in the pornographic work of the Marquis de Sade. She suggests that pornography, like mainstream fictions of romantic love, belongs to the timeless, locationless area outside history and geography where mystifying universals are born. As she writes, "pornography reinforces the false universals of sexual archetypes because it denies, or doesn't have time for, [. . .] the social context in which sexual activity takes place" (16). This is why Carter sees most pornography (including traditional sentimental literature) as an extension of the propagandistic techniques of the moral and political establishments: "[M]ost pornography remains in the service of the status quo [. . .] because its elementary metaphysic gets in the way of real life and prevents us seeing real life" (17). But Carter opens the door to a possible subversive use of potentially pornographic material if and when the writer or artist "moves out of the kitsch area of timeless placeless fantasy [. . .] in order to affect the reader's perception of the world" (19). Remarkably, Carter's notion seems to fit Jehenson and Wells' view of the cultural politics involved in Zayas' deployment of "holy masochism" in *Desengaños*. They argue that Zayas employs the graphic aesthetics of martyrdom to move away from "a reflection model of storytelling" (arguably the model of male-authored sentimental novellas) to "a mediation model that contests the dominant meanings of her honor code society" (195).[5]

5. Jehenson and Wells draw on Caroline Bynum's study of hagiographic discourse and on Deleuze's conceptualization of the distinction between sadism and masochism : "Deleuze associates the former with the father, the latter with 'an intermaternal order' (63), with a world in which 'the father will have no part' [. . .] On the psychological level, then, masochism is seen as negating paternal power and the paternal legacy. On the theological level, 'holy masochism' also allies itself symbolically with the feminine and with the maternal. Caroline Bynum, in *Jesus as Mother: Studies in the Spirituality of the High Middle Ages*, emphasizes the prevalence of iconographic and literary images of the consoling and maternal Christ. She shows how, following upon the evangelist Matthew and his description of Jesus as a hen gathering her chicks under her wing (23:37), hagiography popularized the image of Jesus as Mother, presenting a suffering, lactating Christ whose blood nourishes and saves souls and to whom the desolate turn for comfort" (197). Of *Desengaños*,

To be sure, I would agree with those who argue that the sensationalism of hagiographic discourse plays a conservative and propagandistic role in seventeenth-century Spain (Maravall). However, Zayas seems to appropriate the aesthetics of "holy masochism" to expose the violence of the patriarchal system in a language that erases the "proper distance" from which the reader or spectator of Calderonian and Lopean dramas can safely enjoy the suspense of spectacular actions and the rhetorical exchanges of archetypal characters on matters of love, marriage, honor, and loyalty. While the popular Lopean and Calderonian plays focus on the tough moral and political choices that must be made to protect the purity of genealogical lines and the integrity of the social body, *Desengaños* brings home the sacrificial dimension of marriage and the honor code by foregrounding the obscene (off-the-scene) excesses of patriarchal violence. Lisa Vollendorf writes, "Zayas' aesthetic binds bodies to politics [. . .] Her body-bound aesthetic literalizes the impulses behind social control" (213). In this sense, Zayas' work approximates Carter's provocative notion of moral pornography: "A moral pornographer might use pornography as a critique of current relations between the sexes [. . .] Such a pornographer would not be the enemy of women, perhaps because he might begin to penetrate to the heart of the contempt for women that distorts our culture even as he entered the realms of true obscenity as he describes it" (Carter 19–20).

Briefly stated, whether they are inspired in the graphic aesthetics of martyrdom and *vanitas* art or in sensationalist scenes of monstrosity and crime in contemporary pulp fiction and yellow journalism, Zayas' anatomical close-ups succeed in disrupting the proper distance imposed by the objectifying tradition of sentimental literature. The conventional image of the eroticized feminine object characteristic of love poetry, sentimental novellas, and baroque dramas suddenly collapses in the presence of violated bodies, of ripped and decomposing flesh that spills blood, excrement, and pus and breeds maggots.[6] This shift in perspective is indeed consistent with Carter's

---

Jehenson and Wells observe, "[T]he new order of the cloister for whom the women renounce the world at the end of their storytelling, is systematically equated with this protective, loving, and forgiving maternal bridegroom [. . .] The representation of God as Mother in the hagiographic tradition is never part of the Judgment scene or of the castigation of sinners. Reference is made instead to communitas, to a fellowship of souls bonded in love" (197).

6. "Unlike the distancing optic of the male authors, the focus for Zayas's hagiographic discourse as for the pornographic discourse is at close range on a female body that is debased and tortured [. . .] Instead of presenting an artificial body, Zayas

thoughts on the political work of the "moral pornographer," which is to terrorize our imagination by creating powerful artistic reminders "of the mutilations our society inflicts upon women and the guilt that exacerbates this savagery" (23).

Carter's conceptualization of the moral pornographer as a "terrorist of the imagination" is strongly evocative of Ann Radcliffe's impassioned defense of the aesthetics of "terror" in her 1826 article "On the Supernatural in Poetry." Radcliffe established a sharp distinction between her life-affirming and awakening tales of terror and the male-authored narratives of horror, which she saw as paralyzing and deadly: "[T]error and horror are so far opposite, that the first expands the soul, and awakens the faculties to a high degree of life; the other contracts, freezes, and nearly annihilates them" (quoted by Winter 53). With respect to Zayas, whether we focus on her view of marriage and the house as instruments of torture employed against women (Williamsen), on her body-bound aesthetic (Vollendorf), on her appropriation of the imagery of "holy masochism" (Jehenson and Wells) and the Christian spectacle of salvation (Greer), or on her gusto for macabre scenes that inspire terror, it seems fair to say that the scandalous work of this baroque writer anticipates crucial aspects of the literary and critical tradition of the female gothic, especially the systematic exploration of the links between kinship and terror in the work of such eighteenth- and nineteenth-century authors as Ann Radcliffe, Mary Shelley, and Charlotte Perkins Gilman, as well as more recent novelists and storytellers, such as Shirley Jackson.

Eros, Pathos, and the Anamorphic Body

The detailed image of the commodified body of Zelima in the opening paragraphs of *Desengaños* is one of the most conventionally voyeuristic representations of the feminine object that we can find in Zayas' work. The emblematic significance of this initial display of female anatomy and exoticized clothing can hardly be overstated. The erotic spectacle of Zelima's exquisite body covered in exotic garments literally pulls the audience together for the storytelling celebration (the Sarao). In the presence of the eroticized feminine object, the internal audience of *Desengaños* emerges as a desiring intersubjective community of viewers and listeners. Zelima is first introduced to

---

presents what Elin Diamond calls an 'orificial' one, wholly open in its suffering and pain" (Jehenson and Wells 192–93).

them (and us) as a human commodity, a domestic slave who, dressed in the proper Moorish costume, displays the looks of a princess of Algiers, a queen of Fez or Morocco, or a sultana of Constantinople. This is before she reveals herself as a high-ranking Christian lady in disguise at the beginning of Desengaño 1. The passage of the introduction in which the young slave dressed in princess costume is presented as eye candy in front of a crowd of envious women and salivating men is well worth quoting in its integrity:

> A los últimos acentos de los postreros versos salió Zelima de la cuadra, en tan diferente traje de lo que entró, que a todos puso en admiración. Traía sobre un camisa de transparente cambray, con grandes puntas y encajes, las mangas muy anchas de la parte de la mano; unas enaguas de lama a flores azul y plata, con tres o cuatro relumbrones que quitaban la vista, tan corta, que apenas llegaba a las gargantas de los pies, y en ellos unas andalias de muchos lazos y listones de seda muy vistosos; sobre esto un vaquerillo o albuja de otra telilla azul y plata muy vistosa, y asida al hombro una almalafa de la misma tela. Tenía la aljuba o vaquerillo las mangas tan anchas, que igualaban con las de la camisa, mostrando sus blancos y torneados brazos con costosos carcajes o brazaletes; los largos, ondeados y hermosos cabellos, que ni eran oro ni ébano, sino un castaño tirando a rubio, tendidos por las espaldas, que le pasaban de la cintura una vara, y cogidos por la frente con una cinta o apretadorcillo de diamantes, y luego prendido a la mitad de la cabeza un velo azul y plata, que toda la cubria: la hermosura, el donaire, la majestad de sus airosos y concertados pasos no mostraba sino una princesa de Argel, una reina de Fez o Marruecos, o una sultana de Constantinopla. Admirados quedaron damas y caballeros, y más la hermosa Lisis, de verla, y más con arreos que ella no había visto, y no acertaba a dar lugar al disfraz de su esclava, y así, no hizo más de callar y admirarse (como todos) de tal deidad, porque la contemplaba una ninfa o diosa de las antiguas fábulas. Pasó Zelima hasta el estrado, dejando a las damas muy envidiosas de su acabada y linda belleza, y a los galanes rendidos a ella, pues hubo más de dos que, con los clavos del rostro, sin reparar en ellos, la hicieron señora y poseedora de su persona y hacienda, y aun se juzgara indigno de merecerlo. Hizo Zelima una reverencia al auditorio, y otra a su señora Lisis, y sentóse en dos almohadas que estaban situadas en medio del estrado, lugar prevenido para la que había de desengañar. (123–24) [As the sound of the last lines was fading, Zelima emerged from the next room in such different

> costume from the one she had been wearing that it amazed everyone. She wore a blouse of transparent chambray, all lazy with the sleeves opening wide at the wrist. Her skirt was of fold brocade with silver and blue flowers and ornaments so dazzling that they were almost blinding. It was so short it scarcely reached the turn of her ankle. On her feet she wore sandals adorned with elaborate silk ribbons and bows. Covering everything, she wore an overskirt of a very beautiful filmy blue and silver fabric, and clasped at her shoulder was a mantle of the same material. The garment had sleeves even wider than the sleeves of her blouse and revealed her nicely rounded white arms bedecked with costly bracelets. Her beautiful long wavy hair was neither gold nor ebony but a light chestnut. It cascaded down to far below her waist and in front it was secured by a diamond clip that held a blue and silver veil to shroud her head. Her beauty and grace, and the majesty of her light and stately step, bespoke of a princess of Algiers, a queen of Fez or Morocco, a Sultana of Constantinople. Ladies and gentlemen alike were thunderstruck. The beautiful Lisis, seeing Zelima in raiment she'd never seen before, could not take in her slave's disguise. She simply sat in silence, amazed (like everyone else) by such a divine creature. Zelima did look like a nymph or a goddess from some ancient tale. As she moved toward the platform, she made the ladies feel envious of her splendid beauty and held the gentlemen in her sway. There were more than a few gentlemen who, regardless of the brand upon her face, wished to make her their wife, mistress of their persons and all their possessions and, even so, felt unworthy of winning her. Zelima made a bow to her audience and then to her mistress Lisis. She took a seat on two pillows positioned in the middle of the platform, the special place appointed for the person who was to tell a disenchantment. [Boyer translation 41–42]].

This elaborate description of Zelima as a dazzling spectacle of evanescent folds is a quintessentially baroque (re)construction of the poetic feminine object. Zelima is not just a body in costume but *the* body *as* costume, inseparable from the markers of economic, social, and cultural transactions. Zelima's white skin, her cascading wavy hair, her well-rounded arms, and her adorned feet are as much a part of the spectacle of folds as her pricy bracelets, the ribbons and bows on her sandals, the veil that envelops her head, her transparent blouse, the diamond clip that secures her hair, and the mark of slavery on her face. This description of a Christian lady disguised as a slave dressed up as a Moorish princess goes well beyond the conventional objectification of the female body in the tradition of Neoplatonic literature. Whereas the Petrarchan and pastoral conventions represented the female body in eroticized fragments (face, neck, lips, feet, etc.), the blinding display of flashes of fabric and flesh in the Zayesque spectacle of folds turns it into a series of accessories and markers of economic, social, and libidinal exchange indistinguishable from garments and adornments.[7] Just as important, Zelima's fashion show is explicitly marked in the narrative as her "taking-up the position" or "striking the pose" of the first storyteller of the Sarao: "She took a seat on two pillows positioned in the middle of the platform, the special place appointed for the person who was to tell a disenchantment" (Boyer translation 42). How fitting it is that the exquisitely detailed description of Zelima's costume should precede her self-fashioning discursive performance in the first *desengaño* of the collection.

There are many other instances in the novella collection in which female bodies are displayed before the desiring gaze of masculine characters. Desengaño 6 includes some of the most paradigmatic passages in this respect. Much of the novella is built on a sustained identification with the voyeuristic position traditionally associated with masculine fantasies. A young man poses as a female servant (Estefanía) to gain access to the forbidden feminine spaces where he can enjoy the company of the naive and unguarded Laurela, the object of his desire. The following paragraph illustrates the intensity of the voyeuristic drive of the narrative: "Se fueron, y Estefanía con su señora, asistiéndola hasta que se puso en la cama, gozando sus ojos, en virtud de su engaño, lo que no se le permitiera menos que con su engañoso disfraz, enamorándose más que estaba, juzgando a Laurela aún más linda desnuda que vestida" (309) (Everyone retired, and Estefanía went with her mistress, attending to her until she was in bed. Her [his] eyes enjoyed sights, by virtue of her [his] deception, that would not have been permitted were it not for her [his] deceiving disguise. She [he] fell even more deeply in love, finding

7. We could use this scene to make the point that cultural theorists of postmodernity miss the mark when they conceptualize our present as an age inhabited by posthumans (Hayles) who, for the first time in history, are ready to regard their bodies as "fashion accessories" (van Dijck). As I mentioned earlier, the treatment of the body as a "fashion accessory" is integral to the baroque philosophy of the Jesuit Baltasar Gracián. At least in this sense, we can say that the conceptual lines that currently separate the postmodern from the modern are overstated. Significantly, these distinctions tend to ignore or gloss over the products of baroque culture (see the discussion on "perfected nature" in the introductory section).

Laurela more desirable naked than dressed). While there is no question that the reader is pulled into the voyeuristic position from which Estefanía/Esteban steals forbidden glances of the nude body of Laurela, the theatrical recourse of the disguise complicates the libidinal economy of these passages by adding a charge of multidirectional (potentially homosexual) desire to the entire situation. Laurela's lady friends and servants find it amusing that a woman could be passionately in love with another woman: "[A]unque en todas ocasiones [Estefanía] le daba a entender su amor, ella y todas lo juzgaban a locura, antes les servía de entretenimiento y motivo de risa, siempre que la veían hacer extremos y finezas de amante, llorar celos y sentir desdenes, admirando que una mujer estuviese enamorada de otra" (309) (Despite the fact that Estefanía would seize every opportunity to express her love to her, she and everyone else thought it was folly. It was a source of amusement and laughter, to see her display the repertoire of the lover, weeping from jealousy and lamenting disdains. They were amazed that a woman could be so much in love with another woman).

Laurela's seemingly metrosexual allure and the amorous advances of her "lady lover" are perceived not as a threat to the social body but merely as expressions of harmless folly and opportunities for carnivalesque laughter. Even the patriarch don Bernardo dismisses Estefanía's passionate love for his daughter as a situation more fit to joke about than to be regarded as a serious threat.[8] The contrast with the treatment of male homosexuality in Desengaño 7 could not be more pronounced. If female homosexuality "does not exist" other than as an expression of harmless folly in Desengaño 6, the threat of male homosexuality is only too real in *Mal presagio casar lejos* (Marriage Abroad: Portent of Doom). The dead serious treatment of male homosexuality as a marker of "foreign evil" in Desengaño 7 proves particularly problematic for critics who might agree with Marina Brownlee's call for a "relational feminism" that should stand ready to concern itself with everything that the patriarchal power has condemned to a position of marginality ("Postmodernism and the Baroque in María de Zayas" 119).[9] The homosexual affair culminates in some of the most pornographic scenes of the collec-

8. In terms of the libidinal economy of the narrative, don Bernardo himself is placed in a delicate position when he is repeatedly shown chasing Estefanía with amorous designs of his own.

9. The unambiguous aristocratism of Zayas' work and her disdainful representation of servants and racial others, most notably in Desengaño 4, *Tarde llega el desengaño,* would also seem to get in the way of Brownlee's political ideal of a relational feminism.

tion, including, as we shall see, the sadistic spectacle of the bleeding of doña Blanca.

Jehensen and Wells are among the critics who have paid close attention to the libidinal economy of *Desengaños.* They have noted that eroticized presentations of the conventional feminine object give away to disturbing close-ups of ruptured flesh in scenes of female martyrdom. Going back to the initial display of the feminine object in the introduction of Desengaño 1, we could say that if Zelima represents the *engaño,* a crowd-pleasing spectacle made up of nothing but layers of deception, then subsequent scenes of carnage (the decomposing flesh of doña Inés, the headless corpse of doña Ana, the bleeding bodies of doña Mencía and doña Blanca, etc.) are the graphic images of the *desengaño,* the tragic reality of injustice, violence, and victimization of women hidden behind layers of social and cultural deception. Jehensen and Wells explain the presence of this contrastive imagery in terms of a shift from eros to pathos, a shift that would ultimately promote a sympathetic identification with the position of the female victims: "Voyeuristic identification gives way, instead, to sympathetic identification—pathos replaces eros—and the objectification of women gives way to the presentation of woman's subjectivity, emphasizing her fears, pain, and helplessness, and her superior courage of endurance. In other words, the women enacting these spectacles become *exempla*" (193).

While I find this interpretation illuminating, I am nonetheless inclined to think of the shift from eros to pathos less in terms of a replacement or transcendence of the voyeuristic point of identification than in terms of a perspective oscillation or, rather, an anamorphic superimposition of points of view. This would explain why the theoretical line between eros and pathos is often difficult to draw in practice. The scene of the rape of doña Inés at the hands of the desperate don Diego would be a case in point. Deprived of her will thanks to a diabolical spell, the married lady is reduced to the status of a lifeless prop with which the rapist fulfills his sexual fantasies.

> [F]orzada de algún espíritu diabólico que gobernaba aquello, se levantó de su cama, y poniéndose unos zapatos que tenía junto a ella, y un faldellín que estaba con sus vestidos sobre un taburete, tomó la llave que tenía debajo de su cabecera, y saliendo fuera, abrió la puerta de su cuarto, y juntándola en saliendo, y mal torciendo la llave, se salió a la calle, y fue en casa de don Diego, que aunque ella no sabía quién la guiaba, la supo llevar, y cómo halló la puerta abierta, se entró, y sin hablar palabra, ni mirar en nada, se puso dentro de la cama donde es-

taba don Diego, que viendo un caso tan maravilloso, quedó fuera de sí; mas levantándose y cerrando la puerta, se volvió a la cama, diciendo:—¿Cuándo, hermosa señora mía, merecí yo tal favor? Ahora sí que doy mis penas por bien empleadas. ¡Decidme, por Dios, si estoy durmiendo y sueño este bien, o si soy tan dichoso que despierto en mi juicio os tengo en mis brazos! A esto y otras muchas cosas que don Diego le decía, doña Inés no respondía palabra; que viendo esto el amante, algo pesaroso, por parecerle que doña Inés estaba fuera de su sentido con el maldito encanto, y que no tenía facultad para hablar, teniendo aquéllos, aunque favores, por muertos, conociendo claro que si la dama estuviera en su juicio, no se los hiciera, como era la verdad, que antes pasara por la muerte, quiso gozar el tiempo y la ocasión, remitiendo a las obras las palabras; de esta suerte la tuvo gran parte de la noche, hasta que viendo ser hora, se levantó, y abriendo la puerta, le dijo:—Mi señora, mirad que es ya hora de que os vais. Y en diciendo esto, la dama se levantó, y poniéndose su faldellín y calzándose, sin hablarle palabra, se salió por la puerta y volvió a su casa. (277–78) [Driven by some diabolic spirit that controlled her behavior, she rose from her bed and put on the shoes that were there and a petticoat that lay with her clothes on a stool. She took the key she kept under her pillow and set out, opening the apartment door and closing it after her, unlocking the front door and entering the street. She made her way to don Diego's house; she had no idea what was guiding her but it knew where to take her. Finding don Diego's door ajar, she entered. Without saying a word or noticing a thing, she crawled into bed beside don Diego. When he saw this marvelous event he was beside himself. He got up to close the door and returned to bed saying: "How, my beautiful lady, did I merit such favor? Now I consider all my efforts well rewarded. Tell me, for the love of God, whether I'm asleep and dreaming this marvel or am I so fortunate as to be awake and in my right mind as I hold you in my arms?" Doña Inés replied not a word to these questions or to anything else don Diego said. When the lover noted her unresponsiveness he became sad because the cursed spell seemed to have rendered doña Inés as if unconscious and without the ability to speak. He enjoyed her favors, yes, but they were empty favors. He realized that in her right mind the lady would never have granted them to him, and that was true, she would rather have died. Be that as it may, he decided to make the best of the occasion and the time by turning words into action. He lay with her for the most part of the night.

When he saw it was time for her to leave he got up and opened the door, saying to her: "My lady, it's time for you to go." The moment he said these words she got up, put on her petticoat and her shoes and without uttering a word departed. [Boyer translation 187]]

While these lurid passages are contextualized within an unambiguous condemnation of don Diego's blind passion and his willingness to resort to sorcery to satisfy his monstrous desire, it also seems clear that the scene retains a sense of voyeuristic fascination sustained by a partial identification with the rapist's point of view—his puzzlement, his excitement, his sadness when he realizes that doña Inés is unable to engage in conversation in her trancelike state, even his seemingly sincere disappointment that she would not willingly surrender her body to him. The line between voyeuristic objectification and sympathetic identification with the subjective position of the victim seems impossible to draw here. This is one reason why, as Whitenack has pointed out, Desengaño 5 seems particularly problematic from the perspective of the argument of Jehensen and Wells.

As I mentioned earlier, one of the most deeply disturbing scenes of the novella collection occurs in Desengaño 7, when doña Blanca is bled to death by two patriarchs, one of whom (her homosexual husband) turns "sympathetic" during the very act of the killing. The libidinal economy of this spectacle of murder is further complicated by the specular positioning of doña María, who watches the tragic scene through a peephole (a conventional voyeuristic position if there ever was one), while identifying most sincerely with the suffering and powerlessness of the victim.

> Mandando salir fuera todas las damas y cerrando las puertas, mandaron al sangrador ejecrcer su oficio, sin hablar a doña Blanca palabra, ni ella a ellos, mas de llamar a Dios la ayudase en tan riguroso paso, la abrieron las venas de emtrambos brazos, para que por las pequeñas heridas saliese el alma, envuelta en sangre, de aquella inocente víctima, sacrificada en el rigor de tan crueles enemigos. Doña María, por el hueco de la llave, miraba, en lágrimas bañada, tan triste espectáculo. A poco rato que la sangre comenzó a salir, doña Blanca se desmayó, tan hermosamente, que diera lástima a quien más la aborreciera, y quedó tan linda, que el príncipe, su esposo, que la estaba mirando, o enternecido de ver la deshojada azucena, o enamorado de tan bella muerte, volviéndose a su padre con algunas señales piadosas en los ojos, le dijo: ¡Ay señor, por Dios, que no pase adelante esta crueldad!

> [. . .] Porque os doy mi palabra que, cuanto ha que conozco a Blanca, no me ha parecido más linda que ahora. (363) [They sent all her ladies out and closed the door. Then they ordered the leech to do his duty. They never said a single word to doña Blanca nor did she say anything to them. She only prayed to God to attend her at this final moment. They opened the veins in both arms so that through those tiny wounds the soul of the innocent victim might ooze forth, dripping blood, sacrificed to the cruelty of such harsh enemies. Doña María, bathed in tears, watched the sad spectacle through the keyhole. The moment the blood began to flow, doña Blanca fainted. She was so beautiful the sight would have filled her worst enemy with pity. She looked so lovely that the prince, her husband, could only stare at her. Perhaps he felt affected by the sight of the stripped lily, perhaps he was enchanted by such a beautiful death, at any rate, he turned to his father with tears of compassion in his eyes and said: "Alas, my lord, for God's sake, do not permit this cruel act to proceed [. . .] I swear to you that as long as I've known Blanca she's never looked lovelier than she does now. [Boyer translation 267–68]]

The notion of a replacement of eros by pathos through which the objectification of women would give way to the presentation of woman's subjectivity is certainly suggestive; yet this idea poses a definitive temporal rupture between the time of voyeuristic objectification and the time of sympathetic identification with the victim's subjective point of view. I argue that the previously quoted passages disallow the opening of this temporal rift, insofar as the victim (in this case doña Ana) is always already prefigured in the narrative as a martyr in the waiting, a lamb, an innocent dove (*mártir, corderilla, inocente palomilla*). My claim is that the audience's certainty with respect to the inevitability of the imminent tragedy hovers over Zayas' novellas, impressing itself as a stain of pathos in the more conventional voyeuristic scenes, even if we have to wait for the *desengaños* to unfold to their prefigured pathetic conclusion before we have access to the full impact of the tragedy (its specificity).[10] The quoted passages also show that the voyeuristic

10. Franco Moretti (1983) has underscored the key role that temporality plays in the structuring of pathos. Linda Williams points out, "Moretti has argued, for example, that literature that makes us cry operates via a special manipulation of temporality: what triggers our crying is not just the sadness or suffering of the character in the story but a very precise moment when characters in the story catch up with and real-

impulse of the initial scenes of objectification does not completely dissipate even in the midst of fully developed scenes of victimization and martyrdom. The lingering residue of the objectifying libidinal economy is thus suggested as the stain in the picture of pathos. The notion that the victimized body of doña Blanca could occupy simultaneously the position of the object of the voyeuristic gaze, the tortured body, and the sublime relic is, of course, deeply disturbing. Yet this might, after all, be the point of "moral pornography," if we can reach back to Carter's provocative notion: to terrorize our imagination by creating powerful artistic reminders "of the mutilations our society inflicts upon women and the guilt that exacerbates this savagery" (23).

Needless to say, there are many risks involved here, not the least of which is the reduction of feminine characters to archetypes in the guise of Justines and Juliettes, that is, innocent martyrs and monsters who commit all the crimes of which honest women are falsely accused. Carter makes this point very effectively in her discussion of the life of Juliette in chapter 3 of *The Sadeian Woman.* While this is not the place to discuss the presence of these monsters in women's clothing in Zayas' work, it should be noted that they are invariably presented as enemies of the community of women, standing on the side of the victimizing patriarchs.

To conclude, I view Zayas' bodyworks as anamorphic figures that resist our critical attempts to make sense of them from univocal or totalizing explanatory schemes. The anamorphic quality of these images of eroticized, violated, and sublime bodies is reinforced by the narratees' discussions of individual and social responsibilities, motivations, guilt, and innocence at the end of each tale. These postscripts incorporate a myriad of perspectives, including traditionally masculinist views as well as feminist or protofeminist denunciations of masculine cruelty, along with a range of voices that position themselves somewhere in between. My suggestion is that Zayas' collection of novellas may be thought of as a trap for the reader in the sense that Lacan

---

ize what the audience already knows. We cry, Moretti argues, not just because the characters do, but at the precise moment when desire is finally recognized as futile. The release of tension produces tears—which become a kind of homage to a happiness that is kissed goodbye. Pathos is thus a surrender to reality but it is a surrender that pays homage to the ideal that tried to wage war on it" (11). Herein lies the subversive potential of pathos according to Moretti. Williams' reflections on pathos in sensationalist cinematic fantasies intersect with Jehenson and Wells' interpretation of *Desengaños,* especially their understanding of the function of the graphic aesthetics of "holy masochism," and also with Angela Carter's discussion of pornography in *The Sadeian Woman.*

speaks of Holbein's anamorphic portrait of the French ambassadors as "a trap for the gaze." As we have seen, the idealizing and objectifying distance that is built into conventional images of femininity is disrupted by Zayas' close-ups of the incontinent materiality of victimized flesh. Alternately, the shift in perspective may occur when the sexualized image of the feminine object is transformed into a devotional relic, that is, a prodigious sign of divine presence. Hence, the meaning of these bodies changes depending on whether we look at them from a secular earthbound perspective (in which case we see the devastating effects of a man-made history of violence, predation, corruption, and immorality) or whether we fix our gaze on the eternal realities of providential history.

Conversely, the reader may be caught up in the destabilizing vertigo produced by the oscillation between a view that sustains his or her subjective position vis-à-vis the idealized object (the *engaño*) and the irruption of a normally hidden perspective that shows an oozing mess or, alternately, a sublime body filled with spiritual grace (the *desengaño*). In true anamorphic fashion, once we have seen the stain in the picture, this blot becomes an inherent component of the scene, as a reminder of the arbitrariness of our interpretive choice. The structurally subversive edge of *Desengaños* might ultimately arise from this unsettling sense that no matter what point of view we could decide to embrace from within the multiplicity of choices offered by the narrative and highlighted in the conversational postscripts, the fact is that once we have experienced the vertigo of perceptual oscillation, the illusion of transparency can never be fully reconstituted. Try as we might, we can never shake the impression that what completes the picture is the presence of our own desiring gaze.

We may look at Zayas' bodyworks as voyeuristic attractions, spectacles of "holy masochism," scenes of abject terror, or perhaps something else. But I would argue that they may not be fully reduced to one or the other. They are all these things simultaneously. This type of epistemological oscillation and the built-in resistance to narrative closure are defining features of the work of other major baroque authors and artists, such as Cervantes, Góngora, and Velázquez. At the same time, the perspectivistic drive of *Desengaños* and its turning of the woman's body—and ultimately the social body—inside out is another way in which Zayas' baroque style seems to approximate the narrative tradition(s) of the gothic and, generally speaking, the aesthetics of the fantastic as conceptualized by such critics as Rosemary Jackson and Eric Rabkin.

FOUR

Monsters from the Deep: Lozano's *La cueva de Hércules* and the Politics of Horror

Myths of Origin and Ancient Enemies

On September 21, 2004, Spanish ex-president José María Aznar delivered his inaugural address as Georgetown University's distinguished scholar in the practice of global leadership. His highly publicized speech outlined "seven theses on today's terrorism." Aznar congratulated the bipartisan commission on the September 11 terrorist attacks for taking the lead in defining the enemy of the democratic world: Islamic terrorism. According to the Spanish ex-president, this fundamental recognition comes with a call to military action: "All ambiguity has been removed as to what we must do, in our capacity as democratic societies, to combat our main enemy, the Islamic terrorism." Aznar acknowledged that there are other dangers out there (he mentioned the Basque separatists of the Euskadi Ta Askatasuna, or ETA), but he argued that Islamic terrorism represents a unique threat to "our" democratic freedoms, in that it seeks not simply to take over our governments but to destroy our societies and ways of life and to enslave us all. Referring specifically to the March 11 bombing in Madrid perpetrated by Al Qaeda, the ex-president warned against those who would want to tie the Madrid massacre to recent political and military conflicts, such as the "Iraq crisis." Instead, he urged Americans to recognize that Al Qaeda's terrorist attacks are part of an ancestral war that goes back to the Muslim invasion of Spain in the year 711: "[T]he problem Spain has with Al Qaeda and Islamic terrorism [. . .] has nothing to do with government decisions. You must go back no less than 1,300 years, to the early 8th century, when a Spain recently invaded by the Moors refused to become just another piece in the Islamic world and began a long battle to recover its identity" (http://www3.georgetown.edu/president/aznar/inauguraladdress.html).

The suggestion here is that the members of Al Qaeda involved in the

Madrid bombing of March 11, 2004, are the historical heirs of the Muslim troops that defeated don Rodrigo, king of the Visigoths, in the year 711. The statement also implies that there is a Spanish identity that preexists the historical events of the early eighth century and that must be defended against the recurrent attacks of terrorist aggressors. While these assumptions have been discredited by historians and cultural critics from Américo Castro to Javier Tusell, they are still deeply rooted in the patriotic imagery displayed by conservative political forces in Spain. Tusell wrote in his reaction to the ex-president's words, "Spanish culture cannot be understood without the often conflictive—productive at times—coexisting of three religions. But there are those who repudiate multiculturalism for the benefit of a reemerging Spanish nation in the face of its presumed assassins" (*El Pais*, September 27, 2004, my translation).

In his "American speech" on terrorism, Aznar places the Spanish nation right at the center of a transhistorical war between Western civilization and its ancient Islamic enemy. This scenario of a worldwide war fits well with the messianic rhetoric that legitimizes neoconservative projects of preemptive military aggression. George Bush's justification of the U.S. invasion of Iraq as a means of exporting freedom and democracy to the Middle East in his 2003 State of the Union address is a good example: "Americans are a free people, who know that freedom is the right of every person and the future of every nation. The liberty we prize is not America's gift to the world; it is God's gift to humanity" (quoted by Mariscal 275).

George Mariscal is among those who have noted that the messianic overtones of Bush's State of the Union address sound eerily familiar to scholars working in the early colonial period.[1] Beyond the questions raised by Bartolomé de Las Casas in the context of his well-known sixteenth-century debates with Sepúlveda over the right to war, the fact is that by the late 1500s, the rhetoric of messianic imperialism permeates the political establishment of absolutist Spain, supported in part by the spectacular "discoveries" of Spanish historiography. The genealogical concerns of the late Middle Ages and the early Renaissance became increasingly invested in messianic images of Spain that accompanied "the expansive dreams of Castilian politics" (Tate 18).[2] The

---

1. See Mariscal's compelling essay "Bartolomé de Las Casas on Imperial Ethics and the Use of Force" (2006).

2. See also the studies by Alexander Samson and, more recently, Mercedes García Arenal.

revisionist zeal of the "organic" historians of the late 1400s and the 1500s resulted in a systematic rewriting of the past of the Iberian Peninsula and the consolidation of a national mythology of ancient origins and historical destiny of which Spaniards, especially Castilians, could be proud.

"España, la ilusión que nos une" (Spain the illusion that unites us) is the current slogan of the Spanish neoconservative political block known as Partido Popular, or PP. In a clear case of unintended irony, the slogan of the ex-president's party could easily qualify the discursive products of early modern historiographers. The new and improved image of Spain as an ancestral nation of superior destiny emerged with built-in enemies, much like Aznar's own "illusion that unites us." In fact, it might not be an exaggeration to say that Aznar's Spain was invented by the emerging class of organic intellectuals of the modern state in its imperialist version.

While medieval chroniclers, including the Alfonsine compilers of the *General Estoria* (General History) and the thirteenth-century archbishop known as Toledano, were happy to play up the Greco-Roman connection in their genealogical accounts, historians working under the auspices of the emerging absolutist monarchy sought to establish the existence of an ancestral Spain going all the way back to the biblical time of Noah and his direct line of descendants. This mythical Iberian monarchy would have thrived under the guidance of Castile long before the emergence of the classical civilizations of Greece and Rome. Hence, by the end of the fifteenth century and throughout the 1500s, the Greco-Roman tradition was increasingly downplayed or altogether rejected in the chronicles of Ruy Sánchez, Fabricio de Vagad, Margarit i Pau, Annius de Viterbo, Antonio de Nebrija, and Florián de Ocampo, among others.

The historiographic fate of Hercules may be considered symptomatic of the changing perceptions of antiquity in the cultural and political environment of the nascent Spanish state. In the last decades of the fifteenth century, the Greco-Roman Hercules, once a welcomed founding figure, was abruptly demoted to the status of a foreign invader. This angle is played up by Antonio de Nebrija, who notes that Spain had been "a magnet to the invader" and "the prey and booty of foreigners" (Tate 14) up to the time of the consolidation of the absolutist monarchy under Fernando and Isabel. As Robert Tate pointed out in his informative article "Mythology in Spanish Historiography of the Middle Ages and the Renaissance" (1954), "the phrase 'Hispania tota sibi restitute est,' with which [Nebrija] greets the victories of their Catholic Majesties, implies in its context not only the ejection of the Moors but also a reconstitution of the totality of the Peninsula, a recovery of self, a purification from external encroachments and alien influences" (14–15).[3] In Nebrija's work, as in Annius' *Commentaries,* the classical Hercules of the twelve labors is an antagonistic figure, a piratical aggressor who makes his unwelcome appearance at the end of a long chain of ancient monarchs.[4] Curiously, Annius' mythology of pre-Greek origins incorporated an older Hercules, a son of Osiris and Isis and grandson of Cam, who would have visited Spain many generations before the invader. The figure of the Egyptian Hercules introduced in the *Commentaries* would become very popular among sixteenth-century historians associated with the study of astrology and other ancient sciences. Nebrija's disciple Florián de Ocampo and his followers would uphold and build on the "discoveries" of Annius, which afforded Spain an illustrious lineage going back to Noah's descendants. This ancestral genealogical line would have passed on the sciences of the universe to the Spaniards long before the time of the classical civilizations of Greece and Rome (Tate 16).[5]

Seventeenth-century author Cristóbal Lozano draws from this modern historiographic tradition while making some key adjustments that turn Hercules into a necromancer or "great sorcerer" ("grande mágico") and that transform (or convert) his ancient science into "the devil's craft" ("arte del demonio"). The theologian attributes to the dark powers of Hercules the self-fulfilling prophecy of the destruction of Spain at the hands of Muslim aggressors. Lozano's refurbishing of the legends associated with Hercules, don Rodrigo, the enchanted cave of Toledo, and the fall of Spain in *David Perseguido* (David Persecuted) and especially in *Los reyes nuevos de Toledo* (The New Monarchs of Toledo) contributes to the consolidation of the historiographic myth of "a reemerging Spanish nation in the face of its presumed assassins" (to quote from Tusell's commentary of Aznar's Georgetown speech).

---

3. Much of the overview of Spanish historiography presented here comes from Robert Tate's compelling article. Tate's discussion underscores the emergence of propagandistic notions of Spanish integrity in the context of the absolutist monarchy.

4. Quite telling is Annius' description of the Greek Hercules as a piratical aggressor: "pyrata maximus non iusti belli" (quoted by Tate 13).

5. For a lucid discussion of the work of Florián de Ocampo, see Alexander Samson's "Florián de Ocampo, Castilian Chronicler and Habsburg Propagandist: Rhetoric, Myth, and Genealogy in the Historiography of Early Modern Spain" (2006).

Remarkably, Lozano's version of the legend of the enchanted cave in *Los reyes nuevos de Toledo* is strongly reminiscent of a well-established streak of horror fiction that is built around anxieties of invasion and pollution, from Sheridan Le Fanu's "Green Tea" and Bram Stoker's *Dracula* to Dean Koontz's *Phantoms* (1983) and the countless films dealing with infection and alien invasion, including *The Invasion of the Body Snatchers*, the *Alien* and *Species* series, and a recent string of B movies on subterranean evils. Scholars who study modern horror fantasies have noted that many of these narratives strive "to separate out the symbolic order from all that threatens its stability" (Barbara Creed 70). Whether they focus on universal fears of pollution and the dissolution of boundaries between the clean and proper body and the abject (Julia Kristeva) or emphasize the historically specific content of the repressed that makes its dreaded return (Franco Moretti), cultural theorists have pointed out that horror fantasies reenact the fundamental conflict between self and other at the individual and collective levels, or as Ken Gelder phrases it, the conflict between "the archaic (the 'primal', the 'primitive', the 'frenzied subject of excess') and the modern (the 'struggling moral subject', rational, technological)" (3). The threat of the return of the real and the dissolution of our safeguards is a favorite theme in horror fiction down to Oliver Hirschbiegel's recent remake of *The Invasion of the Body Snatchers.* The unsavory character of the ambassador makes this point with stereotypical Russian flair in his tongue-in-cheek conversation with the young psychiatrist played by Nicole Kidman: "I say that civilization is an illusion, a game of pretend. What is real is the fact that we are still animals driven by primal instincts" (*The Invasion* [2007]).

The battle between civilization and instinct easily moves into the terrain of Christian morality. Le Fanu's "Green Tea" (1869) is a paradigmatic example of a classic horror tale in which the Christian protagonist loses the battle of the mind to the Ancient Enemy: "About four years ago I began a work, which had cost me very much thought and reading. It was upon the religious metaphysics of the ancients [. . .] [This is] not good for the mind—the Christian mind. I mean, Paganism is all bound together in essential unity, and with evil sympathy, their religion involves their art, and both their manners, and the subject is a degrading fascination and a Nemesis for sure. God forgive me! It thoroughly infected me" (23). The poisoning of the Christian Western self that is chronicled in Le Fanu's story affects the body of Mr. Jennings as well as his mind and is simultaneously attributed to contact with ancient paganism and the ingestion of substances that come from the East, green tea in particular.

Gelder's definition of horror as the conflict-filled meeting place between the archaic and the modern and Mr. Jennings' warning against the unholy touch of ancient paganism in "Green Tea" are useful to illuminate what is at stake in Lozano's seventeenth-century tale of boundary crossing, as is Stephen Arata's discussion of Victorian anxieties of reverse colonization in Bram Stoker's *Dracula*. In opening the door to the ancient world, don Rodrigo, the last monarch of the Visigoth kingdom, had invited in an ancestral force whose "very presence seems to presage its doom" (as Arata says about Dracula's arrival in London). The invader comes from not only another place (the cave of Hercules, the mountains of Transylvania) but also another time, since it is an undead relic from the "unchristian" past.

The cover of the DVD version of *Van Helsing*, one of the many filmic reelaborations of the Dracula mythology, reads as follows: "Deep in the mountains of 19th century Carpathia lies the mysterious and mythic land of Transylvania, a world where evil is ever-present [. . .] The immortal Dracula (the Ancient Enemy) will stop at nothing to unleash his master plan of subverting human civilization and ruling over a world of havoc, fear and darkness." These words resonate with Lozano's story of Muslim invasion and also with Aznar's picture of the present "war on terror." After all, the current war against Al Qaeda is—in Aznar's version—the same ancestral conflict between our Western nation and the Ancient Enemy from the East. The face of the monster may change, as in Joe Chapelle's 1998 adaptation of Koontz's *Phantoms:* it may look like a black mass that comes up through the sewage and pipe systems, a possessed dog foaming at the mouth, or a predatory species that attaches to our head and sucks our brains out. But we know that these are all manifestations of the same Ancient Enemy: "chaos, chaos in the flesh" (as the character played by Peter O'Toole puts it). Incidentally, the forces of order in Chapelle's film are science, reason, technology, Christian morality, and the American military.

Ken Gelder's definition of horror seems appropriate to discuss the war against the Ancient Enemy in Le Fanu's "Green Tea," Stoker's *Dracula*, and Chapelle's adaptation of *Phantoms*, as well as in Lozano's *La cueva de Hércules* and Aznar's "Seven Theses on Today's Terrorism." Don Rodrigo unleashed a new dark age of horrors by reopening the door to the "unchristian" past of Toledo, much like Harker had helped transfer the ancient monster from deep inside the Carpathian mountains to Victorian London, "where, perhaps for centuries to come he might, amongst its teeming millions, satiate his lust for blood and create a new and ever widening circle of semi-demons to batten on the helpless" (*Dracula*, quoted by Arata 166).

Ultimately, the problem for the Visigoth kingdom of don Rodrigo, Harker's Victorian England, and Lozano's Christian Toledo is also the problem faced by Aznar's Western European Spain. The essential problem is time, which makes closure impossible. "Time is on my side," whispers the narrator at the beginning of Gregory Hoblit's *Fallen*. This is the voice of a good guy (played by Denzel Washington) in his own life story (or so we are initially led to believe). At the end of the movie, however, we are hit with the sudden realization that the voice to which we have been listening throughout the film is, in fact, that of the Ancient Enemy himself. "Time is on my side," he hums at the film's closing. In true Freudian fashion, historical time is on the side of the other; or, to put it differently, the repressed always returns to the same place, because it is what we are. Manuel Aguirre may have said it best in his commentary on Victorian horror: "the struggle with the dark Other is not one between two opposing principles Good and Evil, but between [. . .] a close-up Here and an excluded There, between a society false to itself and an aspect of its denied Truth" (144).

About Time: A Tale of Two Nations

Few events have inspired more legendary literature than the historical defeat of the Visigoths at the hands of the Muslim troops in the year 711. The many legends associated with the fall or loss of Spain feature compelling characters, such as the enigmatic and tragic figure of the king don Rodrigo, the irresistible femme fatal Florinda, and the treacherous count don Julian, complete with images of barbaric invaders. The fundamental question that structures these narratives is, why did God permit the loss of Spain? The fall of the Christian Visigoth kingdom at the hands of Islamic infidels seems to make little sense from the perspective of Christian providential history. This is why most legends associated with the loss of Spain have to resort to the Old Testament logic of divine punishment. The historical events are thus reduced to the status of moral exempla, while political, military, and social issues are converted into matters of family values.

We witnessed a redeployment of the Old Testament logic of divine punishment in our own day when Christian right-wing leaders Jerry Falwell and Pat Robertson stated during a highly publicized interview on the *700 Club* that the horror of September 11 was God's way of punishing the United States of America for its tolerance of abortionists, liberals, feminists, gays, and lesbians. The language of Falwell and Robertson does not stray far from the explanation of the fall of Spain provided by Cristóbal Lozano in *El rey don Rodrigo* (King Don Rodrigo) included in *David Perseguido y Alivio de Lastimados* (Persecuted David and Relief of the Injured [1652]): "Con mil estragos de religión y costumbres se hallaba el imperio gótico, cerca de los años de setecientos y once [. . .] Tener irritado a Dios con la desenvoltura, enojado al Cielo con la desobediencia y ofendida hasta la tierra con tanta maldad: esto fué la causa que España se perdiese" (52) (The Visigoth Empire was plagued by the corruption of religious values and behavior in the years preceding the seven hundred and eleventh [. . .] To have irritated God and infuriated the Heavens with disobedience and to have offended even the land with such wickedness: this is what caused the loss of Spain).

As in the stories of punishment of the chosen people in the Old Testament, these theologically inspired interventions reduce antagonistic historical agents (the Al Qaeda terrorists of 9/11, the Muslim invaders of 711) to the status of instruments of God's wrath. In the case of Lozano's narrative in *El rey don Rodrigo,* we would have to add the treacherous count don Julian and the female temptress Florinda to the list of instruments of the providential punishment. Lozano writes about Florinda, also known as Caba: "Ella fué sólo instrumento para tomar Dios el azote y ejecutar los castigos" (52) (She was just an instrument of God's whip for the execution of his punishment).

In this version of the tale, Florinda is raped by don Rodrigo, but this does not mean that she is without fault. In the passage leading to her rape, the theologian establishes a direct parallel between Florinda and the biblical figure of Bersabe, David's temptress. The voyeuristic bathing scene shows don Rodrigo stealing curious glances of the naked body of Florinda, who plays vanity games with other noble ladies:

> [B]rindadas de la sonora y cristalina fuente, no sólo dieron al agua, calurosas, las manos, sino que tambien quisieron bañarse las partes que el telar adorno cubre y disimula. Como se juzgaban solas, la más melindrosa se negó al recato, apostando entre ellas sobre cual se aventaja a la blancura: propio de damas, cuando en tales juegos se entretienen y divierten [. . .] Acechábalas curioso [el rey] desde una celosía, donde sin más información que sus mismos ojos (que la juzgó bastante), sentenció para su mal, que era Florinda la más ventajosa en gracias, en blancura y en aseo. ¡Oh, el mal que causa el poco recato en

una mujer hermosa y el no reparar primero que se desnude si hay quien pueda verla! ¡Oh, cuantos han amancillado descuidos de hermosuras poco atentas! Baste el de Bersabé pues a un rey como David le hizo dar de ojos: con que no hay que espantar que el de la Caba le haga al rey Don Rodrigo despeñarse [. . .] Y así, si hay dama, o doncella, que, poco recatada o de propósito da ocasión y gusta que la vean, no se lamente después si viere acuestas el daño y el honor perdido. (54–55) [Invited by the sonorous and crystalline fountain, not only did they dip their warm hands in the water but wanted to bathe those parts that clothes must hide and cover over. Since they thought they were alone, even the most shy among them rejected modesty, competing with one another over who had the fairest skin: this is customary among women who entertain themselves with such playful distractions [. . .] The king observed from behind a lattice where, relying on nothing but the evidence provided by his own eyes (which studied her closely), he came to judge her the most gifted in graces, fairness, and cleanliness. Oh, the damage that is caused by the lack of modesty of a beautiful woman who does not stop to think that someone might be watching her before undressing! Oh, how many have been lost by the carelessness of inattentive beauties! If a king like David could not avert his eyes from Bersabe, we must not be surprised if the carelessness of Caba caused King don Rodrigo's downfall [. . .] And thus, if a lady or maiden provides the occasion to be seen, whether by lack of modesty or because she likes to be looked at, she must not later complain about injuries or loss of honor.]

This passage invites the reader to inhabit the voyeuristic position from which the king secretly enjoys the eroticized bathing scene. Florinda's tragic fate has been sealed by her own playful vanity and carelessness. Lozano's final warning to all women out there amounts to a preemptive and potentially universal justification of rape. There is no doubt as to who occupies the position of the object and whose will matters here: "Abrigó el hermoso objeto en toda la voluntad" (55) (He wrapped his entire will around the beautiful object).

Count don Julian will learn about the king's rape of his daughter in a letter written in her own handwriting. The narrative downplays the significance of don Rodrigo's offense, suggesting that the count's treachery has little to do with his daughter's rape: "[A]unque la Caba callara su afrenta y no incitara a su padre a la venganza, no por eso dejara el conde traidor de pasar adelante con sus tratos" (59) (Even if Caba had silenced her affront and had not incited her father to avenge it, this does not mean that the treacherous count would not have moved forward with his dealings). Don Julian puts together a coalition of conspirators and traitors ("traidores") in southern Spain with the intention of dispossessing the king of his rightful crown for the benefit of his dynastic rival Witiza. He then crosses over to the African continent to enlist the Muslim neighbors to his cause. This is the final act of treachery that would ultimately seal the fate of Spain despite don Rodrigo's heroic efforts to protect his kingdom and the Christian faith.

In the end, the king will see the light, repent his sins, and save his soul. Unfortunately, it would be too late for Spain, which would have to wait nearly eight centuries for its own salvation. The loss of Spain at the hands of bloodthirsty barbarians ("barbara canalla") is chronicled with uncontained emotion in Lozano's apocalyptic discourse: "[Q]uedó España perdida, despobladas sus ciudades, cautivos sus hijos, saqueadas sus riquezas, vueltas en llanto sus glorias, [. . .] la fe cristiana extinguida, muertos sus ministros, desechos sus santuarios, derribadas sus iglesias [. . .] ¡La pluma tropieza en tanto cuerpo difunto como puebla la campaña!" (64–65) (Spain was lost, its cities depopulated, its children enslaved, its riches looted, its glories converted into laments, [. . .] the Christian faith extinguished, its ministers dead, its sanctuaries destroyed, its churches in ruins [. . .] The pen stumbles upon the countless corpses left on the battlefield!).

While Lozano devotes a few passages to the legend of the enchanted cave in *El rey don Rodrigo*, the king's exploration of the mysterious subterranean landscape of Toledo is overshadowed here by the events surrounding don Rodrigo's fixation with Florinda and don Julian's treachery. Lozano will revisit this legendary material a few years later in *Los nuevos reyes de Toledo* (1667), in which don Rodrigo's crossing of the ancient boundary will come to the fore. Much of Lozano's narrative is a reelaboration of the medieval legends associated with the cave and enchanted palace of Toledo, but the seventeenth-century theologian turns the legendary cave into the unholy repository of ancient paganism, "all bound together in essential unity and with evil sympathy" (to use Mr. Jennings words in "Green Tea").[6] This

6. *La cueva de Hércules* may be considered a precursor of gothic horror and romantic aesthetics because of its atmospheric and expressionistic quality and its fixation with medieval legends, enclosures, and ancient ruins. In fact, in the context of Spanish literary history and criticism, the bulk of Lozano's legends are often qualified as preromantic or protoromantic. According to Joaquín Entrambasaguas, Lozano greatly influenced such well-known romantic authors as Espronceda, Zorrilla, and Fernández y González.

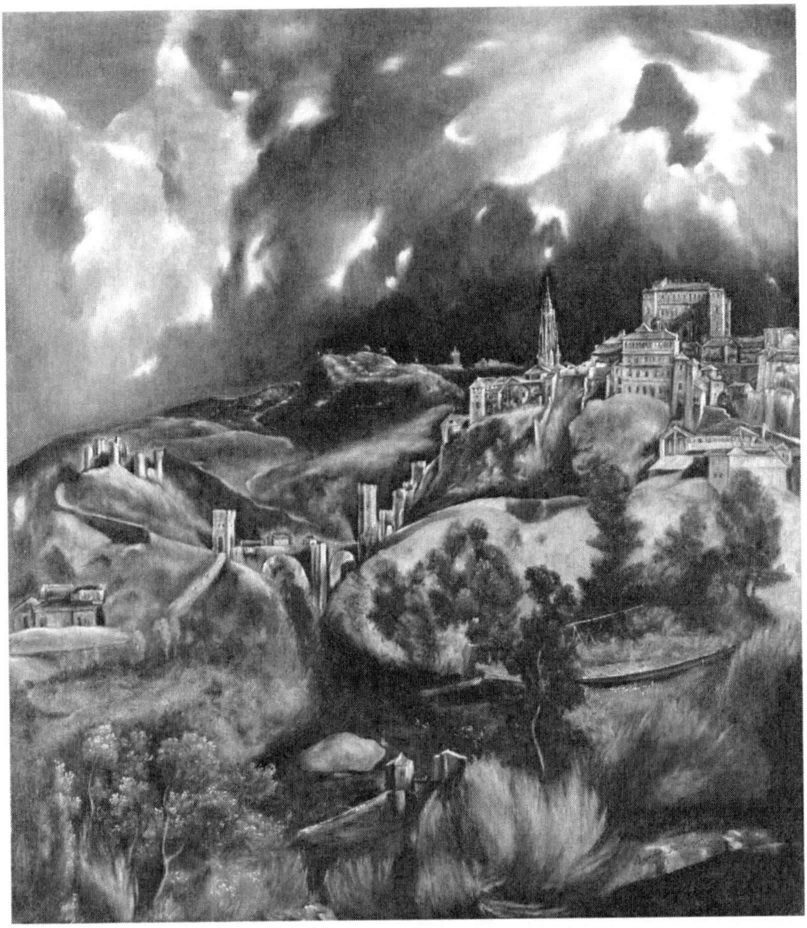

Illustration 4. El Greco's *Vista de Toledo.* (Image from the Metropolitan Museum of Art.)

dark cavernous landscape is the counterpart of the City of Light, the spiritual luminary of Catholic Spain immortalized in El Greco's paintings (see Illustration 4).

Ruiz de la Puerta has studied different versions of the bewitched cave and palace of Toledo. He pointed out that there are plenty of medieval references to an enchanted structure in such texts as the *Crónica General* of 1344. Yet he also notes that the association of this fabulous structure with the practice of sorcery takes center stage in more recent accounts, from the late fifteenth century on. More important, at the hands of early modern authors, the legendary material associated with the cave of Toledo appears to conflate with memories of the famous medieval School of Translation: "Los escritores de los siglos XVI y XVII nos hablan de la cueva como estudio de la Magia, y la mayor parte de ellos no hacen sino tomar las ya conocidas tradiciones relativas a la cueva, la leyenda del rey don Rodrigo, y mezclarlas con el recuerdo de la escuela de traductores. En general, se encuentra en ellos la convicción de Toledo como lugar de magos, y la cueva como su recinto de enseñanza" (67) (Sixteenth- and seventeenth-century authors speak of the cave as a school of sorcery, and most of them do nothing but repeat known rumors related to the cave and the legend of don Rodrigo, which they mix with the memory of the School of Translation. In general, they remain convinced that Toledo was a city of sorcerers and the cave its school).

These observations may help us understand the significance of Lozano's attribution of the loss of Spain to the self-fulfilling prophecy of Hercules, as well as his conversion of the mythical hero into a great ancient master sorcerer who would have refurbished the cave for the teaching of the dark arts. The narrative makes this point repeatedly: "Hércules, el famoso, la reedificó y amplió, sirviéndose de ella como de real palacio y leyendo allí la Arte Mágica" (The famous Hercules refurbished it and expanded it, using it as royal palace for the study of the magical art). If these references to the science of the Egyptian Hercules and his teachings of sorcery are, in fact, metonymically tied to the memory of the School of Translation that flourished in Toledo during the twelfth and thirteenth centuries, as Ruiz de la Puerta suggests, then the activities of the medieval multicultural center of Iberian culture could be attributed to the evil designs of the Ancient Enemy.

Lozano reinvents the enchanted cave as an unholy receptacle that contains the relic(t)s of virtually all forms of political, cultural, and ethnic difference. These relic(t)s are envisioned as manifestations of the same transhistorical unchristian anti-Spanish enemy, whether they be the remnants of ancient paganism, Muslim and Jewish presence, or sixteenth- and seventeenth-century Moriscos. Hence, the narrative creates a metonymic link between the legendary stories of ancient relics safeguarded by the evil spells of Hercules and his pagan followers and the more recent rumors about jewels and riches presumably hidden by Morisco traitors: "Que las hay grandes [cosas en la cueva], y aún quizá tesoros, no lo dudo, pues en partes menos guardadas y secretas, donde vivieron los moros, sabemos y lo vemos cada día que se han hallado y descubierto joyas y riquezas de sumo valor. Luego teniendo los bárbaros un receptáculo como éste, y con candados, como suelen de sus hechicerías, ¿quién duda que al ganarles la ciudad y al expelerlos de ella, cuando dándolos por cristianos solo en el nombre, y hechos solos de su ley, los arrojaron de España; quién duda digo que encerrarían en lo más profundo de esta cueva la mayor parte de sus tesoros?" (209) (That there are great things in the cave, perhaps even treasure, I do not doubt, for there are locations not quite as guarded and secret, where the Moors once resided, where riches and jewels of great value have been found. And so, having the barbarians a receptacle such as this, guarded with their spells as they often do, who is to doubt that when the city was taken from them and they were expelled from Spain—as they were Christians in appearance only and were given to their Law—who is to doubt, I say, that they must have hidden in the depths of this cave most of their riches?).

The propagandistic dimensions of Lozano's framing of the legend of the bewitched cave are most evident in his justification of the Hapsburgs' campaigns of racial cleansing. The theologian manages to conflate the Moors, Muslims of earlier centuries, with the Moriscos, new Christians expelled in 1609–14, while drawing a metonymic link with the ancient palace of Hercules and his cultivation of sorcery. The compression of historical time inside the mythical landscape of the cave results in the creation of an allegorical figure of radical antagonism that can be activated to describe the lurking presence of ancient, medieval, and modern enemies of Spain. These mythical and historical enemies are associated directly or indirectly with the devil's craft: "La experiencia nos enseña lo mucho que con arte del demonio alcanzan los nigrománticos" (211) (Experience shows how much these necromancers can do with the devil's art). This is why we must be vigilant to make sure the door to the unchristian past is never reopened.

We find similar appeals to keeping our doors closed in such classic horror tales as Arthur Machen's "The Great God Pan" (1894) and the aforementioned "Green Tea" by Sheridan Le Fanu. In Machen's story, Dr. Raymond laments his accidental opening of the door to the "house of life," which is a gateway into prehistoric cosmic time: "[W]hen the house of life is thus thrown open, there may enter in that for which we have no name, and human flesh may become the veil of a horror one dare not express" (148). "The Great God Pan" has been hailed by Lovecraft as a masterpiece of horror and one of the best examples of the modern anxiety he famously named *cosmic fear*. As I noted earlier, "Green Tea" redirects this epochal anxiety toward the pre-Christian past. Mr. Jennings' contact with the metaphysics of the ancients poisons his mind beyond the possibility of recovery. The proposed cure for Mr. Jennings' disease is the surgical clogging or sealing of the organ of sight responsible for this unwarranted and wholly destructive contact with the relics of the past. The good doctor says, "I should have first dimmed and ultimately sealed the inner eye which Mr. Jennings had inadvertently opened" (41). The gateway to the past must be sealed to prevent the Ancient Enemy from poisoning our Christian world. This is precisely Lozano's fundamental lesson in *La cueva de Hércules.* The pagan, Muslim, and Jewish past of Toledo (and, by extension, Spain) must be expelled from the daylight, literally pushed underground, buried in the name of Christian reason incarnate in history.

We could say that Hercules' cave, Dr. Raymond's "house of life," and Mr. Jennings' "inner eye" are different names for the passage that brings us into contact with the abject (the part of ourselves that we are most committed to rejecting or denying) via a descent into what Barbara Creed calls the foundations of the symbolic construct. Arguably, the drive to revisit the original site of exclusion of the abject is the ultimate testimony of the fragility and arbitrariness of our foundational constructs (their permanent crisis). In essence, the more we repeat the ritualized act of exclusion, the more locks we place on the door, the more we realize that complete and final separation from the unclean other is ultimately impossible.

The compulsion to reenact the foundational act of exclusion is signified in *La cueva de Hercules* by the many locks that are placed on the door that separates the City of Light from the darkness of the cave: the cave's opening was "cerrada con una tapa de hierro, llena de candados" (212) (covered with an iron door full of locks). Reportedly, each new monarch added his own locks to this subterranean place: "Cada rey que sucedía en la Corona, especialmente los godos, añadían a tal palacio nuevas cerraduras" (211) (Each new king that inherited the crown, especially the Visigoths, placed new locks on the door to the palace). We are told that the door to the cave and palace of Hercules remains securely locked in Lozano's own time: "[P]ermanece cerrada for muchas y justas causas" (209) ([It] remains closed for many just reasons). But we may ask ourselves whether the reinforced door can truly be trusted to forever protect Lozano's Spain, especially if, as Aguirre argues, the struggle with the dark other is nothing more than a conflict "between a society false to itself and an aspect of its denied Truth" (144).

Remarkably, the door to the cave of Hercules is located inside a Christian church. The difficulty of disentangling the history of Christianity from the "messiness of antiquity" is also evidenced by the multiple functions of the cavern. According to Lozano, the cave would have been a privileged site for the celebration of pagan rituals and the teaching of sorcery, but he also acknowledges that it seems to have been utilized as a Christian temple and sacred graveyard during the time of the Roman persecutions. Thus, the theologian cannot help but remind us that the new, purified Toledo, the symbol of the spiritual ideals of the Counter-Reformation, stands on a burial ground where pagans, Jews, Muslims, and Christians rest side by side. It is tragically ironic that the cave's main entrance—literally, its point of origin ("principio")—should be located inside the church of San Ginés or Saint Genesius, a temple devoted to the memory of a legendary Roman actor who renounced his own pagan past in order to embrace Christian martyrdom: "Yace esta cueva y principio de ella en la iglesia parroquial de San Ginés, casi en lo más alto de la ciudad. Tiene la puerta por de dentro de la misma iglesia, la cual hoy permanece cerrada, por haberse así dispuesto por muchas y justas causas" (209) (The entrance to the cave is located in the parochial church of Saint Genesius, near the top of the city. The door is in the inside of the church, and it has been decided that it should remain closed for many just reasons).[7] To add to the mix, the historical records of the city suggest that Toledo's cavernous underground may have been the site of choice for the administering of procedural inquisitorial torture. The city's premiere Web site for all things related to the "Toledo subterráneo" (subterranean Toledo) underscores this tragic irony with its own legendary accents: "[L]os sótanos de Toledo no sólo servían a los alquimistas, magos y nigromantes que ejercían allí sus artes ocultas. También servían para castigarles cuando la terrible Inquisición les descubría" (http://go.to/leyendasdetoledo) (Toledo's underground served not just alchemists, sorcerers, and necromancers who practiced their occult arts. It was also used to punish them when they were discovered by the terrible Inquisition).

A comparison of Lozano's version of the legend or legends of King don Rodrigo and the enchanted cave of Toledo with the packaging of the same mythical material in Miguel de Luna's 1592 chronicle *Historia verdadera del rey don Rodrigo* (The True History of King don Rodrigo) may help us understand what is at stake in the culture wars of the sixteenth and seventeenth centuries. While this is undoubtedly a conflict about space (inside vs. outside, our place vs. theirs), the point I am trying to make here is that it is also a des-

7. The popularity of this third-century Roman martyr in seventeenth-century Spain is evidenced in the frequent fictionalization of his life and death in plays, such as Lope's *Lo fingido verdadero* (1608) and Lozano's own narrative version of the legend in his incomplete posthumous collection *El gran hijo de David más perseguido, Jesucristo, Señor Nuestro* (The Great Son of David Most Persecuted, Jesus Christ, Our Lord). Lozano's version of the legend can be found in the second volume of the collection *Historias y leyendas,* edited by Joaquín Entrambasaguas (129–36).

perate fight for historical time. That *Historia verdadera* should be Lozano's closest source is in itself an interesting fact, since historians have identified its author, Miguel de Luna, as one of the Morisco "translators" who forged the infamous *libros plúmbeos,* or "lead books," of Granada, a collection of "archeological discoveries" that were presented in the late 1500s as documents recorded by early Christians in the first century. These forgeries were intended to rewrite Christian history by painting a positive image of Islam that could be attributed to the views of the original Christian communities.[8]

The lead books recently made the Spanish news when the Vatican returned them to Granada in the year 2000. Just a few months earlier, on the floor of the Andalusian parliament on November 19, 1999, the parliamentary group of Izquierda Unida—Los Verdes (United Left—The Greens) had presented a motion that included the following *exposición de motivos* (exposition of motives or facts): "En el último tercio del siglo XVI en Granada seguía vigente la división entre cristianos viejos y cristianos nuevos, es decir, entre moriscos y no moriscos y ya se vislumbraba 'la solución final' a la castellana que a principios del siglo XVII se pondría en marcha en todos los reinos unificados por los Reyes Católicos. Ello [. . .] hizo que, muy posiblemente, un grupo de moriscos cultos granadinos (con la nobilisima causa de conseguir la libertad) utilizasen la imaginación en su lucha contra la intolerancia del nuevo estado basado en la uniformización de la lengua, la religión y las costumbres [. . .] Desde 1595 'aparecieron' veintidós libros plúmbeos que son, según el doctor Miguel José Hagerty, 'el último testimonio escrito en la lengua árabe de la civilización andalucí' " (*Diario Ideal de Granada,* June 18, 2000) (In the last third of the sixteenth century, the division between old and new Christians—that is, between Moriscos and non-Moriscos—was still in place, and one could see the Castilian "final solution" in the horizon, which would be set in motion in all the kingdoms unified under the Catholic Monarchs at the beginning of the seventeenth century. This [. . .] possibly drove a group of cultured Granadinian Moriscos to mobilize their imagination (for

8. For a detailed examination of the circumstances surrounding the apparition of the lead books in the late sixteenth century and their controversial history, see Juan Sánchez Ocaña, *El Sacro Monte de Granada: Imaginación y realidad,* published in 2007 by the Ayuntamiento de Granada. Sánchez Ocaña's book contains an extensive appendix, including a series of compelling images and newspaper clippings, and also a useful bibliographical section, going back to seventeenth-century descriptions of the *libros plúmbeos* and subsequent pronouncements on the subject of their authenticity. See also Francisco Márquez-Villanueva, "La voluntad de leyenda de Miguel de Luna," *Nueva Revista de Filología Hispánica* 30, no. 2 (1981): 359–95.

the very noble cause of achieving freedom) in order to fight against the intolerance of the new state, which was founded on a uniform language, religion, and culture [. . .] Twenty-two lead books "appeared" since 1595, which, according to Doctor Miguel José Hagerty, are "the last testimony of the *Andalusí* civilization written in the Arabic language"). That the *libros plúmbeos* are being discussed in political circles at the turn of the twenty-first century shows that the ideological wars that inspired them have found fertile ground in our day.

If the lead books "translated" by Miguel de Luna and Alonso del Castillo were meant as an intervention in the political and cultural debates on and around the official status of new Christians in the unified kingdoms, *Historia verdadera* is an attempt to penetrate the historiographic circles in which the history of Spain was being (re)written by organic intellectuals. Márquez Villanueva (1981) and Bernabé Pons (2001) have pointed out that Luna's text is a deliberate statement against the historiographic myths of gothic origins, the so-called *mito neogótico* that feeds the official doctrine of Philip II. Miguel de Luna's strategy involves claiming, once again, the role of the translator of an Arabic original. Thus, *Historia verdadera* is said to chronicle the fall of the last of the Visigoth monarchs from the unbiased perspective of an Arabic historian by the name of Abulcácim Tárif Abentarique.[9]

The events that interest us here are narrated in the first book of part 1, titled "Historia de la Conquista de España" (History of the Conquest of Spain). Luna favors the term *conquest* over the notion of "loss" to qualify the defeat of don Rodrigo and the Visigoths at the hands of the Muslim troops. In contrast to Lozano's sympathetic portrayal of don Rodrigo's troubles, the Morisco author draws a thoroughly negative picture of the Visigoth monarch as a murderous usurper, an adulterous rapist, an inept leader, and a cowardly traitor who turns against his own family, victimizes his people, and abandons his troops. In the absence of attenuating circumstances, such as Florinda's immodesty and her father's gratuitous disloyalty, don Rodrigo emerges as an effigy of tyranny destined to be succeeded by able leaders, such as the valorous Captain Tarif and his noble superior Almanzor, who represent the more progressive, tolerant, and benevolent Muslim rule.

---

9. L. F. Bernabé Pons' introductory study to the edition of Luna's *Historia verdadera* published by the University of Granada in 2001 offers an interesting commentary of the text and its context of production and consumption. This "preliminary study" draws a compelling picture of the culture wars of the late 1500s and Luna's place in them.

Luna suggests that the defeat of don Rodrigo and the establishment of the Muslim political and cultural orders is not a disruption of Spain's history but its culmination. To be sure, this is not the tragic beginning of a long and terrible cycle of punishment that would come to an end with the cleansing triumph of the Catholic Monarchs over the last Moorish king of Granada in 1492 and the final expulsion of tens of thousands of new Christians in the early seventeenth century. Instead, Luna's *Historia verdadera* is a message of hope for the Moriscos of the late sixteenth century. Faced with increasingly intolerant images of Spain as a Catholic nation in which "the other races" are out of time, Luna fights back with his own, Morisco pronouncement: this is our time.[10] If I could borrow from Walter Benjamin's evocative imagery in "Theses on the Philosophy of History," Luna exhumes the ruins of the past not to protect the present but to save the future; and what better place to look for talismanic relics than amid the ruins of Toledo's interred history?

A brief summary of this episode of *Historia verdadera* will underscore the centrality of time to Luna's revisionist history of the fall of don Rodrigo. Having heard the news of the sacks perpetrated in the southern provinces by a small contingent of North African troops led by Captain Tarif and Count

10. Following Márquez Villanueva's lead, Luis F. Bernabé Pons argues, "Miguel de Luna tiene ante sí como blanco de sus dardos el mito neogótico que, conformado desde siglos atrás, era la doctrina official de la España de Felipe II. Enlazados los reyes cristianos con aquellos godos que se habían visto sorprendidos en la fortaleza de sus reinos por una inaudita traición, todo lo que cayera fuera de esa línea trenzada con los hilos de la religión quedaba adjudicado a la categoría de los enemigos de España y de Dios. Para esta forma de ver las cosas [. . .] los árabes únicamente habían supuesto en la Península el castigo a la desventura de los godos y un incómodo lapsus en el triunfo de la auténtica esencia de España; de la misma manera sus descendientes debían seguir siendo mirados como un elemento ajeno a la sociedad hispana, sospechoso de infidelidad religiosa y política e imposibilitado de ser integrado en el cuerpo social español" (XLV) (Miguel de Luna has before him as the main target of his darts the neogothic myth that, constructed centuries earlier, was the official doctrine of the Spain of Philip II. As the Christian monarchs were tied to those Visigoths who had been surprised in their strong kingdom by an unimaginable act of treachery, everything that fell outside this line of religious continuity was automatically classified in the category of enemies of Spain and God. From this point of view, the Arab presence in the Peninsula was simply the punishment for the excesses of the Visigoths and an uncomfortable lapse in the triumph of the authentic essence of Spain; in the same way, the descendants of the Arabs ought to be seen as a social element foreign to the Spanish society, suspect of religious and political infidelity and excluded from the possibility of integration into the Spanish social body).

don Julian, don Rodrigo looks to secure his territories against further invasions. But the king recognizes that he has virtually no chance against the superior military prowess and political savvy of his enemies, especially given the ruinous state of his kingdom, for which he is directly responsible: "[S]abía muy bien su posibilidad y tambien sabía la poca fuerza de sus Reynos, respecto de aver mandado derribar por el suelo las fortalezas, y castillos y deshecho las armas" (22) (He knew very well his possibilities and was also aware of the diminished strength of his kingdom since he had ordered the destruction of fortresses and castles and the disposal of weapons). In a desperate attempt to even the playing field, following the advice of one of his closest aids, Archbishop Toriso, don Rodrigo leads a treasure-hunting expedition into the enchanted Tower of Toledo, an ancient structure located on the eastern edge of the city.[11] To access the tower, they must go through a cave that is situated directly underneath it. The cave's entrance displays a mysterious warning/invitation at the top of its secured door: "El Rey que abriere esta cueba y pudiere descubrir las maravillas que tiene dentro, descubrirá bienes, y males" (23) (The king who shall open this cave and uncover the wonders that it contains will find goods and evils).

As they set foot inside the cave, the king and his men hear a loud clatter and are soon confronted by a bronze statue of massive proportions. The statue pounds on the ground with a mace. A fearful don Rodrigo pleads with the effigy until the bronze colossus ceases its pounding. To the left of the statue, the king's people discover a canvas that conveys the message "Rey desdichado, por tu mal has aquí entrado" (24) (Wretched king, you have entered at your own peril). To its right, they can see other inscriptions that read, "Por las extrañas naciones serás poseído y tus gentes malamente castigados" (24) (You shall be possessed by foreign nations and your people severely punished). Carved on the statue's back, they see the words "A árabes invoco" (24) (I call on the Arabs). On its chest is "Mi oficio hago" (24) (This is my obligation).

Visibly shaken by these somber omens, don Rodrigo gives orders to leave the underground passageway at once. The bronze statue resumes its rhythmic

11. Incidentally, Tárif Abentarique (the forged Arabic author) says he uses Archbishop Toriso as an eyewitness source for this section of his chronicle: "[N]o dejaré de contar por extenso, lo que della me contó este arzobispo Toriso, habiéndose hecho del bando del conde don Julián en nuestro campo, como persona que se halló presente" (23) (I will not leave aside what the archbishop Toriso related to me, after he joined don Julian on our side as an eyewitness).

blows as they exit the cave. Don Rodrigo orders the sealing of the cave's entrance, in a futile attempt to erase the memory of what they have seen: "[Y] poniendo silencio sobre lo que avia visto, volvieron a cerrar la torre y cegar la puerta de la cueva con mucha tierra para que de un prodigio y mal agüero como éste no quedase memoria alguna en el mundo" (And imposing silence on what they had seen, they closed the door to the tower and covered the cave's entrance with mounds of dirt, so that the world would have no memory of the prodigious omen). At the stroke of midnight, the structure of the ancient tower comes crushing down amid a terrible uproar. The king asks his advisers to ascertain the exact meaning of what they have seen: "[El Rey] mandó juntar hombres sabios, para determinar con certidumbre lo que significavan aquellas letras, y haviendo conferido, y estudiado sobre ellas, vinieron a declarer, que aquella vision, y estatua de bronce, significava el tiempo [. . .] El epitafio en sus espaldas, que dize A arabes invoco, significaba, que andando el tiempo España avia de ser conquistada de los Arabes" (25) ([The king] ordered to gather men of wisdom to establish with certainty the meaning of these symbols, and having conferred and after careful examination, they came to declare that the said vision of the bronze statue signified time [. . .] The epitaph on its back, which states, "I call upon the Arabs," meant that with the passing of time, Spain would have to be conquered by the Arabs).

While Lozano's "orthodox" version of the events offers richer details and a certain atmospheric quality that may be connected with a baroque and/or protogothic sense of narrative suspense, the theologian's key adjustment comes in the form of a critical omission. As we have seen, in Luna's *Historia verdadera*, the prodigious statue that prophesies the Arabic conquest of Spain is explicitly identified—even certified—as an effigy of time: time in the flesh. Remarkably, this essential bit of information never makes it into Lozano's refurbishing of the story. To be sure, the enigmatic messages "A árabes invoco" and "Mi oficio hago" are still present in Lozano's version, but the precise "identity" of the bronze statue on which the words are imprinted is never disclosed.

The absence of a final declaration concerning the "identity" of the statue, along with the attribution of the prophesy of the destruction of Spain to the craft or science of the Egyptian Hercules, allows for a radical reinterpretation of the events: "A una manga o cabo de esta cueva, [. . .] como tan grande mágico, hizo labrar Hércules un palacio encantado, en el que puso ciertos lienzos y figuras con algunos caracteres, alcanzando por su ciencia que había de verse España destruída por aquella gente bárbara y extraña" (211) (In one of the cave's galleries, [. . .] Hercules, the great sorcerer, built a bewitched palace, where he placed some canvases and figures imprinted with certain signs, prognosticating through his science that Spain would face certain destruction at the hands of a barbarous and foreign people). Not surprisingly, the great sorcerer's prognostication of the destruction of Spain at the hands of foreign barbarians would have nothing to do with the progress of historical time in Lozano's version of the legend. Instead, the theologian attributes the ancient prophesy of the Egyptian Hercules and its fulfillment to the counterhistorical designs of the devil: "La experiencia nos enseña lo mucho que con arte del demonio alcanzan los nigrománticos" (211) (Experience shows how much these necromancers can do with the devil's art).

Briefly stated, the sixteenth-century Morisco and the seventeenth-century theologian anchor their respective accounts of the tragic exploits of don Rodrigo on radically different views of the past, present, and future of Spain. Luna's *Historia verdadera* explains the Muslim conquest of the declining Visigoth kingdom as a traumatic, but ultimately logical, event, which is fully coherent with the progress of history. By contrast, Lozano's baroque tale works on the assumption that the nine centuries of Muslim presence on Iberian soil from 711 to 1492 and beyond (to the 1609–14 expulsion of the Moriscos) is nothing more than a parenthetical interruption of history's linear progression. Lozano's reframing of the legendary material in "properly Christian terms" allows for the closing of the circle of demonic cyclic time. In a sense, the time between 711 and 1492 is literally thrown back into the enchanted cave, redefined as the anomalous time of the bewitched.

Luna's text allows for an understanding of the Arabic conquerors as agents of history who would bring forth the next step in the political and cultural evolution of the Iberian Peninsula, but in Lozano's tale, the Arabs and their legacy (all the way up to 1609) are reinterpreted as a terrible curse that somehow came from an ancient unchristian past. This mythical notion is tied to the modern historiographic "discoveries" that allow the Habsburg's monarchy (and, today, the political forces represented by Aznar) to draw a seamless line of continuity between the Visigoth kingdom of the early eighth century and the absolutist state of the late 1400s. The suggestion is that the long and rich historical period that goes from 711 to 1492 must be treated as a parenthesis of demonic time that was tragically opened by an act of foreign aggression and closed with the proclamation of Spain's Catholic destiny under King Ferdinand and Queen Isabella. The closing of the parenthesis of demonic time is represented in Lozano's tale as the sealing of the bewitched cave where the Ancient Enemy must forever be contained.

According to Manuel Aguirre, as Christian mythology takes over the Western world, "the cycle gradually yields to the line [. . .], but the older cyclic time does not disappear; just as Christianity demoted pagan deities to the rank of demons, so it preserved the older conception of time in a deranked way as that time-structure which befitted devils" (117–18). In this sense, the modern terror that we associate with what Lovecraft termed *cosmic fear* is very closely tied to the post-Tridentine anxieties expressed in *La cueva de Hércules.* I am talking about the fear that Christian time may itself be, as Aguirre says, "bound, fore and aft, by a much vaster, cosmic time of Elder Things" (175); the fear that they might return; the fear that the truly real is the nightmare and that our City of Light(s) is but a dream, as in Julio Cortázar's *La noche boca arriba* (The Night Face Up).

This fundamentally modern fear is at the heart of countless horror tales dealing with the polluting power of relic(t)s, from Machen's "The Great God Pan" and Le Fanu's "Green Tea" to Stoker's *Dracula* and Lovecraft's "The Call of Cthulhu," as well as a host of cinematic offerings, including Guillermo Del Toro's *Cronos* (1992) and a string of more recent B movies, such as *Phantoms* (1998), directed by Joe Chapelle; *The Cave* (2005), directed by Bruce Hunt; *The Cavern* (2006), directed by Olatunde Osunsanmi; *Beneath* (2007), directed by Dagen Merril; and *Catacombs* (2007), codirected by Tomm Coker and David Elliot. The imagery of the "terror that lives below" (to quote from the DVD cover of *Beneath*) has not changed much. Caves and other subterranean passages continue to unsettle us as much as the relic(t)s that are contained in them. Hence, the words on the cover of the DVD version of the 2007 *Catacombs* could easily describe the basic story line of Lozano's subterranean gallery of baroque horrors: "Below the City of Lights exists a World of Darkness, [a] 200-mile labyrinth of limestone tunnels under the city that's lined with the remains of 7 million people."

In Lozano's version of the legends of don Rodrigo and the bewitched cave of Toledo, the underground galleries also run the length of the city: "Va la cueva por debajo de la tierra, tan dilatada y larga, que no sólo coge el espacio que hay hasta el cabo de la ciudad, sino que sale de ella por término de tres leguas" (209) (The cave runs beneath the ground, and it is so dilated and large that it extends not just the length of the city but three leagues beyond it). If *Catacombs* immerses its spectators in a dark landscape of ancient subterranean galleries populated by relic(t)s running the length of the City of Lights (Paris in this case), *The Cave* offers a series of scenes that come even closer to the imagery displayed in *La cueva de Hércules,* beginning with the familiar warning "Prohibited Area / Off-Limits" and continuing with the images of the cave's entrance. To access the underground structure, one has to go through a trapdoor located inside a Christian church. The subterranean galleries of the cave are lined with majestic columns and richly decorated walls, as in the ornamented passageways of the cave of Hercules: "Su fábrica es magnífica, notable y primorosa, compuesta de muchos arcos, pilares y columnas y adornada toda de labradas y menudas piedras" (209) (Its structure is magnificent and remarkably beautiful, built with many archways, pillars, and columns and decorated with finely carved stones).

Referring to the peculiar placement of the cave's trapdoor inside a Christian temple, one of the characters in *The Cave* offers a suggestive explanation for the location of the entrance, which might apply just as well to the cave of Hercules: "They built the church to seal the cave as a display of God's protective power." In other words, the structure of the Christian temple is a container erected to prevent the Ancient Enemy from crossing over into our world of light. In the film, the characters involved in this initial conversation mention local legends that narrate terrible battles between heroic Christian knights and ancient demons lurking in the depths of the cave. "Did they win?" asks one of the explorers. The response to this question is a tragic premonition of things to come: "European legends always have sad endings." As if to corroborate this premonitory warning, the film ends on an unsettling note: "At first I thought it could only survive in the cave environment, but now I am not so sure. I think it wants to get out." As the camera gives us an extreme close-up of the scientist's mutating eyes just before she merges into the crowd, we realize that the Ancient Enemy has somehow survived and now walks our modern cities.

It is not difficult to see a connection between the paranoid structure of horror fiction going back to Lozano's *La cueva de Hércules* and the modern political imaginary that continues to produce oversimplified images of sociohistorical and cultural conflicts: the "war on terror," "good versus evil," "us versus them." According to Manuel Aguirre, our Western modernity is hampered by an entropic desire to wall ourselves inside ever-narrowing conceptions of self and reason. This observation may not be as shocking when we consider that the two key symbolic constructs of the modern age are the subject and the nation-state, both of which emerged first and foremost as the insides of borders meant to protect us from the other side. These modern "illusions that unite us" (to refer once again to the slogan of Aznar's neoconservative party) are also the illusions that isolate and separate us from an increasingly intolerable other. In the case of Lozano's post-Tridentine Toledo and Aznar's modern Spain, this dark other emerges as an undead relic or relict, a remnant of our unchristian history that will not stay properly buried.

Afterword

THE SEVENTEENTH-CENTURY ILLUSION of a purified Christian Spain demands a sacrificial cleansing: the expulsion of the Moriscos and the cleaning up of the past. The danger today is that the European Spain of the twenty-first century could make similar demands on itself. This is the point that Alex de la Iglesia makes in *El día de la bestia* (Day of the Beast [1995]), in which the agents of "the Door [or Gate] to Europe" (*la Puerta de Europa*) murder immigrants, homeless, and undesirables in the streets of the Spanish capital. The killers leave the same warning/proclamation/invitation in every crime scene: "Limpia Madrid." (Clean Up Madrid). De la Iglesia's comedy of horrors effectively dramatizes Manuel Aguirre's insight that "the struggle with the dark Other is not one between two opposing principles Good and Evil, but between [. . .] a close-up Here and an excluded There, between a society false to itself and an aspect of its denied Truth" (144).

The crowds of Christmas shoppers who are oblivious to the epidemic of hate crimes spreading through the streets of Madrid in *El dia de la bestia* are reminiscent of the grotesque masses of soulless zombies in George Romero's *Dawn of the Dead* (1978). "They are us!" says one of the survivors as the zombies approach the glass doors in the famous mall scene of Romero's horror classic. As Barbara Creed noted, the fear of zombies is the fear of the "abject body without a soul" (65). Could this explain the uneasiness one feels looking at the plastinated cadavers of Body Worlds as well as the mindless crowds of Christmas shoppers in *El día de la bestia*?

Doors that do not stay shut are among the most common props in the theatrics of mass-consumed horror.[1] The door ajar proves irresistibly dangerous; it frightens us while simultaneously awakening our curiosity about the

1. So W. H. Rockett argued in "The Door Ajar: Structure and Convention in Horror Films That Would Terrify" (1982).

lurking monsters that might inhabit the other side and their "excessive enjoyment." Conventional horror fantasies reenact redemptive rituals of sin and punishment, wish fulfillment and repression. They allow us to experience the raw emotions and primal instincts of the "dark side" before the monsters are killed, expelled, or contained so that we may return to the luminous integrity of our fortified homeland. But what if our homely safeguards began to feel like prison walls, as in Zayas' *Desengaños;* or pathetic failures of the imagination, as in Cervantes' *Novelas ejemplares;* or curious epitaphs on empty crypts, as in Medrano's *La silva curiosa*? What if what we really fear is not the darkness of the cave but the bright desert of the world? Is this not the baroque horror vacui that haunts the (post)modern subject in Alejandro Amenábar's *Abre los ojos* (Open your Eyes [1997])? The enlightened dream of the perfectly clean city with which the film opens and closes is an iconic image of literary dystopias and sci-fi movies, from *A Brave New World* to *The Matrix*.

The protagonist of *Abre los ojos* is a clean-cut CEO dressed for success in the global economy. His Madrid apartment is as indistinctively functional as an airport terminal, the perfect nonplace. César has nothing to worry about, nothing to do but wait for his life sequence to unfold, to "see what happens." His life resembles that of the baggage-free ticketed traveler recorded in the prologue of Marc Augé's *Non-places: Introduction to an Anthropology of Supermodernity* (1995): "He was enjoying the feeling of freedom imparted by having got rid of his luggage and at the same time, more intimately, by the certainty that, now that he was 'sorted out,' his identity registered, his boarding pass in his pocket, he had nothing to do but wait for the sequence of events. [. . .] [A]ll there is to do is to 'see what happens.' [. . .] [A]lone at last" (2–6). Yet there are intrusions. A dejected sexual partner insists that César know her name. A country from the Middle East defies the global "homogenization of needs and consumption patters" (Augé 5) by clinging "unreasonably" to antidemocratic demands: "When an international flight crosses Saudi Arabia, the hostess announces that during the overflight the drinking of alcohol will be forbidden in the aircraft. This signifies the intrusion of territory into space. Land = society = nation = culture = religion: the equation of anthropological place, fleetingly inscribed in space. Returning after an hour or so to the non-place of space, escaping from the totalitarian constraints of place, will be just like a return to something resembling freedom" (Augé 116).

Augé's traveler is relieved to return to the nonplace of space, where he enjoys a semblance or simulacrum of freedom. In Amenábar's film, however, César's nonplace has been irreversibly polluted by an intruder, who continues to tamper with his programmed life sequence until the simulacrum no longer holds. The protagonist then has to confront the true face of the monster: César, alone, in the infinite desert of the world. César begs to wake up from the dream escape turned nightmare, but can he? Or will he simply awake into another simulated life sequence, another haunted dream, another empty city?

Works Cited

Abre los ojos (1997). Dir. Alejandro Amenábar.

Aguirre, Manuel. *The Closed Space: Horror Literature and Western Symbolism*. Manchester: Manchester University Press, 1990.

Alarcón, Daniel Cooper. *The Aztec Palimpsest. Mexico in the Modern Imagination*. Tucson: University of Arizona Press, 1997.

Alcalá Galán, Mercedes. "Estudio." *La silva curiosa*. By Julián de Medrano. New York: Peter Lang, 1998.

Alemán, Mateo. *Guzmán de Alfarache*. Ed. Benito Brancaforte. Madrid: Cátedra, 1981.

Allegra, Giovanni. "Introducción." *Jardín de flores curiosas*. By Antonio de Torquemada. Madrid: Castalia, 1982.

Anales de Madrid. Reinado de Felipe III. Años 1598 a 1621. Ed. Ricardo Martorell Téllez-Girón. Madrid: Estanislao Maestre, 1931.

Anonymous. *Cantar de Mio Cid*. Francisco Marcos Marín. Madrid: Alhambra, 1985.

Anonymous. *Libro de cosas notables que han sucedido en la ciudad de Córdoba. Dos sucesos de terror. Cuentos del siglo de oro*. Ed. Félix Navas López and Eduardo Soriano Palomo. Madrid: Castalia Prima, 2001.

Anonymous. *Prodigioso suceso que en Ostraviza tierra de el Turco a sucedido este presente año de 1624, de que estan los Turcos muy atemorizados por las declaraciones que entre ellos sacaron deste presagio, en que hallan por estas señales, y otras muchas que an sucedido años antes (que en otra Relacion segunda se verá) la ruyna y perdicion que se espera de la Casa Otomana, y sus secuaces; en aumento de nuestra santa Fee, con el favor de Dios nuestro Señor, de su Sanctidad nuestro Papa Urbano VIII. Y el Catolico Rey Filipo 4. Coluna y defensa nuestra*. Sevilla, Juan de Cabrera, 1624. Real Academia de la Historia, Madrid, Papeles de Jesuítas. 112–24.

Anonymous. *Relacion cierta, y verdadera, del mas estupendo, y espantoso caso que se ha oído, sucedido en la Ciudad de Cordova por Junio deste presente Año de 1672. Hazese relacion de un desalmado hombre, que en una noche de casado degolló a su muger, a su suegra, una niña, y dos parientas de su esposa*. Córdoba, Herederos de Salvador de Cea, S.A., 1672. British Library, Londres, 1072g. 26 (27).

Anonymous. *Relacion verdadera de un mõstruoso Niño, que en la Ciudad de Lisboa nació a 14, del mes de Abril, Año 1628, la cual en una carta ha embiado de Madrid Sebastiã de Grajales Ginoves a un Mercader desta Ciudad, junto con la efigie verdadera del dicho monstruo, la qual se sacó de una que enviaron a la Majestad del Rey nuestro Señor*. Barcelona, Esteban Liberós, 1628. Biblioteca de Catalunya, Barcelona, Folletos Bonsoms 2905.

Arata, Stephen. "The Occidental Tourist: Dracula and the Anxiety of Reverse Colonization." *The Horror Reader*. Ed. Ken Gelder. New York: Routledge, 2000. 161–71.

Augé, Marc. *Non-Places. Introduction to an Anthropology of Supermodernity.* Trans. John Howe. London: Verso, 1995.

Avalle-Arce, Juan Bautista. "Persiles and Allegory." *Cervantes* 10 (1990): 1–17.

Aznar, José María. "Seven Theses on Today's Terrorism" (http://www3.georgetown.edu/president/aznar/inauguraladdress.html).

Bacon, Francis. *The New Organ.* Eds. Lisa Jardine and Michael Silverthorne. Cambridge: Cambridge University Press, 2000.

Baena, Julio. *Discordancias Cervantinas.* Newark: Juan de la Cuesta, 2003.

Baena, Julio. "Spanish Mannerist Detours in the Mapping of Reason: Around Cervantes' *Novelas Ejemplares.*" *Reason and Its Others: Italy, Spain, and the New World.* Eds. David Castillo and Massimo Lollini. Nashville: Vanderbilt University Press, 2006. 204–20.

Baquero, Ana. "Los espacios de la maravilla en la novela corta áurea." *Loca Ficta: Los espacios de la maravilla en la Edad Media y Siglo de Oro.* Ed. Ignacio Arellano. Madrid: Iberoamericana, 2003. 57–68.

Barnes-Karol, Gwendolyn. "Religious Oratory in a Culture of Control." *Culture and Control in Counter Reformation Spain.* Eds. Anne Cruz and Mary Elizabeth Perry. Minneapolis: University of Minnesota Press, 1992. 51–77.

Barona, Juan de. *Relacion autentica y verdadera, en la qual se trata y da cuenta de un testimonio que levantó un Cavallero en la Ciudad de Amberes, este año a una señora muy principal (que estava casada con un caballero, ya hõbre mayor en días) porque no quiso conceder a sus torpes amores, y la vengança que la dicha señora tomó del dicho cavallero, cortandole la cabeça en su misma cama, la qual va dividida en dos Romances curiosos. Compuestos por el licenciado Juan de Barona.* Barcelona, Estevan Liberos, 1616. Biblioteca Nacional, Lisboa, Res. 254/29.

Barthes, Roland. *Mythologies.* Trans. Annette Lavers. New York: Hill and Wang, 1972.

Bataillon, Marcel. *Erasmo y España.* Trans. Antonio Alatorre. Mexico D.F.: Fondo de Cultural Económica, 1986.

Battistini, Andrea. "The Telescope in the Baroque Imagination." *Reason and Its Others: Italy, Spain, and the New World.* Eds. David Castillo and Massimo Lollini. Nashville: Vanderbilt University Press, 2006. 3–38.

Baudrillard, Jean. *Simulacra and Simulation.* Trans. Sheila Faria Glaser. Ann Arbor: University of Michigan Press, 1994.

Beckford, William. *Vathek.* Ed. Roger Lonsdale. London: Oxford University Press, 1970.

Beneath (2007). Dir. Dagen Merril.

Benedict, Barbara. *A Cultural History of Early Modern Inquiry.* Chicago: University of Chicago Press, 2001.

Benjamin, Walter. *The Origin of German Tragic Drama.* London: New Left Books, 1977.

Benjamin, Walter. "Thesis on the Philosophy of History." *Illuminations.* Ed. Hannah Arend. Trans. Harry Zohn. New York: Schocken Books, 1969.

Bernabé Pons, L. F. "Estudio preliminar." *Historia Verdadera del rey don Rodrigo.* By Miguel de Luna. Granada: Universidad de Granada, 2001.

Blackwood, Algernon. "The Willows." *The 13 Best Horror Stories of All Time.* Ed. Leslie Pockell. New York: Warner Books, 2002.

Blanco Aguinaga, Carlos. "Cervantes y la picaresca. Notas sobre dos tipos de realismo." *Nueva revista de filología hispánica* 11 (1957): 313–42.

Bono, James. "Perception, Living Matter, Cognitive Systems, Immune Networks: A Whiteheadian Future for Science Studies." *Configurations* 13 (2005): 135–81.

Brownlee, Marina. "Postmodernism and the Baroque in María de Zayas." *Cultural Authority in Golden Age Spain*. Eds. Marina Brownlee and Hans Gumbrecht. Baltimore: Johns Hopkins University Press, 1995. 107–27.

Brownlee, Marina. *The Cultural Labyrinth of María de Zayas*. Philadelphia: University of Pennsylvania Press, 2000.

Bucki-Glucksmann, Christine. *Baroque Reason: The Aesthetics of Modernity*. Trans. Patrick Camiller. London: University of Teesside, 1994.

Buffalo News, May 7, 2006.

Bynum, Caroline. *Jesus as Mother: Studies in the Spirituality of the High Middle Ages*. Berkeley: University of California Press, 1982.

Calabrese, Omar. *Neo-Baroque: A Sign of the Times*. Princeton: Princeton University Press, 1992.

Calderón de la Barca, Pedro. *El alcalde de Zalamea*. Ed. Angel Valbuena Briones. Madrid: Cátedra, 1990.

Calderón de la Barca, Pedro. *El médico de su honra*. Ed. Angel Valbuena Briones. Madrid: Espasa-Calpe, 1965.

Calderón de la Barca, Pedro. *El pintor de su deshonra*. Ed. Angel Valbuena Briones. Madrid: Espasa-Calpe, 1965.

Carilla, Emilio. *Manierismo y barroco en las literaturas hispánicas*. Madrid: Gredos, 1983.

Carroll, Noël. *The Philosophy of Horror Or Paradoxes of the Heart*. New York: Routledge, 1990.

Carter, Angela. *The Sadeian Woman. An Exercise in Cultural History*. London: Virago Press, 1979.

Casalduero, Joaquín. *Sentido y forma de* Los trabajos de Persiles y Sigismunda. Buenos Aires: Editorial Sudamericana, 1947.

Cascardi, Anthony. "The Genealogy of the Sublime in the Aesthetics of the Spanish Baroque." *Reason and Its Others: Italy, Spain, and the New World*. Eds. David Castillo and Massimo Lollini. Nashville: Vanderbilt University Press, 2006. 221–42.

Castillo, David. *(A)Wry Views: Anamorphosis, Cervantes and the Early Picaresque*. Purdue Studies in Romance Literatures 23. West Lafayette, IN: Purdue University Press, 2001.

Castillo, David. "Baroque Landscapes: Traveling West through the Desert of the World." *Poiesis and Modernity in the Old and New Worlds*. Eds. Anthony Cascardi and Leah Middlebrook. Hispanic Issues. Nashville: Vanderbilt University Press (forthcoming).

Castillo, David. "Clarividencia tangencial y excentricidad en *El licenciado vidriera:* nueva interpretación de un motivo clásico." *Estas primicias del ingenio. Jóvenes cervantistas en Chicago*. Eds. Francisco Caudet and Kerry Wilks. Madrid: Castalia, 2003. 55–71.

Castillo, David. "Exemplarity Gone Awry in Baroque Fantasy." *Revista Canadiense de Estudios Hispánicos* 33, 1. *La constitución del barroco*. Número monográfico. Eds. José Jouvé-Martín and Renée Soulodre La France (forthcoming).

Castillo, David. "Gracián and the Art of Public Representation." *Rhetoric and Politics: Baltasar Gracián and the New World Order*. Eds. Nicholas Spadaccini and Jenaro Talens. Minneapolis: University of Minnesota Press, 1997. 191–208.

Castillo, David. "Horror (Vacui): The Baroque Condition." *Hispanic Baroques. Reading Cultures in Context*. Eds. Nicholas Spadaccini and Luis Martín-Estudillo. Nashville: Vanderbilt University Press, 2005. 87–104.

Castillo, David, and William Egginton. "The Perspectival Imaginary and the Symbolization of Power." *Indiana Journal of Hispanic Literature* 8 (1996): 75–93.

Castillo, David, and Massimo Lollini. "Introduction: Reason and Its Others in Early Modernity (A View from the South)." *Reason and Its Others: Italy, Spain, and the New World.* Eds. David Castillo and Massimo Lollini. Nashville: Vanderbilt University Press, 2006.

Castro, Américo. *De la edad conflictiva. Crisis de la cultural española en el siglo XVII.* Madrid: Taurus, 1972.

Catacombs (2007). Dir. Tomm Coker and David Elliot.

The Cave (2005). Dir. Bruce Hunt.

The Cavern (2006). Dir. Olatunde Osunsanmi.

Cervantes Saavedra, Miguel de. *Don Quijote de la Mancha.* 2 vols. Ed. John Jay Allen. Madrid: Cátedra, 1998.

Cervantes Saavedra, Miguel de. *Entremeses.* Ed. Nicholas Spadaccini. Madrid: Cátedra, 1982.

Cervantes Saavedra, Miguel de. *Novelas ejemplares.* 2 Vols. Ed. Harry Sieber. Madrid: Cátedra, 1990.

Cervantes Saavedra, Miguel de. *Los trabajos de Persiles y Segismunda.* Ed. Carlos Romero Muñoz. Madrid: Cátedra, 1997.

Céspedes y Menéses, Gonzalo. *Varia fortuna del soldado Píndaro.* Ed. Arsenio Pacheco. Madrid: Espasa-Calpe, 1975.

Chartier, Roger. *The Culture of Print. Power and the Uses of Print in Early Modern Europe.* Trans. Lydia Cochrane. Cambridge: Polity, 1989.

Checa, Jorge. "Cervantes y la cuestión de los orígenes: escepticismo y lenguaje en *El Coloquio de los perros.*" *Hispanic Review* 68, 3 (Summer 2000): 295–317.

Chicago Tribune, July 31, 2005.

Childers, William. "The Baroque Public Sphere." *Reason and Its Others: Italy, Spain, and the New World.* Eds. David Castillo and Massimo Lollini. Nashville: Vanderbilt University Press, 2006. 165–85.

Childers, William. *Transnational Cervantes.* Toronto: University of Toronto Press, 2006.

Cortázar, Julio. "La noche boca arriba." *Aproximaciones al estudio de la literatura hispánica.* Eds. Edward Friedman, Teresa Valdivieso, and Carmelo Virgillo. Boston: McGrew-Hill College, 1999. 50–56.

Creed, Barbara. "Kristeva, Femininity, Abjection." *The Horror Reader.* Ed. Ken Gelder. New York: Routledge, 2000. 64–70.

Cronos (1992). Dir. Gillermo del Toro.

Cruz, Anne. "*La bella malmaridada:* Lessons for the Good Wife." *Culture and Control in Counter-Reformation Spain.* Eds. Anne Cruz and Mary Elizabeth Perry. Minneapolis: University of Minnesota Press, 1992. 145–70.

Cruz, Sor Juana Inés de. "A su retrato." *Aproximaciones al estudio de la literatura hispánica.* Eds. Edward Friedman, Teresa Valdivieso, and Carmelo Virgillo. Boston: McGrew-Hill College, 1999. 163.

Daston, Lorraine. "Marvelous Facts and Miraculous Evidence in Early Modern Europe." *Wonders, Marvels, and Monsters in Early Modern Culture.* Ed. Peter Platt. Newark: University of Delaware Press, 1999. 76–104.

Daston, Lorraine, and Katherine Park. *Wonders and the Order of Nature, 1150–1750.* New York: Zone Books, 1998.

DeLamotte, Eugenia. *Perils of the Night: A Feminist Study of Nineteenth-Century Gothic.* New York: Oxford University Press, 1990.
Deleuze, Gilles. *The Fold: Leibniz and the Baroque.* Trans. Tom Conley. Minneapolis: University of Minnesota Press, 1993.
Del Río Parra, Elena. *Una era de monstruos. Representaciones de lo deforme en el Siglo de Oro español.* Madrid: Iberoamericana, 2003.
Denver Catholic Register, March 1, 2006.
Descartes, René. *The Passions of the Soul.* Trans. Stephen Voss. Indianapolis: Hackett, 1989.
Diario Ideal de Granada, June 18, 2000.
Díez Borque, José María. *El teatro en el siglo XVII.* Madrid: Taurus, 1988.
Díez Borque, José María (ed.). *Teatro y fiesta en el Barroco.* Barcelona: Ediciones del Serbal, 1986.
Egginton, William. "Gracián and the Emergence of the Modern Subject." *Rhetoric and Politics: Baltasar Gracián and the New World Order.* Eds. Nicholas Spadaccini and Jenaro Talens. Minneapolis: University of Minnesota Press, 1997. 151–69.
Egginton, William. *How the World Became a Stage: Presence, Theatricality, and the Question of Modernity.* Albany: State University of New York Press, 2003.
Egginton, William. "Reason's Baroque House (Cervantes, Master Architect)." *Reason and Its Others: Italy, Spain, and the New World.* Eds. David Castillo and Massimo Lollini. Nashville: Vanderbilt University Press, 2006. 186–203.
El día de la bestia (1995). Dir. Alex de la Iglesia.
Ettinghausen, Henry. "Sexo y violencia: noticias sensacionalistas en la prensa española del siglo XVII." *Edad de Oro* 12 (1993): 95–107.
Ettinghausen, Henry. "The News in Spain: *Relaciones de sucesos* in the Reigns of Philip III and IV." *European History Quarterly* 14 (1984): 1–20.
Fallen (1998). Dir. Gregory Hoblit.
Findlen, Paula. "Possessing Nature." *Museums, Collecting and Scientific Culture in Early Modern Italy.* Berkeley and Los Angeles: University of California Press, 1994.
Fischer, Ulrich. "When Death Goes on Display." *Catalogue. Anatomy Art. Fascination Beneath the Surface.* Heidelberg: Institute of Plastination, 2000. 233–37.
Forcione, Alban. *Cervantes and the Mystery of Lawlessness: A Study of "El Casamiento engañoso y El coloquio de los perros."* Princeton: Princeton University Press, 1984.
Forcione, Alban. *Cervantes' Christian Romance: A Study of* Persiles y Sigismunda. Princeton: Princeton University Press, 1972.
Forcione, Alban, and Tilbert Diego Stegmann. "El Persiles." *Historia y Crítica de la literatura española.* Vol. II, *Siglos de oro: renacimiento.* Barcelona: Crítica, 1980. 651–60.
Foucault, Michel. *Madness and Civilization. A History of Insanity in the Age of Reason.* Trans. Richard Howard. New York: Vintage Books, 1988.
Fuentelapeña, Antonio de. *El ente dilucidado. Tratado de Monstruos y Fantasmas.* Ed. Javier Ruiz. Madrid: Editora Nacional, 1978.
Galilei, Galileo. *Siderius Nuncius*, a cura di Andrea Battistini. Letteratura Universale Marsilio. Venice: Marsilio, 2001.
García Arenal, Mercedes. *Messianism and Puritanical Reform: Mahdis in the Muslim West.* Leiden: Brill, 2006.
García de Enterría, María Cruz. *Catálogo de los pliegos poéticos españoles del siglo XVII en el British Meseum de Londres.* Pisa, 1977.

García Sánchez, Franklin. "Génesis de lo fantástico en la literatura hispánica." *Teoría semiótica. Lenguajes y textos hispánicos.* Ed. Miguel Angel Garrido Gallardo. Madrid: Consejo Superior de Investigaciones Científicas, 1984. 325–31.

García Sánchez, Franklin. "Orígenes de lo fantástico en la literatura hispánica." *El relato fantástico. Historia y sistema.* Eds. Antón Risco, Ignacio Soldevila, and Arcadio López. Salamanca: Ediciones Colegio de España, 1998. 85–114.

Gelder, Ken. "Introduction: The Field of Horror." *The Horror Reader.* Ed. Ken Gelder. New York: Routledge, 2000. 1–10.

Gilbert, Sandra, and Susan Gubar. *The Madwoman in the Attic. The Woman Writer and the Nineteenth-Century Literary Imagination.* New Haven: Yale University Press, 1979.

Gilman, Ernest. *The Curious Perspective. Literary and Pictorial Wit in the Seventeenth Century.* New Haven/London: Yale University Press, 1978.

Gracián, Baltasar. *Obras completas.* Madrid: Aguilar, 1944.

Gracián, Baltasar. *The Art of Worldly Wisdom. A Pocket Oracle.* Trans. Christopher Mauer. New York: Doubleday, 1992.

Greer, Margaret. *María de Zayas Tells Baroque Tales of Love and the Cruelty of Men.* University Park: Pennsylvania State University Press, 2000.

Gumbrecht, Hans. "Form without Matter vs. Form as Event." *MLN* 111 (1996): 578–92.

Hayles, Katherine. *How We Became Posthuman. Virtual Bodies in Cybernetics, Literature and Informatics.* Chicago: University of Chicago Press, 1999.

Hart, Thomas. "Renaissance Dialogue into Novel: Cervantes's *Coloquio.*" *MLN* 105, 2 (1990): 191–202.

Hobbes, Thomas. *Leviathan.* Ed. Richard Tuck. Cambridge: Cambridge University Press, 1991.

http://go.to/leyendasdetoledo.

The Invasion (2007). dir. Oliver Hirschbiegel.

Jackson, Rosemary. *Fantasy: The Literature of Subversion.* London: Methuen, 1981.

Jackson, Shirley. *The Haunting of Hill House.* New York: Penguin Books, 1959.

Jehenson, Yvonne, and Marcia Wells. "María de Zayas's Wounded Women: A Semiotic of Violence." *Gender, Identity, and Representation in Spain's Golden Age.* Eds. Anita Stoll and Dawn Smith. Lewisburg: Bucknell University Press, 2000. 178–202.

Kantorowicz, Ernst. *The King's Two Bodies: A Study in Mediaeval Political Theology.* Princeton: Princeton University Press, 1957.

Kenny, Neil. *The Uses of Curiosity in Early Modern France and Germany.* Oxford: Oxford University Press, 2004.

Kristeva, Julia. *Powers of Horror: An Essay on Abjection.* Trans. Leon Roudiez. New York: Columbia University Press, 1982.

Le Fanu, Sheridan. "Green Tea." *The 13 Best Horror Stories of All Time.* Ed. Leslie Pockell. New York: Warner Books, 2002. 7–41.

Le Goff, Jacques. *The Medieval Imagination.* Trans. Arthur Goldhammer. Chicago: University of Chicago Press, 1988.

Linke, Uli. *German Bodies: Race and Representation after Hitler.* New York: Routledge, 1999.

Lope de Vega, Félix. *El castigo sin venganza.* Ed. José María Díez Borque. Madrid: Espasa-Calpe, 1987.

Lope de Vega, Félix. *Acting Is Believing. A Tragicomedy in Three Acts.* Trans. Michael McGaha. San Antonio: Trinity University Press, 1986.

Lope de Vega, Félix. *Peribañez y el comendador de Ocaña*. Ed. Juan María Marín. Madrid: Cátedra, 1979.
López de Ubeda, Francisco. *La pícara Justina*. Ed. Bruno Damiani. Madrid: Studia Humanitatis, 1982.
Lovecraft, H. P. "The Call of Cthulhu." *The 13 Best Horror Stories of All Time*. Ed. Leslie Pockell. New York: Warner Books, 2002. 346–78.
Lovecraft, H. P. "Supernatural Horror in Literature." *The World's Greatest Horror Stories*. Eds. Stephen Jones and Dave Carson. New York: Barnes and Noble, 2004. 1–65.
Lozano, Cristóbal. *Historias y leyendas*. 2 vols. Ed. Joaquín Entrambasaguas. Madrid: Espasa-Calpe, 1955.
Luna, Miguel de. *Historia Verdadera del rey don Rodrigo*. Ed. Luis F. Bernabé Pons. Granada: Universidad de Granada, 2001.
Machen, Arthur. "The Great God Pan." *The 13 Best Horror Stories of All Time*. Ed. Leslie Pockell. New York: Warner Books, 2002. 91–148.
Maravall, José Antonio. *El mundo social de "La Celestina."* Madrid: Gredos, 1986.
Maravall, José Antonio. *La cultura del barroco: Análisis de una estructura histórica*. Barcelona: Ariel, 1975.
Mariscal, George. "Bartolomé de las Casas on Imperial Ethics and the Use of Force." *Reason and Its Others: Italy, Spain, and the New World*. Eds. David Castillo and Massimo Lollini. Nashville: Vanderbilt University Press, 2006. 259–78.
Márquez Villanueva, Francisco. *Fuentes literarias cervantinas*. Madrid: Gredos, 1973.
Márquez Villanueva, Francisco. "La voluntad de leyenda de Miguel de Luna." *Nueva Revista de Filología Hispánica* 30, 2 (1981): 359–95.
Medrano, Julián de. *La Silva curiosa*. New York: Peter Lang, 1998.
Medrano, Sebastián Francisco de. *Relación de la fiesta, que se hizo a la dedicación de la iglesia parroquia de S. Miguel de los Octoes, fundada en esta villa de Madrid*. [1623]. Rpt. in *Relaciones breves de actos públicos celebrados en Madrid de 1541 a 1650*. Ed. José Simón Díaz. Madrid: Instituto de Estudios Madrileños, 1982. 184–89.
Menéndez Pelayo, Marcelino. *Orígenes de la novela*. Vol. 3. Santander: Aldus, 1943.
Merchant, Carolyn. *The Death of Nature: Women, Ecology, and the Scientific Revolution*. San Francisco: Harper and Row, 1980.
Mexía, Pedro. *Silva de varia lección*. Ed. Antonio Castro. 2 vols. Madrid: Cátedra, 1989.
Mirollo, James. "The Aesthetics of the Marvelous: The Wondrous Work of Art in a Wondrous World." *Wonders, Marvels, and Monsters in Early Modern Culture*. Ed. Peter Platt. Newark: University of Delaware Press, 1999. 24–44.
Molho, Maurice. "Soledades." *Semántica y poética*. Madrid: Taurus, 1988. 39–81.
Monleón, José. *A Specter Is Haunting Europe: A Sociohistorical Approach to the Fantastic*. Princeton: Princeton University Press, 1990.
Moraña, Mabel. "Baroque / Neobaroque / Ultrabaroque: Disruptive Readings of Modernity." *Hispanic Baroques: Reading Cultures in Context*. Eds. Nicholas Spadaccini and Luis Martín-Estudillo. Nashville: Vanderbilt University Press, 2005.
Moretti, Franco. "Dialectic of Fear." *The Horror Reader*. Ed. Ken Gelder. New York: Routledge, 2000. 148–60.
Nelson, Bradley. "A Ritual Practice for Modernity: Baltasar Gracián's Organized Body of Taste." *Reason and Its Others: Italy, Spain, and the New World*. Eds. David Castillo and Massimo Lollini. Nashville: Vanderbilt University Press, 2006. 79–100.
Nerlich, Michael. "On the Philosophical Dimension of El casamiento engañoso and El coloquio de los perros." *Cervantes's "Exemplary Novels" and the Adventure of Writing*.

Eds. Michael Nerlich and Nicholas Spadaccini. Minneapolis: The Prisma Institute, 1989. 247–329.

Nerlich, Michael. *Cervantes's "Exemplary Novels" and the Adventure of Writing*. Eds. Michael Nerlich and Nicholas Spadaccini. Minneapolis: The Prisma Institute, 1989.

NewScientist.com. November 21, 2002.

NewScientist.com. May 21, 2006.

Nieremberg, Juan Eusebio. *Curiosa filosofía*. Madrid: Imprenta Real de Madrid, 1644.

Observer, March 24, 2002.

Ordoñez, Elizabeth. "Woman and Her Text in the Works of María de Zayas and Ana Caro." *Revista de Estudios Hispánicos* 19, 1 (1985): 3–15.

Ortega y Gasset, José. *La deshumanización del arte. Velázquez. Goya*. México: Editorial Porrúa, 1986.

Otto, Rudolf. *The Idea of the Holy: An Inquiry into the Non-rational Factor in the Idea of the Divine and Its Relation to the Rational*. 2nd ed. London: Oxford University Press, 1950.

Pascal, Blaise. *Pensées*. New York: E. P. Dutton, 1958.

Perry, Mary Elizabeth. "Magdalens and Jezebels in Counter-Reformation Spain." *Culture and Control in Counter-Reformation Spain*. Eds. Anne Cruz and Mary Elizabeth Perry. Minneapolis: University of Minnesota Press, 1992. 124–44.

Phantoms (1998). Dir. Joe Chapelle.

Piña, Juan de. "La cueva encantada." *Literatura fantástica y de terror española del siglo XVII*. Ed. Joan Estruch. Barcelona: Fontamara, 1982.

Poe, Edgar Allan. "The Fall of the House of Usher." *The World's Greatest Horror Stories*. Eds. Stephen Jones and Dave Carson. New York: Barnes and Noble, 2004. 183–201.

Quevedo, Francisco de. *El Buscón*. Ed. Pablo Jauralde Pou. Madrid: Castalia, 1990.

Rabkin, Eric. *The Fantastic in Literature*. Princeton: Princeton University Press, 1976.

Radcliffe, Ann. "On the Supernatural in Poetry." *New Monthly Magazine and Literary Journal* 16 (1826). "Original Papers." London: Henry Colburn, 1986. 145–52.

Rallo Gruss, Asunción. "Las misceláneas: Conformación y desarrollo de un género renacentista." *Edad de Oro* 3 (1984): 159–80.

Ramírez, Juan Antonio. *Corpus Solus. Para un mapa del cuerpo en el arte contemporáneo*. Madrid: Ediciones Siruela, 2003.

Redondo, Agustín. "Les 'relaciones de sucesos' dans l'Espagne du Siècle d'Or: Un moyen privilégié de transmission culturelle." *Cahiers de l'UFR d'Etudes Ibériques et Latino-Américaines* 7 (1989): 55–67.

Rey Hazas, Antonio. "Género y estructura de *El Coloquio de los perros* o cómo se hace una novela." *Lenguaje, ideología y organización textual en las* Novelas ejemplares. Ed. José de Bustos Tovar. Madrid: Universidad Complutense, 1983. 119–43.

Richardson, Ruth. *Death, Dissection and the Destitute*. London, Routledge, 1987.

Riley, E. C. "Cervantes, Freud, and Psychoanalytic Narrative Theory." *Modern Language Review* 88, 1 (1993): 1–14.

Risco, Antonio. *Literatura fantástica de lengua española*. Madrid: Taurus, 1987.

Rockett, W. H. "The Door Ajar: Structure and Convention in Horror Films That Would Terrify." *Journal of Popular Film and Television* 10, 3 (Fall 1982): 130–36.

Rocky Mountain News, February 27, 2006.

Rodríguez Cacho, Lina. "La selección de lo curiosos en 'silvas' y 'jardines': notas para la trayectoria del género." *Criticón* 58 (1993): 155–68.

Rodríguez de la Flor, Fernando. *Barroco: Representación e ideología en el mundo hispánico (1580–1680)*. Madrid: Cátedra, 2002.

Rodríguez de la Flor, Fernando. "On the Notion of a Melancholic Baroque." *Hispanic Baroques: Reading Cultures in Context*. Eds. Nicholas Spadaccini and Luis Martín-Estudillo. Nashville: Vanderbilt University Press, 2005. 3–19.

Rodríguez de la Flor, Fernando. *Pasiones frías. Secreto y disimulación en el barroco hispano.* Madrid: Marcial Pons Historia, 2005.

Ruiz de la Puerta, Fernando. *La cueva de Hércules y el palacio encantado de Toledo.* Madrid: Editora Nacional, 1977.

Samson, Alexander. "Florián de Ocampo, Castilian Chronicler and Habsburg Propagandist: Rhetoric, Myth, and Genealogy in the Historiography of Early Modern Spain." *Forum for Modern Language Studies* 42, 4 (2006): 339–54.

Sánchez Ocaña, Juan. *El Sacro Monte de Granada: Imaginación y realidad*. Granada: Ayuntamiento de Granada, 2007.

Sánchez Ortega, María Helena. "Women as Source of 'Evil' in Counter-Reformation. Spain." *Culture and Control in Counter-Reformation Spain*. Eds. Anne Cruz and Mary Elizabeth Perry. Minneapolis: University of Minnesota Press, 1992. 196–215.

Sarduy, Severo. *Obra completa*. Ed. Gustavo Guerrero y Francois Wahl. 2 vols. Madrid: Ediciones Unesco, 1999.

Schramm, Percy. *Las insignias de la realeza en la Edad Media española*. Madrid: Instituto de Estudios Políticos, 1960.

Schwarz, Hillel. *The Culture of the Copy. Striking Likeness, Unreasonable Facsimiles.* New York: Zone Books, 1996.

Scotsman. August 1, 2003.

Shelley, Mary. *Frankenstein or The Modern Prometheus*. Ed. Maurice Hindle. New York: Penguin Books, 2003.

Soul Journey. December 26, 2004.

Spadaccini, Nicholas, and Jenaro Talens. "Introduction. The Practice of Worldly Wisdom: Rereading Gracián from the New World Order." *Rhetoric and Politics: Baltasar Gracián and the New World Order*. Minneapolis: University of Minnesota Press, 1997.

Spadaccini, Nicholas, and Jenaro Talens. *Through the Shattering Glass: Cervantes and the Self-Made World*. Minneapolis: University of Minnesota Press, 1993.

Stoker, Bram. *Dracula*. Ed. Nina Auerbach and David Skal. New York: W. W. Norton, 1997.

Stoker, Bram. "Dracula's Guest." *The 13 Best Horror Stories of All Time*. Ed. Leslie Pockell. New York: Warner Books, 2002. 149–62.

Tate, Robert. "Mythology in Spanish Historiography of the Middle Ages and the Renaissance." *Hispanic Review* 22, 1 (1954): 1–18.

Todorov, Tzvetan. *The Fantastic*. Trans. Richard Howard. Cleveland: Press of Case Western Reserve University, 1973.

Torquemada, Antonio de. *Jardín de flores curiosas*. Ed. Giovanni Allegra. Madrid: Castalia, 1982.

Turner, Bryan. "Introduction." *Baroque Reason: The Aesthetic of Modernity*. By Christine Bucki-Glucksmann. London: University of Teesside, 1994.

Tusell, Javier. *El País*. September 27, 2004.

Van Dijck, José. "Bodyworlds. The Art of Plastinated Cadavers." *Configurations* 9, 1 (2001): 99–126.

Van Helsing (2004). Dir. Gareth von Kallenbach.

Vollendorf, Lisa. *Reclaiming the Body: María de Zayas' Early Modern Feminism.* Chapel Hill: University of North Carolina Department of Romance Languages, 2001.

Von Hagens, Gunther. "Anatomy and Plastination." *Catalogue. Anatomy Art. Fascination Beneath the Surface.* Heidelberg: Institute of Plastination, first printing 2000. 11–38.

Walpole, Horace. *The Castle of Otranto. A Gothic Story.* Ed. W. S. Lewis. New York: Oxford University Press, 1982.

Wells, Marcia. "María de Zayas y Sotomayor and her 'novela cortesana': A Reevaluation." *Bulletin of Hispanic Studies* 55 (1978): 301–10.

Wetz, Franz Josef. "The Dignity of Man." *Catalogue. Anatomy Art. Fascination Beneath the Surface.* Heidelberg: Institute of Plastination, first printing 2000. 239–58.

Whitenack, Judith. "'Lo que ha menester': Erotic Enchantment in *La inocencia Castigada.*" *María de Zayas: The Dynamics of Discourse.* Eds. Amy Williamsen and Judith Whitenack. Madison: Fairleigh Dickinson University Press, 1995. 170–91.

Williams, Linda. "Film Bodies: Gender, Genre, and Excess." *Film Quarterly* 44, 4 (1991): 2–13.

Williamsen, Amy. "Challenging the Code: Honor in María de Zayas." *María de Zayas: The Dynamics of Discourse.* Eds. Amy Williamsen and Judith Whitenack. Madison: Fairleigh Dickinson University Press, 1995. 170–91.

Winter, Kari. *Subjects of Slavery, Agents of Change: Women and Power in Gothic Novels and Slave Narratives, 1790–1865.* Athens: University of Georgia Press, 1992.

Winter, Kari. "Relic(t)s." Unpublished.

Yllera, Alicia. "Introducción." *Desengaños amorosos.* By María de Zayas. Madrid: Cátedra, 1983.

Zayas, María de. *The Disenchantments of Love.* Trans. Patsy Boyer. Albany: State University of New York, 1997.

Zayas, María de. *Desengaños amorosos.* Ed. Alicia Yllera. Madrid: Cátedra, 1983.

Zayas, María de. *Novelas amorosas y ejemplares.* Ed. Julián Olivares. Madrid: Cátedra, 2000.

Žižek, Slavoj. *Tarrying with the Negative. Kant, Hegel, and the Critique of Ideology.* Durham: Duke University Press, 1993.

Žižek, Slavoj. *The Ticklish Subject. The Absent Centre of Political Ontology.* London: Verso, 1999.

Index